Life Is Not a Rehearsal

David Brudnoy

Life

Is Not

a Rehearsal

A Memoir

DOUBLEDAY

New York *London* *Toronto* *Sydney* *Auckland*

PUBLISHED BY DOUBLEDAY
a division of Bantam Doubleday Dell Publishing Group, Inc.
1540 Broadway, New York, New York 10036

DOUBLEDAY and the portrayal of an anchor with a dolphin are
trademarks of Doubleday, a division of Bantam Doubleday Dell
Publishing Group, Inc.

Book design by Paul Randall Mize

Library of Congress Cataloging-in-Publication Data
Brudnoy, David, 1940–
Life is not a rehearsal: a memoir/David Brudnoy.—1st ed.
    p.   cm.
1. Brudnoy, David, 1940–   .   2. Radio broadcasters—
United States—Biography.   3. Gay men—United States—Biography.
I. Title.
PN1991.4.B78A3   1997
791.44′028′092—dc20
[B]   96-16574
CIP

With love, to Ward, who saved me

Life is but an illusion; the dreams of night are real.
—Japanese novelist EDOGAWA RAMPO

It's not that I'm afraid of dying. I just don't want to be there when it happens.
—WOODY ALLEN, "Death (A Play),"
from *Without Feathers*

Life is not what you find; it's what you create.
—An American proverb, origin unknown

Contents

Preface

Death, or death's shadow, visited me three times, uninvited, during a six-month period, though I could also say that the invitation was my doing and that my survival owed as much to dumb luck as to the intervention of my dear friend Ward Cromer, to whom this book is dedicated. I want to tell you about my life, and about what I've learned about myself and about disease and friendship and celebrity and a number of other things that transpired during that half-year and afterward. While I often touched on sexuality, including homosexuality and, from the early 1980s, on AIDS during a quarter-century of writing for newspapers and magazines and broadcasting on radio and television, I hadn't written about my own experiences in these matters anywhere except for one magazine article, which appeared in April 1995 in *National Review*. My private life was kept just that—private. What happened in mid-November 1994 turned me overnight, whether I liked it or not, into an AIDS "celebrity."

In New England, for more than twenty-five years I had been a fixture in the media—a "survivor," as one newspaper column put it years ago; "inescapable," as an old pal more cynically phrased the matter. And my public doings were truly inescapable, provided you read the local press, watched local TV shows, or listened to talk radio. Especially if you listened to talk radio. But nothing that had long been known about me prepared those who thought they knew me for the news that appeared on the front pages of the local dailies.

On the national scene I am known primarily as a political writer with a conservative or libertarian perspective. That facet of my life began with a front-page story in *National Review* in 1968 on the emerging problematic aspects of what by then had come to be called black power. I also functioned for a while on *CBS Morning News,* doing television point-counterpoint with Susan Cheever. I had begun college teaching in the mid-1960s, and although I continued to teach in a number of universities for several years, I moved gradually into a broadcast media career, both in New England and nationally, first as a television commentator and writer and then as a radio host and lecturer. Since my politics were (and are) right of center, the usual stereotypes were applied to me. My image was that of a mainline conservative activist and essayist in the William F. Buckley, Jr. pattern. The customary reticence of that era, long before more than a handful of people had dared to speak publicly of their homosexuality, led me to segment my life: in the public sphere I seemed to be a garden-variety conservative with libertarian tendencies; in private, in the late 1960s and early 1970s I simply lived my romantic (or sexual) life offstage. In those days people rarely asked anyone whether he was homosexual; it was considered too awkward a topic to discuss, and unless someone exhibited stereotypical mannerisms, others assumed that everybody around them was straight. Only once in my first several years on television did a colleague—our noon news anchorwoman, Marilyn Salenger—mention the matter. She said, "I assume that you're homosexual." I said, "I assume that you're wrong." She wasn't, but in the mid-1970s I was hardly alone in preferring to keep that aspect of my life out of public conversation.

In the fall of 1994 I began a process that directed me toward intertwining my private and public lives. As a gifted healer put it, I began to zip up the two strands of my life into one: united, forthright, unprettified. I don't tend generally to pay attention to psychics or astrologers or healers; I don't sleep under a pyramid or fondle crystals or scream primally, or for that matter scream at all. A "rational skeptic" would be how most people who know or know of me would describe me. Nonetheless, Deb Mangelus, this healer, somehow sensed what I was going through, both in my physical health and in my unwillingness on a conscious level to come fully to grips with my physical decline. I'm so dubious about the nonrational approaches to knowledge—astrology, numerology, psychic intuition, and the like—that I feel a bit goofy even considering this. Still, perhaps part of what helped me survive a medical condition that had doctors about to give up on me entirely involved that uniting of my public and private lives, at least to some degree. This may sound like a slogan from some Coming Out 101 syllabus, but I wonder: as soon as my entire life was public knowledge and I had nothing to hide and no desire to do so, I began to recover. And I've never looked back with nostalgia at the not-so-good old days.

What began in the late summer of 1994 as a gradual slide into serious illness led rapidly to the first of my three brushes with death. With a gratifying, if only temporary, recovery came the complete national public revelation of my sexual orientation and of my disease syndrome. The fact that I am homosexual had over the past two decades and step by tiny step become pretty much known in New England, although in the national arena the subject rarely arose. The AIDS diagnosis, however, which I had been given several years earlier, I had kept from all but a few carefully chosen friends. When I arrived at Massachusetts General Hospital on October 25, 1994—doctors have since told me that I was probably no more than fifteen or twenty minutes away from death—my story turned into fodder for a massive media onslaught, a feeding frenzy.

It is a common assumption that conservatives are rarely homosexual and even more rarely contract AIDS. Of course this is ridiculous, but *I* say "ridiculous" because I am all three and I know many other conservatives and libertarians who, sad to say, have died from AIDS and many who struggle with it. But the story, as pitched to some Hollywood producer, amounted to this: conservative celebrity is gay and has AIDS. This image reduced me to a bizarre cliché, and in part I have written this book to liberate myself, and those readers who come to it with that stereotype, from a reductionism that clouds our minds to understanding and perpetuates myths about sexual orientation, about the perceived connections between sexuality and politics, and, not insignificantly, about how one lives with a fatal disease syndrome and makes the best of it.

When the *New York Times* covered my return to the airwaves in January 1995 after what had appeared to be an inescapable trajectory toward death, I turned into the best-known person with AIDS in New England; as my friend the nutritionist Dr. Judith Wurtman put it, I became Magic Johnson without the jump. News of my illness had literally dominated the local press for weeks in November and then appeared to moderate and evanesce, only to take hold again on the national level in the wake of an article about me in the *New York Times*. At eleven o'clock on Saturday evening, before the Sunday *Times* was available outside New York, my phone (the number is unlisted) rang; a producer for ABC's *Day One* was on the line, asking if I would agree to give his program the first television rights to my story. I asked, What story? What are you talking about? The producer said that he had just read this terrific piece by John Tierney in tomorrow's *Times* and did I want him to read it to me on the telephone? I was far from having completely recovered my energy and was more asleep than awake, so I said I could wait till morning to read it. By that time, early on Sunday, my radio producer, Kevin Myron, had been called by the other networks, and the push was on to get the odd tale of David Brudnoy, homosexual conservative-libertarian talk host with AIDS, on one or two or more of the weeknight television magazine shows.

Soon ABC, CBS, NBC, and *People* had all done features on me; *Time, USA Today,* and some regional newspapers that I had never seen before quoted me. The crunch was on. I got caught up in this media frenzy and in my expanded and rather flattering celebrity raced off to Chicago, taking Kevin along to maneuver me—I still needed a cane to walk, and fatigue was my constant companion—through O'Hare, in and out of a limousine, and then into Harpo Productions. I was to appear on *Oprah* with Olympic diving medalist Greg Louganis, who had just announced that he was gay and had AIDS. Nobody who chooses to go into the gilded fishbowl of television, and the even more intimate, revealing context of talk radio, can survive by being shy, diffident, "aw, shucks." I'm none of that, and I enjoyed the national exposure for its intrinsic pleasures and took that exposure as a compensation, however inadequate, for the horrors of what I was experiencing, the beginning of the final acts in the dramatic though not fictional story of a person with AIDS.

In my youth I dreamed of an academic career, quiet, untroubled by controversy, unsullied by media notoriety. We don't often get what we want, as philosopher Mick Jagger put it in his classic song, and sure enough, precisely what I didn't think I wanted is what I most certainly got. After I had returned to my radio program full-time, five hours nightly, five evenings each week, and to teaching media criticism at Boston University, I felt strong enough to begin this book and increasingly intent on writing it. As I have worked on it, I have grown freer in my willingness to share personal memories, less diffident about what only a couple of years ago I would never have expected to reveal in the public sphere. All of which goes a long way toward explaining what I mean by the title of this book. None of us is guaranteed anything on earth except to inhabit it for some span of time. Our grandmothers all told us not to put off until tomorrow what we can do today, and however silly that sounded when we were children, wanting very much to get out of doing whatever the adults were telling us to do, we are better off living each day as if it might be our last. After all, life is *not* a rehearsal; it's the real thing. And once circumstances had stripped me of my anonymity and I had come to accept, even to enjoy, being a public figure on a far more inclusive scale than ever before, I realized that wedding my public and personal life, the politics with the person, could only enlarge an understanding of both.

Still, wanting to tell this story honestly is not the same as losing a sense of propriety, or at least of proportion. I *am* conservative in temperament, restrained in my behavior, and committed to the belief that self-revelation needn't lapse into the kind of warts-and-all confessional writing better left to poets—

or to exhibitionists. After all, it's risky business to go public. For years, gay advocates and AIDS activists have insisted that coming out is a cleansing experience and that no matter how that exposure comes to be, the "outed" person will feel relief, perhaps even a kind of spiritual rebirth. I've grave doubts about that concept, and I've ribbed the "closet police" for their insistence that everybody who is gay or living with AIDS, or both, ought to dash to the nearest microphone to broadcast the news to a presumably waiting world. As for my experience, in which my audience had been far more interested in my medical diagnosis than I would have imagined, I expected that any negative publicity resulting from my "outing," or whatever it should be called, would come from the sort of conservatives who appear to obsess about homosexuality and to froth at the mouth about what they like to refer to as the "politicization" of AIDS. In me, after all, we have a nationally known personality on the right who suddenly "turns out" to be gay and comes down with the "gay plague" to boot. However, conservatives have generally been the most supportive of all who have written to me or spoken about me. Likewise, while I am not religious in any formal sense, the thousands of people who wrote to say that they were praying for me jolted and honored me again and again. The only sustained public scolding of me did not come from Christian or Jewish believers or conservatives unable to imagine that one of their own could also be what good conservatives aren't supposed to be and to have contracted a disease that only those dreadful gay people contract. Fortunately, that sort of response has been rare, perhaps indicating that in the fifteen years of the plague, some learning and a modicum of humane consideration have begun to replace ignorance and hatred and terror.

The more interesting criticism of me came from some writers in the gay press, beginning after I made what I thought was an innocuous comment in early January 1995 on CBS's *This Morning*. I simply said in passing that during my college days at Yale in the early 1960s, many of us lived a kind of double life, and all things considered, it was often somewhat fun. Context is everything, and in that era few career-oriented Yalies and others who intended to pursue careers in the mainstream paraded about as avowed homosexuals. Possibly today's young gay people have an easier time of it, since the love that in those days dared not speak its name now cannot shut up. That wasn't the way things were back then, in the Jurassic age of American understanding (or lack of understanding) of the homosexual experience. And the truth is that I was trying, like most American boys, to live up to society's expectations. Except that I was also inching toward a self-awareness and at last toward a self-actualization that was not precisely the Ozzie and Harriet variety. When gay newspapers and commentators on radio chastised me for not having come out soon enough, for not having become a one-issue gay spokesman, for not having insisted that everybody know of my HIV diagnosis immediately after I knew of it myself, or for God knows what, I began to understand how fractured, even fragile, the gay community (so called) really is.

When I was well enough to respond, I explained that I didn't intend to become a spokesman for gay causes. I was determined not to reduce myself to becoming a one-issue person or a role model for people living with AIDS, and just as determined not to lose perspective: I am, after all, many things other than an AIDS patient. But inevitably, I have in fact become a spokesman for some gay causes and more than occasionally a poster boy of sorts for AIDS. This may sound as if my medications have done a number on my head, as kids in my generation learned to phrase it, but I can truthfully say that I am a happier person, even knowing that my death is a certainty in the not-too-distant future, than when I carried the burden of my diagnosis more or less alone. I still believe that no one should "out" another person and that we are not all of such identical makeup that everyone is better off throwing away the discretions—the pretences, as some say—of his life according to some set pattern. But I have actually enjoyed what I assumed I would detest, becoming in a sense a fully public person. It's not so bad after all, and my life is less a rehearsal now than it ever was before.

Samuel Johnson is quoted by his amanuensis, James Boswell, as saying, "Depend upon it, Sir, when a man knows that he is to be hanged in a fortnight, it concentrates his mind wonderfully." When a person knows full well that he will surely shuffle off this mortal coil sooner than most would expect, not at the end of a hangman's rope but as the conclusion of a breakdown of his immune system, that, too, concentrates the mind wonderfully. With people who know that they'll die soon, convention and good taste may fairly take a back seat to urgency. The prospect of writing a memoir like this, working to complete the task of uniting my public and private lives and throwing caution—some caution, at least—to the wind, has been daunting, more than a bit audacious; but there it is, *here* it is, now or never. I've the feeling that if I keep moving, like the shark who can't stop or he'll drop, maybe I'll avoid succumbing to regrets about spilling it all out on the broad public stage. Another favorite writer, perhaps more accessible to moderns than Dr. Johnson, is that great nineteenth-century Irish gift to the worlds of letters, of wit, and of irony, a kind of affected role model for many gay people, Oscar Wilde. In his novel, *The*

Picture of Dorian Grey, Wilde declared, "There is only one thing in the world worse than being talked about, and that is not being talked about." Fair enough. So, with my mind concentrated on this story, I begin.

DB
Boston
August 1996

Life Is Not a Rehearsal

ONE

The Best Little Boy in the World

Hutchinson is a nondescript, small Minnesota town fifty miles due west of Minneapolis. Flat, bucolic, peaceful, a center for commerce in a farming community inhabited largely by Scandinavian and German immigrants and their children and grandchildren, Hutchinson in the 1920s and 1930s lacked the hidden scandals of a Peyton Place. It was a safe, humdrum village of the sort that was home to the majority of Americans in the early twentieth century, a place familiar to all Americans in the nostalgic paintings of Norman Rockwell. My visits there with my mother and grandmother when I was a child were exciting adventures, opportunities to see the house that my mother had grown up in, at 106 Jefferson Street South, and the office at 10 Main Street North where my grandfather, David Lewis Axilrod, Hutchinson's only physician and its health officer, had practiced medicine. It was there that I saw for the first time such fascinating things as outhouses and farm animals, things that a city child never encountered.

My grandmother Lillian, like Grandfather David, was one of many children. Her father had worked his way across the northern tier of states as a laborer, landing in Wisconsin and then eventually settling in Minnesota. Identified in one photograph as "Rev. David Aronsohn," he was a cantor, among his other occupations, ministering to the handful of Jews whom he encountered throughout the Midwest. My grandfather began his medical practice in Hutchinson, where my uncles Arnold and Harold (nicknamed Hutch, for obvious reasons), and then my mother, Doris Ferne, were born. In the year of my mother's birth, 1910, Hutchinson's population was 2,368, though by 1990 it had burgeoned to over 12,000.

My mother's family moved to Minneapolis in 1920, when Uncle Arnold, not exactly Doogie Howser, M.D., but a precocious boy nonetheless, was admitted to the University of Minnesota at the age of fifteen. Grandma Axilrod told me that she and her husband, who died just before I was born, felt that a fifteen-year-old shouldn't be expected to live away from home, and no matter what my grandfather felt about leaving his medical practice in a community in which he had become beloved, family came first. The house that my grandparents bought at 1201 Penn Avenue North, in a middle-class neighborhood in north Minneapolis, sat just across the street from Lincoln Junior High School, then brand-new. Both my mother and Uncle Hutch went there, and my grandmother helped start its swim team. The house was also a half-block from John Hay Elementary School, which I attended years later, just as I attended Lincoln.

My father, Harry George, was born in 1908 in the state capital, St. Paul, the second of three children of Israel and Esther Brudnoy, who had come from Russia to America in 1905, bringing their firstborn, Simon, with them. Esther soon gave birth to my father and then later to their only daughter, Katherine, known in the family as Chashele or (a lot easier for me) as Kathie. My parents met as students at the University of Minnesota in the late 1920s and married in 1935. Their union typified the inverted pyramid of family size in America during the past century: the parents on both sides came from large families (all four of my grandparents had nine or ten siblings); both my parents came from families of three children; they in turn had only one child.

I remember asking why my parents had stopped with one, and my mother's invariable response that they had done such a good job creating me that there was no point in risking a lesser offspring by having more children. This flattering answer served its purpose—to change the subject gently—though I often yearned for a brother or sister, even if in practical terms being the sole recipient of my parents' love wasn't exactly a burden. We never again took up the subject of why I had not been given a sibling, and to this day I don't know if my parents wanted another child and were unable to have one or if they chose to call it quits with me.

It was the 1940s, and we were a typical family of the time. I knew nothing, I asked little, sensing that I shouldn't, and I understood nothing about the precise manipulations necessary to make a baby. In those days, sex education barely existed in American public schools, and what we kids may have wanted to know simply hung there in the air, unanswered, unasked. Or I should say *usually* unasked. Once, when I was twelve years old, I brought up something tangential, something about the meaning of a word I had seen in *Time* magazine, "homosexual," and my dad's response was gibberish to my ears. I never again asked him anything along those lines. Not having the slightest comprehension of the phenomenon of creating a baby, children in the 1940s could hardly be expected to ask about variations on the theme, among them the variation that eventually defined me, homosexuality. We know now that even infants exhibit sexual behavior, but nobody talked about that sort of thing then.

In 1939, a year before my birth, my father joined the Army Reserves, a fact that my mother never stopped grumbling about, especially since as a dentist my father was immediately inducted into the military when war broke out, leaving his wife and newborn son alone. That I spent nearly three years without a father in residence fulfills one of the hoariest clichés of the etiology of homosexuality in young boys, but if that were the case, it seems to me that tens of millions of American boys, and boys elsewhere—all of those who grew up while Daddy was away at war or grew up with no dad at all—would probably be homosexual.

In most regards, my childhood was ordinary and comfortable. Before my father went overseas, we lived for short periods in Macon, Georgia, and San Antonio, Texas, at or near army bases. When I was just two, my father was sent overseas and my mother and I moved back to her family's Minneapolis house on Penn Avenue, where I lived until I went to college in 1958. Our extended family was all I knew in my boyhood, and living in a big house continually inhabited by a shifting cast of family members seemed unexceptional, as it was for millions of Americans. My mother's brother Hutch lived with us between marriages and his own stint in the Navy, and my grandmother's divorced sister, Jenny, from whom I first heard the dread word "shingles," bunked in more often than not, when she wasn't living in Hutchinson and caring for her wastrel former husband, whose well-being she considered her burden and the appropriate divine punishment for her divorce.

4

I was named after my dead grandfather David, whose photograph held the place of honor on the mantel in our living room. I saw the family resemblance in our prominent ears, and I asked my grandmother over and over to tell me stories about him. He emerged in my private family history as the greatest doctor of all time, and when I found two hidden compartments in my grandmother's desk, unknown even to her until I discovered them, I asked for some memento of my grandfather to hide there. Children love small, dark, secret places, and I was no exception. In the attic I found a large collection of Uncle Arnold's *Tarzan* books, and I loved reading them and dwelling on the cover paintings of the muscular, seminaked hero. I also found a skull, not the skull *of* my grandfather, of course, but his, for some medical school function that I didn't fathom. When I learned about poor dead Yorick's skull, I memorized the relevant line from the play and, using Grandpa Axilrod's marvelously scary skull for theatrical purposes, did my juvenile version of *Hamlet*.

My mother and grandmother, my great-aunt Jenny, and various other relatives who camped at our house throughout the war years spoiled me, giving me unconditional love throughout my childhood. When my father returned from the war, he added to the cozy, enveloping atmosphere of that frenetic, boarding-house-like home. As of the end of the war we also had a live-in maid, Clara Agnes Leahy, whom I never recall having lived without in those early years. She and I made up a conspiracy of two against the "real" adults, as I saw Clara not quite in that category. When I was perfectly horrid I was her tormentor, and when I was the best little boy in the world she was my pal. Clara's room boasted a photograph of a painting of a long-haired man surrounded by bright light and sporting an apple on his chest, also bathed in light. I saw the Sacred Heart of Jesus and had no idea what it was: it looked like an apple to me. I knew it had something to do with Clara's religion, but I couldn't bring myself to ask her about it. It was beautiful, and though I couldn't figure out what the apple was doing on the man's chest, I kept my questions to myself. Clara was the soul of literal-mindedness. When we were told that for daylight saving time we should turn our clocks forward at two A.M., Clara waited until two A.M. to change hers. I recall staying up with her one year until the magic moment when the clock could be set for the transformation into daylight saving time, and doing it again when the clocks were turned back. A child's literal apprehension of the world is probably a universal phenomenon, but with Clara I shared that affection for things as they were said to be.

Periodically Clara took me downtown to the imposing, almost byzantinely beautiful Basilica of Saint Mary, the first basilica in North America, not to convert me to Catholicism but because we both found our little expeditions away from 1201 Penn Avenue a fine escape from the "real" adults. More important, Clara introduced me to philately, creating an enduring interest that became my prime hobby, and I gazed with wonder at her collection of a series of Vatican stamps showing the popes, glowing on gold foil paper and looking so forbidding in their medieval gowns. Pope Pius XII, whose photograph Clara exhibited next to that of the beautiful long-haired man with an apple on his chest, so resembled our family's rabbi that I was totally confused.

Clara also introduced me to her stamp dealer, who became, as a wise guide to the best use of my pennies, my adviser on how to start a stamp collection. I was a pack rat from my earliest days, and collecting—anything, actually, though certainly beautiful stamps—came naturally to me. My collection

6

centered on U.S. stamps, from which I began to learn about American presidents, inventors, literary heroes, and such, a painless way of developing a love of history. I learned something about value as well, understanding that I could probably buy one first-rate stamp or several second-rate stamps but, on a limited budget, not both. I learned how to read stamp catalogues, how to distinguish between common errors, which didn't enhance a stamp's value, and rare errors, which appeared in stamps that I could read about in catalogues but couldn't afford. I don't want to make too much of this, but I think I began to develop an appreciation for fineness in manufacture and design, for proportionality, for what Clara liked to call the "just so" of things. I became one of nature's neatniks: I liked books lined up by height, stamps inserted into my album with precise margins between them, pictures that I cut out of magazines posted perfectly on my walls to make a pleasing arrangement.

Stamp collecting introduced me to a certain organizational method, and I think that this propensity to order and set patterns was reflected in due course in my political orientation, if not, perhaps, my sexual orientation. From Clara and our dealer I learned something about household economy, about making choices with limited funds, and about beauty even in small bits of colored paper. I spent hours bathing in the beauty of those tiny pieces of paper; I have my stamp collection to this day, though most of my other collections—kids' books, rocks, butterflies impaled on cardboard, athletic equipment, my first encyclopedia, and much of the rest—long ago passed into the hands of younger cousins. I even discarded a lifetime supply of *National Geographic* magazines, a subscription begun for me by my great-uncle Harris Axilrod, Grandpa David's brother. One picture particularly, in an issue in 1951 or 1952, captivated me in my early adolescence: it showed a strapping young African native, naked and covered with white powder, sitting on the shoulders of an older tribesman in a ritual of becoming a man. How I could part with that I don't know, since it was the first photographic image, at least the first I remember, that aroused me sexually.

I was not aroused sexually by stamps, nor, certainly, by our dealer, the proprietor of Art's Stamp Shop, a minuscule hole in the wall on a secondary street in downtown Minneapolis. But to me the stamp shop was paradise: all those gorgeous stamps, drawers upon drawers of them, a lifetime of Art's expertise, a treasure trove for Clara and me, a shrine almost, to which we went every week, to learn, to gaze, to buy. I wonder now, though I had no inkling of it then and doubt that Clara did either, if this thin, toothy, gentle fellow who owned the stamp shop was homosexual—the first, if my suspicion is correct, of my acquaintance. Art did nothing untoward; he exhibited no stereotypical gestures—not that I would have recognized a stereotypical gesture at that point—but he was a bachelor devoted to his little business, avuncular and kindly to a small boy who had more interest than money, and he was as considerate of me as of Clara, who had more to spend and much more knowledge of what she was spending on. Perhaps I'm wrong, and Art wasn't gay. I knew nothing of his personal life, but I loved being around him and always felt as if in some way, which I was incapable of analyzing, Art regarded me as a friend. Clara had given me stamp collecting as my first great avocation and she had given me Art, and my devotion to her was vast—alternating not infrequently, granted, with the perverse viciousness at which children are so adept. Before Clara came to live with us at the end of the war, she had worked for an airline, and my proudest possessions well into my teens included the plastic airline plate, cup, knife, fork, and spoon set she bestowed on me.

In my preteens, I learned that my mother had suffered what today would be called a minor nervous breakdown (whatever "minor" means) during my father's absence and had been sent to Los Angeles for several months to live with an uncle who was active in various entertainment fields and who introduced her to his show business friends, among them Rudy Vallee, the singer. I have a photograph of her accompanied by a handsome blond man and other smiling adults, dated 1944, though I've no recollection of her absence during the better part of that year. No doubt Grandma Axilrod substituted just fine for her. One of my grandmother's sisters, Bertha, lived with her husband, Abe Rudolph, three blocks from our house, and still another, glamorous Great-aunt Betty, often stayed with us in between visits to the coasts, as she liked to refer to Los Angeles and Miami, where in my imagination I had her living in palaces, just like in the movies. Bertha and Abe, Betty, and an apparently inexhaustible cast of characters made up the ever-changing but always large population of our family compound. Everybody pampered me; of course, I deserved to be pampered: I was the best little boy in the world, bright, pleasant, obedient (except sometimes), affectionate, and the youthful center of everybody's attention at 1201 Penn Avenue North.

I am told, in what has become family lore, that when my dad returned from the war in late 1945, shortly after the bombings at Hiroshima and Nagasaki, this man of whom I had no memory at all was anxious to meet me, or remeet me, but I was apprehensive. Who was this person to come into *my* house and get in the way of *my* wonderfully supportive relatives, especially my *mother?* I am told that the morning after his return I tiptoed into my mother's bedroom to confront this person in her bed, who asked, "Would you like to see my medals?" I was too young to remember him, so what could be a better icebreaker with a five-year-old than to show him a box full of showy round metal things attached to colorful ribbons? My Oedipal moment passed quickly, and the father's incorporation into his son's cozy life was thereafter total.

My father's parents lived two blocks away, though I have no recollection, save for a couple of photographs, of my grandfather Brudnoy, who died in 1946. I learned of this while playing with some neighborhood children, and the news was incomprehensible. What did "died" mean? Who had experienced this "dying" thing? I wasn't permitted to attend his funeral, nor the ritual gathering of friends and family for the seven days following. Grandpa Brudnoy was almost as much a mystery to me as Grandpa Axilrod. But Granny Brudnoy is a vivid memory. A Russian lady of the old school, she provided an endless supply of ginger ale while she poured tea from a huge samovar, placing a sugar cube between her teeth as she drank. I might have learned Russian and Yiddish from her, or German from Grandma Axilrod, but in those days the craze to be fully assimilated took precedence over our current penchant for transgenerational cultural learning. My father spoke a bit of Yiddish, though he was American-born, but my mother, the child of parents fully Americanized already, learned no German or Yiddish from hers. Though I had two grandmothers within minutes of each other, one at home, the other nearby, I failed to learn the languages of my ancestors but grew up with the confidence that comes naturally to a child absolutely certain of being completely loved.

My Aunt Kathie lived with her mother, providing another adoring lady to fuss over me. When I was eight she taught me to waltz, and we wowed 'em at her wedding. But before she married and moved away, Kathie often took me to movies, unintentionally setting me on a path of movie mania. We both loved Esther Williams swimming films; I thrilled at the Busby Berkeley–type precision swimming routines, and I remember noticing the smiling men who were the foils for Esther Williams's star turns. In the era before television became pervasive, a boy's entrance into fantasy and imagination depended on radio, with its adventure tales, its mystery stories, and its sometimes brilliant comedy; on books, like my uncle's collection of Edgar Rice Burroughs adventures; and on the glories of the movies. When I wasn't going downtown to "adult" movies with Aunt Kathie, I went with my neighborhood buddies to Saturday matinees at the local theater. I loved the serials, especially if they featured handsome, heroic men rescuing endangered damsels, though I cared less about the damsels than about the heroes.

My mother, ever the prude, forbade my father to take me to see *The Barefoot Contessa,* with Ava Gardner, in 1954. Marilyn Monroe was strictly off limits, too. But for me, an undiscussed pleasure at the movies was watching not the screen goddesses but the supporting gods. And the starring gods, too. I remember more or less fixating on the print ads for *The Story of Robin Hood* in 1952, looking repeatedly at the image of Richard Todd naked to the waist, though the movie itself kept Robin fully dressed. I even mentioned the disjuncture to my parents, who evidently thought nothing of my interest in the bare-chested, income-redistributionist hero of Sherwood Forest. This fascination with handsome men on the movie screen was a fairly blatant clue to my nature, but not one that resonated consciously with me or with my folks. The cinema became, and

11

remained, my passion and my socially acceptable journey into fantasy.

Except for my intermittent tyrannizing of Clara, I was the perfect child, less a troublemaker than most children, more the obedient son and, I think, a clever manipulator of the weakness of adults, of their propensity to believe that a smiling child reflects a happy child. I learned that David means "beloved" in Hebrew, and felt that I had been appropriately named. What is childhood but the experience of innocence, of parental care, putting together experiences that form a memory book of facts, fantasies, desires, like the pictures in a photo album that show the development of a child's life: birthday parties, summer vacations, the notable moments of youth? These were my memories in the years before family life in America began to evaporate at a frightening rate.

Surely family life for some, perhaps for many, has always been hard, but I felt I had it all: grandmothers, aunts, uncles, cousins, great-uncles, and great-aunts, my mother's cousins and my father's, a gorgeous mother and a handsome father, a neighborhood full of kids my own age, a place in the world that nobody could take away from me. We had several lilac trees in our back yard, and I would become almost drunk with delight smelling them, and when they were in season I enjoyed crushing the magenta flowers in my hand and rubbing the residue all over my face; I became a lilac child in all but name. And I had Clara, my respite from the "real" adults and my ally. Years later, in the mid-1970s, I gave her a posthumous tribute by using her name as my byline when I wrote a TV column in *Boston* magazine. Edward L. Bernays, renowned as the father of American public relations, wrote to the magazine to say that "Miss Leahy's television column is the best I have ever read," which pleased me and my editor no end. However, as I was working as a TV commentator at the time, my behavior was more than slightly unethical, insofar as I was writing about the field I worked in and the people I worked with. Obviously I couldn't let anybody know that Clara Agnes Leahy was yours truly, or that the letter from the great Mr. Bernays was a bouquet to *me*. I gave up the column when pangs of guilt triumphed over my small perversity, but I think that taking such pleasure in pulling the wool over the eyes of the magazine's readers reflected a very minor art that I had perfected years before: being one thing on the surface and another just beneath. I think my pal Clara would have enjoyed the joke.

Two blocks away from our house lived my father's older brother, my uncle Si, and his wife, Fanny, and my cousins David Michael and Rachel. David, just shy of two years older than I, had been named by his parents after nobody in particular, but my mother, prone to lingering resentments and over-reaction, held on to a small kernel of resentment because her sister-in-law had "stolen" the name of my mother's father, which she intended to use for her first son. So there were two David Brudnoys in the neighborhood, and since Big David preceded me in every grade and with every teacher and was always good and I was sometimes naughty, I never went through an entire year in school without some condescending, irritated teacher telling me that "the *real* David Brudnoy would never do something like *that.*" Yes, I *was* the best little boy in the world, but my big cousin David, whom I idolized, was somehow ever so much better, and people often referred to me, with that unmistakably significant raised eyebrow, as the "other" David Brudnoy. I fell chronologically between David and his sister, Rachel, who tended to adore me, which was some compensation for my adulation of the flawless David, the prince, the perfect David.

My mother's oldest brother, Arnold, lived across town with his wife, my other Aunt Fanny, and his children, Barbie and David—another David, this one named fully after our shared dead grandfather, David Louis Axilrod—with whom I was friendly but not in daily proximity. And my mother's other brother, Hutch, finally married for the last time; by his wife, Clarice, I got two cousins by marriage, Dick and Diane. Our family was so huge, or so it seemed to my juvenile mind, that I wasn't always sure who was who, which cousins were on my mom's side and which on my dad's.

These tribes of relatives spread throughout Minnesota, Iowa, and Wisconsin. In Superior, Wisconsin, lived the eldest of two sons of yet another of my mother's cousins, a boy who became—unknown to anybody, since I didn't know how to express what I felt about him—a truly idolized paragon. This boy, who was tall, muscular, sandy-haired, and wiry, treated me and his younger brother like worms, but because he was older, in addition to being a skilled fisherman and, by the standards of my emerging aesthetics, beautiful, I was wrapped up in adoring him. When we visited our Wisconsin family we would go to the lake to fish. I spent as much time as possible hovering around my big cousin, who usually tried to get me and his kid brother, who was my age, off his back.

In hindsight I realize that I wasn't singled out for his disdain; his brother and I were children in his eyes, and he wanted to hang around with his peers. Since I had no siblings and didn't grow up knowing that a two-year gap in age between young brothers is an eternity, I kept trying to bridge that gap, only to be firmly and repeatedly slapped down by the big guys. My Wisconsin cousin and my cousin David Michael Brudnoy had terrific friends whom I wanted to be around; at best they tolerated me. David Michael's closest pals were two brothers, who with their sister made up the Lebedoff triplets. David and Johnny Lebedoff were geniuses, I concluded, as was David Michael, and my happiest moments were when they condescended to take me with them, once at three in the morning to climb to the top of a ski run to watch the first total solar eclipse of my lifetime. On Sundays I sometimes caddied for my father, who always lost to his brother Si, at that very golf course–cum–ski run. On that magic morning of the eclipse I was in heaven, permitted to go along with the older boys, whom I passionately wanted to be like in every way.

In later life, as a teacher and a media figure, I acted as a mentor to many young men (and some women), and I believe that it is often this way: the kid who wanted older boys to guide him and sought out these sophisticates later becomes the sophisticate whom younger people seek out for guidance. I doubt that any kid goes throughout his entire life without a same-sex crush at some time, and generally these things leave no marks. But when I was hospitalized and fighting for my life in 1994, I had a dream about my Wisconsin cousin filled with erotic moments, with him touching me and me reaching out to feel his chest, none of which had happened in reality. A childhood wish revived itself unexpectedly, and very possibly the lingering effects of nine days in a coma on morphine somehow intensified dreams that seemed to be actual memories, not fantasies. Obviously I was floating through a reverie of sensual gratification that I could have sought only unconsciously when I was a child but that in my drug-induced receptivity to vivid images packed a powerful wallop. I am not trained in psychology, but I believe that dreams have meaning, and mine for several days during my recovery weren't of the usual metaphoric kind—

planes falling, buildings tumbling, monsters pursuing me—but insead were explicit, populated by people I had wanted to touch when touching was forbidden. In my dreams I lived my forbidden desires.

I regarded my family life not only as completely normal but also as perfect, until I reached the ripe old age of four and a half and my mother came up with the brainstorm of sending me to a day school run by an ultra-Orthodox congregation a few blocks from our house. I returned home in tears, crying to her that I was going to hell for riding my tricycle on Saturdays. That was all it took for her to end my sole experience in captivity to religious zealots. But the Jewish religion, shorn of extremes, continued to play a role in my life. My mother, who had been raised in small-town Minnesota until her family moved to Minneapolis, and my father, whose own father considered Zionism, not Judaism, his religion, were torn between wanting to create a Jewish environment for their son and not wanting a devout observation of the rituals to overwhelm me. For my grandmother's sake, we kept kosher at home, but we ate whatever we wanted when in restaurants, especially on Sunday nights, when we went to a movie downtown and dined at either the local Chinese restaurant or the Italian spaghetti house, both garish but exciting to me. I was subjected to the torment of high-holiday services, hour upon hour, up and down, praying, moaning, groaning, as I thought of it, and I loathed every moment. When Catholic friends complained about a mass being long if it ran for an hour, I thought they were wimps compared to us children of Abraham. To this day I dislike long theatricals, bloated movies, unnecessarily wordy speeches. What I thought of in my child's mind as the too-muchness of religious services translated in adulthood into a preference for brevity. I learned later that the playwright George Bernard Shaw, who had also been a theater critic for a London newspaper, declared that theatergoers liked their plays long to get their money's worth, but critics liked the plays short, the better to get home and write their reviews. I side with the critics.

I did like some religious holidays, though. Hanukkah was made much of in the family so that none of us children would get any ideas about Santa Claus and Yuletide trees and such. I liked Passover despite the two-hour-long seders, because when I was the youngest in the family, before Rachel was born, I got to ask the four questions—Why is this night different from all other nights, and so on—and was even allowed one sip of what passed in those days for wine, the sickeningly sweet Jewish ceremonial goo. And at Sukkoth, my aunt Fanny Brudnoy constructed a tabernacle hung with grapes and other fruits in her back yard, and the whole family went there for a party every year. Flashy holidays held their attractions for me—decorations, games, presents (of course), somewhat exotic rituals—but even at an early age I tended to doubt the stories of miracles; my "whys" were not confined to the four questions of the holiday, and my no doubt irritating habit of doubting much if not quite everything made me an unlikely candidate for an observant religious upbringing.

From age eight I was subjected to nearly seven years of Hebrew school, Mondays through Thursdays right after regular school and early on Sunday mornings. In later life, from high school on, I loved learning languages, but Hebrew school was more than language: it was a horror, religious fairy tales from the Old Testament that struck me as implausible. Each year in Hebrew school the stories were altered ever so slightly, and my growing sophistication led me to question why what we had been taught the year before could suddenly take on a whole new interpretation. "Mr. Cohen, I thought the angel really did wrestle Jacob, but now you say it's a parable. What's a parable?" "Enough of that, Dovidle [little David]. Now, class, what did the Lord change Jacob's name to?" I was prone then, as now, to reject inconsistencies, and this odd pedagogy, with its demand that we believe every story without question until the next year's story made last year's obsolete, drove me first to confusion and then to despair. Then *I* drove at least one of my Hebrew teachers to a heart attack, or so it was whispered; I took the heat for this man's hospitalization because of my non-stop badgering, and feeling deservedly guilty for the teacher's heart failure struck me as a kind of divine punishment for my wickedness. I have often thought that the Catholic confessional is an inspired notion, a way to get your guilt off your chest and then get on with the business of transgressing any number of commandments, including the eleventh, of my own devising: thou shalt not make thy teachers ill.

I was not a reformed sinner even after being blamed for the teacher's illness, and one January near the end of my seven-year imprisonment in Hebrew school I got my little gang of trouble-making rascals to drag a discarded Christmas tree into the school. It took about nine seconds for the principal, Mr. Kaiser (whose name struck me as ironic, since my budding interest in history had taught me what a kaiser was), to drag the young heathen Davy out the door and into suspension. The best little boy in the world struck again.

My aunt Fanny Brudnoy's father taught me the appropriate material for my bar mitzvah, and since I was late in losing my soprano voice, I put on a good show that day. My mother, a spiritual though not biological heir of the Puritans, believed that a boy's coming of age shouldn't be celebrated in the presence of liquor, so she insisted that the party on May 30, 1953, should be alcohol-free. I was a bit of a prude then as well, so I was with her on that decision. I noticed that the adults came to and left the party quickly. My bar mitzvah was a turning point in my willingness to do whatever I was told to do, and soon I took to demanding my liberation from the oppressive Hebrew school, where my grades had been cascading downward. Whatever the religious impulse was, or is, I had little of it. I wanted to be set loose from Principal Kaiser's torture chamber (I was given to hyperbole), and I just stopped believing Bible stories. By 1955, when I quit Hebrew school, Howdy Doody was more real to me than Moses's burning bush. What I came to admire in adulthood, the ethics of Judaism, was absent from what was pounded into us in those early grades.

If I had any serious interest in my bar mitzvah aside from acquisitive ones—I was not unaware of the presents that rewarded the boy who went through the ordeal—I've no recollection of it. I knew, of course, that we Jews were in the minority, but as a young child I experienced no hint of hostility to Jews, even in a city that in the 1930s had been a hotbed of anti-Semitism, nor any sense that being Jewish was any more notable than being a boy. I was both and that was that. I learned early on to segment my life: I was Jewish when the occasion warranted, deracinated otherwise. My lack of interest in religion was unconsciously bolstered by my dad, who dutifully observed the occasional high-holiday agonies in the synagogue but otherwise ignored the rituals, though he was and remains a paragon of generosity to both Jewish and secular charities. My mother tried energetically to instill something of the faith in her contrarian son, even attending adult Hebrew language classes to enlarge her sense of the tradition, which as that rarity a Jew in tiny Hutchinson she had missed in her own

19

childhood. I made valiant efforts to be a terror and a terrible student in Hebrew classes, while in regular school my performance was exemplary. I was more than willing to leave the religious stuff to Mom; *I* wanted out.

More school was the last thing I wanted, whether it was learning to play the piano under the intense, unrelenting tutelage of my aunt Fanny or being trapped in Mr. Kaiser's prison. I wanted to collect rocks and stamps and paint fill-in-the-line pictures, and eventually to paint without filling in the lines. In due course my best pal, Danny Ziff, and I came up with one of my semi-notable achievements, printing up counterfeit money on a mimeograph machine (there *was* life before Xerox) and strewing the bills all over downtown Minneapolis from the observatory deck of the Foshay Tower, then the city's tallest. This was more like it: we were self-starters, showing off our artistic skills and irritating people. Danny and I were adept at making what we thought of as inspired messes. And my cousin the *real* David Brudnoy, who almost never did anything that wasn't perfect, fell on one occasion under my perverse spell. David and the Lebedoff brothers and I called the local Cadillac dealer, announced that we were representing the grand emir of Aden—stamp collecting had its instructional virtues, for who but a kid who collected stamps would even know that Aden existed?—and would like to order a dozen Fleetwoods and would appear the next day to finalize the purchase. For our exertions we found ourselves the subject of a newspaper account a few days later. Where are the grand emir's representatives? the article asked. We were famous, so to speak, though we were not identified as the perpetrators. Years passed before David Michael and I had the nerve to tell our parents what we had done. In concocting little bits of larceny, or at least illegality, I was invariably the leader of the pack. A life of crime

20

might have suited me well. I was an inveterate tease, charming, sprightly, sharp, perverse, even while my image remained that of a sweet kid who was the soul of goodness, a willing companion for my mother when she went shopping for clothes, rarely a nuisance at home except when time came to take out the garbage. I was my mother's biggest fan when she did theatricals for charity, her admirer beyond all others when she caught everybody's eye as she danced up a storm; she and Aunt Kathie were mad for square dancing and the polka, and the reflected glow of their beauty and finesse bathed me in pride. But when the urge to do something unwise presented itself, I was demonic.

My mother and grandmothers and elderly great-aunts and Clara and Aunt Kathie raised me and praised me and generally let me get my way, and if I disappointed them by my refusal to take religion seriously, especially what was inflicted on me in Hebrew school, I made up for that by my academic triumphs in public school. I was, however, terrible at most sports, although because I was a little big for my age I was sometimes useful to the better-coordinated boys as a kind of battering ram. I had one big moment one freezing November afternoon, playing football in junior high school, when I caught a long pass and charged off down the field to a touchdown. I wondered whether I was faster than lightning, since nobody seemed to be following me, and I was half aware of people yelling "Idiot!" and "Numbskull!" and such, which I didn't understand until I crossed the finish line for my glorious moment in the sun and realized that I had spun myself around and run to "triumph" in the wrong direction. In sports I was hopeless.

Like a lot of unathletic but brainy kids, I learned how to win by humor and wit and sarcasm, and although I was never quite the egghead pet of the jocks, they tolerated me. Maybe I should have restrained the urge to raise my hand in class at every ques-

21

tion, but the looks of loathing directed my way were never serious enough to require stitches. Boys didn't kill each other over sideways glances in those years, and the occasional bloody nose, delivered by somebody who couldn't stand one more raised Brudnoy hand in every class, was bearable. I was good at what I was good at and that was that, though I wanted desperately to be athletic like the boys I admired, not just the smart-aleck who always had the answer. I could only hope that my abilities would compensate for my gawkiness on the playing field. In reality, of course, they did, but in my mind I was deficient. Something about me wasn't quite right, something didn't quite cohere into a properly rounded boy. I knew there was a lack, a difference, but how extensive the difference was I had no idea then.

Maybe I was too ungainly to be an athlete, like the boys I admired, but I was determined not to be a nerd; though that term didn't exist then, the concept was all too well understood. Once, in junior high school, while we were rehearsing for a play, a girl called me "fairy." Though I didn't understand exactly what she meant, I knew instinctively that this was a terrible thing to be. To this day I still wonder how that girl knew something about me that I didn't yet know about myself. Every kid has been called every name in existence, but the only word that lingered with me, like a stone striking me in the head, was that one. Somehow kids "know," even before in the strictest sense they know, that there are words that both wound and correctly define. I was a "fairy," she said; what was that? What was I?

In junior high school I belonged to everything—the Junior United Nations, the student civic association, the literary club—and I even enjoyed swimming naked in the pool with the other boys. Swimming was the one sport that I could do with at least average competence, and I enjoyed the visuals even though I had no fixed sense that my admiration of the agility and gracefulness of the athletic boys had a deeper significance. Since we lived directly across the street from Lincoln Junior High, at lunchtime I was able to go home, where my grandmother, mother, and Clara and I had as our constant companions the midday soap operas: *Ma Perkins, Helen Trent, Our Gal Sunday*. I remember wondering if a "fairy" was somebody who actually cared about *Our Gal Sunday*, the little girl from the mining town of Silver Creek, Colorado, who married England's richest, most handsome lord, Lord Henry Brynthrop, and went on to endure every imaginable misery on the radio. While other kids were reveling in the din of a junior high school cafeteria, I was swept up by the characters on the radio soaps, captivated by the unimaginable excesses of these continually put-upon people, wondering how they looked, constructing a world of my own out of the voices of actors and the limitless possibilities the characters' situations suggested to me. My heroes were Sky King and the Shadow and Superman; my faves of comedy were Jack Benny, Fred Allen, Burns and Allen, Fibber McGee and Mollie, Amos 'n Andy. Woody Allen got it just right when he said of the 1940s, apropos of his film *Radio Days,* "The whole country was tied together by radio. We all experienced the same heroes and comedians and singers. They were giants." They were giants to me, before we got television in the early 1950s and began our long national love affair with the tube.

I remember many of my teachers, especially those who cottoned to me and encouraged me in my particular abilities. One, Mr. Scott, was tall, muscular, square-jawed, graced by a thick mop of curly black hair, and he stood on solid thighs topped by

23

rounded buttocks. I memorized every feature of his face and his body, and I delighted in his gentle ribbing of us—he called me Mr. Shop, since I was absolutely no good at all in metal, electric, wood, and printing shop. Our teachers were generally old and wore glasses and suits, but Mr. Scott was a *man*—a hunk, in today's vernacular. He was the most awesomely handsome man on earth, I was certain, so unlike the other male teachers, so reminiscent of my heroic, snide cousin in Wisconsin, but Mr. Scott was a mentor, and I wanted to be just like him or with him forever. I think that most of the other boys worshiped Mr. Scott too. Again and again my dreams during my hospitalization in 1994 evoked memories of Mr. Scott and of my Wisconsin cousin, both of whom emerged finally, in my middle age, as acknowledged, albeit retroactive, objects of desire.

Possibly a child without siblings communicates a need, at least a longing, for guidance, which sensitive, caring adults understand and act on. Our neighbor in the house next door provided me with no reveries of longing but did offer his companionship every summer, taking me to the lake near our house so I could swim. My neighbor across the street, Mr. Fleener, principal of Washburn High School, was an avid gardener and let me help him with his gardening. My reward was all the ears of corn I could eat, and my passion was for the multicolored Indian corn that was considered choice in Minnesota but best suited for pigs according to many other Americans. These adults were part of what today we would likely call my extended family. Each helped give me confidence in myself, never transgressing, never asking anything untoward of me. I was not alone among my friends in being a confused child nor, probably, unique in turning out to be gay. And though kids then lacked explicit understanding of youthful sexual yearning, we were compensated by the innocent friendliness of adult men

24

who meant only the best for us. I learned less about gardening or crafts or swimming than I did about relating to men who cared. I know now that back then we were deprived of what gay kids today can find in support groups and with adults who will speak openly with them about sexuality. I was never seduced by anyone, never abused, never treated shabbily by an adult when I was a child, and though I lacked the explicit mentoring that is available today, I got the affection of adults both in my family and outside, which helped me mature.

For years my parents urged me to go to sleep-away camp like the other kids my age. I resisted every summer until they finally gave up. Then, in typical David fashion, I relented and asked them to let me go to Herzl Camp in Wisconsin, the place they had been touting for all the years of my obstinacy. I enjoyed living in the cabin with other boys, even though by then I had begun to take the prize for sheer number of zits per square inch of face, and not surprisingly, I was about as awkward at canoeing and other sports as I was back home at football and baseball. I did, however, make my mark that one summer at camp as leader of a midnight raid on the girls' camp. I recall being stupid with lust, more or less, for the girls, but I think now that I was more interested in the excitement of sneaking out of our cabins and turning into a marauding gang of boys giddy with the adventure of disobeying a rule and searching for panties. For me the pleasure wasn't in bringing the girls' underthings back to the boys' cabins but in being the ringleader of this naughty pack of boys. To break a rule was something I wouldn't dream of doing in public school, but at Herzl I felt almost obliged to see what I could get away with.

I was thrown into a world half mixed—boys and girls played, prayed (God, did we pray!), ate, and did theatricals together—

and half all male: we slept and used bathroom facilities only with our own. This was the first time in my life I was surrounded by hordes of incipiently randy boys, whose attributes I began to notice, whose differences I started to see, and whose relative places on my personal scale of attractiveness I considered with real seriousness. Many of them were knockouts, one or two vaguely resembling a boy I had fixated on when I was in sixth grade, just the year before. A fifth-grader, this boy seemed to me angelic, with huge black eyes under endless lashes, a pale, almost porcelain face framed by a shock of jet-black curly hair. Just the sight of him had an effect on me that exceeded that of any other male, man or boy, till the Year of Mr. Scott. I never learned the boy's name or spoke to him, since I was a big sixth-grader and he was a little boy, one whole grade beneath me, but here I was in close quarters with dozens of boys, and something was happening—nameless, of course, but powerful. I was seeing what I wanted, and I had no fixed idea what, if anything, to do about it.

I also developed a crush on my counselor, Billy, who must have been seventeen or eighteen and had a room of his own at one end of our long cabin and periodically emerged, in whatever he was wearing or half wearing at the time, to hush us up or give us marching orders for the next day or comfort a crybaby. Naturally, when he said that he wanted to come to Minneapolis for a couple of days after camp, I extended an invitation to stay with us. I knew that Grandma's room, Clara's room, and my parents' room were taken, so he would have to bunk with me. I remember that when he visited, he fell asleep immediately, and I did absolutely nothing but stare at him from my felled-tree position, never moving a muscle. He also asked if he could borrow my father's car for a date, and I was chagrined when Dad said no. I felt mortified, as if my father had ruined my friendship, such as it was, with this athletic, charming "older man," but somehow my hero *du jour* managed to find his way to his girlfriend's house without my father's Oldsmobile. How was it, I sometimes wonder, that nobody ever did anything sexual to or with me? Of course I had no idea of what something done to or with me would be, and no name for what I was feeling with greater frequency in the presence of paragons like Mr. Scott and teenage dreamboats like my Camp Herzl counselor.

As I look back on those years, I think that since I had some, though not many, of the attributes of a tough little cookie, adventuresome and filled with a sense of immutable entitlement, I might have enjoyed being hugged by one of those men. The era is often derided as one of unalloyed repression, and certainly my feelings were less than half digested and wholly unexpressed and unexpressible. The very concept of seduction, even of enticement, was alien to me: innocent not only of deeply submerged desire but even more of the very phenomenon that I would later manifest—homosexuality—I could do nothing about the emptiness in my being, since I knew of nothing that could remedy it. My father never had a birds-and-bees discussion with me, nor did any of my uncles, my older cousins, my adored Mr. Scott, or my neighbors. We boys boasted of our knowledge while knowing nothing; we crowed about our successes with girls while scarcely getting up the courage to kiss one; we spread misinformation and devoured the misinformation that others spread to us. But what we didn't have was any context in which to absorb a homosexual feeling, beyond merely imagining that to want to be with another boy or man was a kind of homage to his exemplary virtues.

Everything in our world, in the world of virtually every American boy, was conducive to the expression of stereotypical desire for girls, which became the rhetoric of boys even before puberty and certainly after the onset of those hormonally terrifying days, once the era of routinely loathing girls had begun to ease into the era of loving or at least wanting them. Nothing in our world opened up the possibility of having a fully understood feeling for another boy or man. What to ask? Whom to ask? If there is one constant in the recollections of men my age about their emerging sexuality, it is that the feelings, however intense, swam about in our minds like aimless goldfish in a bowl; there was no matrix via which to absorb and conclude something valuable from them. We were spared the knowingness and premature sophistication of a later generation, and while there is worth in retaining innocence well into adolescence, at the same time we were denied the converse of that innocence: knowledge. I recall that one of the few lessons I took away from Hebrew school that spoke to my juvenile understanding of reality was the tale of the Garden of Eden. God forbade Adam and Eve to taste of the fruit of the Tree of Knowledge of Good and Evil; we students were told that God was testing his human creations' fidelity to the word of their creator. But I went a step beyond, concluding that the sin of Adam and Eve was not just disobeying but rather learning things that their creator, their sole parent, God, wanted them not to know. At only the most superficial, amorphous level, I sensed that there was something or some things that the world I lived in didn't want me to know. Beyond that tentative suspicion I was clueless.

When I had my first wet dream, I was horrified and assumed that somehow I had rushed my peeing; this sticky stuff must be urine before it is properly ready to spill out. Worse, the little mess on me and on my pajamas was accompanied by some odd feelings of pleasure. So I had both soiled myself and my bedclothes and enjoyed the experience, which made the horror worse. I asked nobody about it, not my father, not my cousin David. I wasn't so stupid as to think that I was the only boy on earth who had violated nature in this way, but I knew that I shouldn't talk about it. When finally I realized that I could evoke the feeling without waiting for a dream to do it for me, I mastered the fine art of masturbation, a private pleasure that I felt embarrassed talking about with anyone. The confusions of budding adolescence are not inconsiderable, and for most boys those early teen years are made frightening or at least puzzling more by aspects of sexuality than by anything else.

One event interrupted my idyllic 1950s American boyhood, leaving a residue of anger and unresolved feelings at least as significant in my development as my unformulated sexual feelings. It happened on an ordinary Saturday afternoon, when I arrived home from my usual routine of studying painting at the Walker Art Center and attending a piano recital. As I entered my house, I found my family gathered in the living room, enveloped in a black mood of misery. I looked desperately for my parents, sure that somebody had died. The story came together quickly, as my mother and grandmother explained between sobs that my mother's oldest brother, Arnold, had been arrested and accused of murdering a patient whom he had supposedly impregnated. Uncle Arnold regularly practiced dentistry at night for his working patients who couldn't make daytime appointments, and on those occasions he would work on his patients' teeth without a nurse present, and like many dentists, though not my father, he often used gas as a relaxant and anaesthetic. The charge against him was that he impregnated the woman and that when she came to confront him, he panicked, killed her in his office, and took her body to an alley, where he dumped it. To this day I don't know if the charge was true, but a sensational trial ensued, hyperbolically called the "trial of the century" in the press. The middle-class Jewish Dr. Axilrod was brought to account for the killing of a lower-income gentile woman, giving the trial the irresistible elements of class, religion, sex, and violence. In ten minutes one Saturday afternoon, my unshakable belief in the constancy of life, in the seemingly solid security that my large family had provided for me, shattered. My father and my uncles were veterans of the great war, heroes in my mind, supportive of their children and their wives, good citizens, pillars of the community, blameless. Suddenly they were all dragged into the media feeding frenzy: Arnold's siblings and their spouses, Arnold's wife and children and his mother, my grandmother, all profiled in the press. We who had been taught as children that if something was in the newspaper, it was true, if it was reported on radio or on TV, it was an undeniable fact, quickly saw the negative power of the media. Privacy disappeared in a matter of hours, a kind of gruesome preview of what would happen in my own life decades later.

My family rallied around, of course, and the orthodox version in our homes was that Arnold was entirely innocent. I hoped then and hope now that he was, but day after day, week after week of this trial led to the near-destruction of his family. His wife and children were trailed by reporters anxious for the "human interest" angle; as that term is defined in practice, it often means being inhumane to the families of people on trial. I was perhaps a bit less surprised than many others when the more recent "trial of the century," that of O. J. Simpson, turned into an obscene circus. Nothing that fierce occurred in the Arnold Axilrod case, but for the mid-1950s, what happened was sensational, and it was probably the most notorious murder case in Minnesota history, at least to that date. My mother, who attended the trial daily, was referred to in a newspaper account as "the accused's handsome sister"—I didn't know why my beautiful mother was called handsome, but that was the least of our worries—and every day at session's end, a TV special updating the day's proceedings aired.

If not quite the media event of the Simpson affair, the Dr. Axilrod trial on TV was still a nightmare. We endured well over a month of screaming headlines in the papers, radio commentary (little of it favorable to the accused), and an advertising gold mine for the TV stations. Because my surname was Brudnoy, in the first days of the trial my schoolmates didn't connect me or my parents with it. One teacher, however, made snide remarks about the case on a nearly daily basis, apropos of nothing in our class (world history), but evidently it was a topic of consuming interest to him. I sat in silence, tears held back somehow, as this teacher found occasion to savage my uncle. A dollop of anti-Semitism crept into the newspaper accounts of the event as well, as Arnold's attorney was routinely described as a fixture in the Jewish community, and references to Arnold's ancestry included frequent reminders that his had been Hutchinson's only Jewish family and the "fascinating" information that his wife's family was well known for activism in the Jewish community of Toledo, Ohio.

When at last Arnold was convicted of manslaughter, convicted again on appeal, and then sent to Stillwater State Prison, everyone in our family was left with a never-salved sadness. Knowing nothing of the reality of the legal system and of the intrusiveness and callousness of the media other than what my family had just experienced, I began to develop a passionate disdain for the media and a distrust of lawyers that deflated and in short order completely extinguished my budding interest in studying the law.

My family's anonymity had been stripped away. Innocence as I knew it was now history, and while my family always maintained that my uncle was innocent, more because we wished it were so than because we had any proof one way or the other, I knew at some level that we had all been tainted by the experience, if we were not culpable ourselves of rape and homicide. I thought on the day of the first verdict of my agonies in Hebrew school and remembered that the God of the Hebrew Bible was prone to vengeance, to saddling generations upon generations with the transgressions of a parent: the curse of the blood, as it were. I wondered for a moment if we were all to be victims of the crime that Arnold had or had not committed. And that evening I did something odd, odd for me: I walked up to Beth El Synagogue, two blocks from our house, and went into the sanctuary and (I would not call it prayed) pondered.

Forty years later, in 1995, when the Massachusetts Bar Association honored me with an award for excellence in law-related journalism, my mind wandered back to my uncle's trial, to what I had long felt was wrong with a legal system that seeks to win often at the expense of truth and real justice, and to what the famous Axilrod trial had done to a family—mine. A youngster's perspective is often all or nothing: the law was either our friend or our enemy, the media either served us as the dispenser of truth or it was insidious. We mature and our purview grows subtler and, one hopes, more moderate. But then I lacked the perspective to see both the legal system and the media as of mixed virtue and vice, and I took what my family had been through as representative of those two professions. The memory of all that flashed through my mind as I accepted the bar association's award to the enthusiastic applause of a standing crowd of lawyers. For just a few seconds, I was stunned.

❏ ❏ ❏ ❏

I have seen my father cry only twice. The night after the verdict was handed down was the first. Like everyone in the family, my dad had experienced every moment of the media coverage and some of the trial itself. He had tried to be a strong supporter of my mother and my grandmother, in whose house we lived. But weeks of keeping his emotions in check suddenly gave way to an outpouring of tears. The restraint and the calmness he had demonstrated during those weeks could be maintained no longer. He knew what Arnold's trial had done to my grandmother, to Arnold's wife and children, to my mother, even perhaps to me and to himself, and he sat in our kitchen, his body shaking with emotion, tears flowing. The second time I saw him cry came a few months after my mother died, in 1972, when Dad was visiting me in Boston. As we sat in my living room, the pain of his loss reached into him, and out came the tears. He hadn't cried at Mother's funeral, though he must have when he found her dead of a heart attack in their den. He was stoic on almost all occasions, as he was when we spoke on the telephone in November 1994 and I told him I had AIDS. I can only guess at his private reactions when he was alone, but I am my father's son in many ways, and we both tend to bury our feelings in public and to confront our woes privately.

I grew up believing that all good things were forever, because in my early childhood all things seemingly *were* eternal. Most children in that era had no reason to imagine the setbacks of adulthood, much less a sensational trial that ripped apart a family's sense of confidence. But Arnold's trial and conviction, followed by his years-long imprisonment and what that did to his wife and children and to my grandmother and mother and father, printed an indelible mark on me. I was deficient in athletics, skeptical about what I saw as the fairy tales inflicted on me in Hebrew school, though I was enough a child to hope that miracles happen. Still, I was bright, in some ways precociously so, and at fourteen, having aged rapidly, I began, however tentatively, to comprehend some of the ways things really are. I never thereafter doubted that nothing lasts forever, that the beauty of life is transient and evanescent, that a day of happiness should be cherished as if it were eternity.

A near-idyllic boyhood had crumbled in only as long as it took to explode my childish expectation of eternal happiness. Someone wisely said that whatever your chronological age is, childhood really ends with the death of your parents. Perhaps one might also say that innocence ends with the shattering of illusions. As the trial and its aftermath slid out of the public's attention and became a lasting pain but no longer a daily trauma in my home, I was in my last days of junior high school, about to turn fifteen, and I could hardly wait to get away from my house, from the school across the street at which a callous teacher had made sport of the case. I looked forward eagerly to beginning at North High School, a mile away from home, with new teachers, who might by September have begun to forget my uncle's trial, who might not inflict on me more memories of that family catastrophe. Maybe there I could begin my life again.

TWO

Boola-Boola

When my day of revelation came in mid-November 1994 and the weight of secrecy about my AIDS flew off my shoulders, and when two months later the national press took up the story and I was given more than my Warholian fifteen minutes of fame, people I had known and loved during my adolescence reappeared. It's a hell of a way to renew acquaintances, but the card in the hand I had dealt myself, the one saying Go Directly to Illness, has had its compensations. I learned that I could take and even ask for help without feeling like a failure, and that the connections of the past, which we often toss aside because life has moved on and we have moved on, aren't so easily forgotten. A few of the girls I thought I was in love with in high school reconnected with me. I wince now and then, remembering how unknowing I was during those years, how in the dark I was about my sexual orientation. I meant in no way to deceive any of them—I was busy enough deceiving myself—and we were in an era where the worst offense the average middle-class boy might commit against his girl(s) was to give out false signals, to suggest promises that would very likely not be fulfilled. With an occasional twinge I have found myself thinking about how ignorant I was then, how sincerely but foolishly I did what all the boys did, chasing after girls and feeling ever so much the big man. But as I made contact during this past year with the now middle-aged women who were so much a part of my life then, I felt a glow, owing to the pleasure of experiencing those friendships again.

Some of my male friends also resurfaced, among them one of the boys I admired most in high school, Judson (Judd) Sheridan. A star hockey player, A student in every subject, and devout Methodist who tried on many occasions to convert me, Judd was a paragon of honesty and straight shooting. We had last seen each other in the mid-sixties, when he was a Rhodes scholar and I visited him in England, but when he looked up at the TV and recognized me on *Today* in the dead of winter in 1995, he called Boston University immediately. I was teaching that morning and hadn't seen the feature myself, but even before I left the university Judd and I were on the phone, and within a few weeks of that conversation the Sheridans visited me in Boston. Then Judd did a typically Judson thing: he contacted the other guys I had hung around with, and they too contacted me. By July the gang of three and their wives came to Boston to visit, almost as if on a secular hegira to see a friend of their youth whose stay on earth was likely to be brief.

In senior year at North High School, Judd had been voted most likely to succeed; Sandy Margolis, who played the piano beautifully, was voted our class's most talented. And Jerry Segal, who formed the other corner in this quadrangular friendship, though not distinguished in a yearbook category—he wasn't a joiner—should have been voted most gently winning and most unalarmingly contentious. Judd was a macho man, though we didn't have the term in those days, Sandy was the bantam gymnast and unlikely-looking aesthete, I was the jokester and imitation ladies' man, and Jerry was the sweetest of us all.

One of my Boston friends has told me that when he and his best buddies have their yearly reunion, they enter a time warp, and so did the four of us. Our high school memories were vivid, and our wise-guy goof-off attitude—even Saint Judson had his moments of sheer silliness—filled us up again as if we were teenagers. This was a voyage back into the golden days of our cocky optimism, as if the thirty-seven years since our graduation had compressed into an instant. My aches and pains, my awareness that unless a cure for AIDS was discovered, I would be fortunate to make it to my fifty-sixth birthday, receded unspoken into the background, and time simply flew away. I was the clever boy I had been, as were they, and we recapitulated our adolescent behavior, morphing in our imaginations, if not in our physiques, into the kids we had been. I don't recommend getting a terminal illness to experience this kind of reawakening of friendship, but in my case it was a tremendous compensation. We had loved each other as compatriots; I was filled with gladness when I realized that their affection for me had endured, and that they still cared enough to come thrilled me, nothing less. Whether I would have done the same had one of them been ill, I can't say. Am I as faithful a friend to anybody as these guys were and are to me? I don't know. But I learned from the day I was carted off to Massachusetts General Hospital at the literal brink of death that people cared, and that caring has sustained me.

After the trio and their wives had come and gone from their mission to see me, I looked again at our yearbook and concluded, after suppressing the thought for nearly forty years, that I had most likely had a kind of inchoate yearning for Jerry. Boys in those days were far less aware of their beauty than many are today, and I doubt that Jerry realized how handsome he was. I doubt that *I* fully realized how attractive he was to me. I had yearned for that fifth-grade boy when I was in the sixth grade. I had worshiped Mr. Scott and apotheosized him as if on Olympus. And I had enjoyed going to the high school swim meets to see my sinewy acquaintances do their stuff (the swimmers were a clique unto themselves, and I was only an admirer from afar). But I hadn't yet the sense, though I surely was unconsciously developing the sensibility, to accept the fact that my apparently aesthetic feelings were of a somewhat earthier nature.

Instead, my friendship with Jerry was bound up in a can-you-top-this rivalry. We argued about everything. What's the correct pronunciation of the name of the last czar of Russia? I said Nicholas, Jerry said Nicolai. We argued about the right speed to drive my father's car when we went on pointless expeditions into the deep, deep country, escaping the city and continuing our nonsensical disagreements. We argued about which girl was the best "stacked" and which was the most likely to be confused with a dog. During an informal wrestling match in the gym's mat room one afternoon, Jerry broke my wrist—an accident, of course, but I never forgot it: the cast, the itch, the putrid smell of the plaster when it finally came off. Jerry remembered nothing of that day, and try as I did during our visit so many years later, I couldn't induce him to express the slightest hint of guilt.

For all four of us boys, high school was a snap. We did well in schoolwork and had our little areas of excellence. We were steadfast in our mutual admiration and affection. The word "homosexuality" or any variant of it never came up. Some of us and our female friends were reading *Compulsion,* and we tittered slightly about the suggestions of perversion in the main characters' intense friendship. One of the girls, Sheila (Happy) Berman—who lived up to her nickname—and I tried to figure out just what it was that these two young men may have been doing when they weren't committing murder and covering up their crime.

Such was the state of awareness of homosexuality among bright Minnesota teenagers in the mid-1950s, even though one of our classmates was flamboyantly effeminate. While we didn't talk about it, we all just *knew* that something about him was different, even beyond his sashaying walk and dramatic hand gestures. Like kids of today, we would do anything to appear to be like everyone else. But this boy was *different*—not that we had a more sophisticated or intuitive vocabulary to define the difference. We didn't harass him, we just avoided him. Whatever he was, we wanted nothing of it. Even I, who would have profited from getting to know him, wouldn't dare say hello. Difference itself was a contagion that we feared. I am often amazed by the courage of young gay kids today, proclaiming themselves, insisting on being taken on their own terms. In my youth our only terms were "normality" and the most studious avoidance imaginable of any behavior that transgressed an unspoken but fully comprehended line. My pals and I were not cruel, not usually, but for us, as for the entire generation, terror was unequivocally and easily defined: being thought different.

Like other boys, I went through the torments of the Age of Horniness: uncontrollable erections in class, just when the teacher asked me to go to the blackboard and write something. I wondered if these pedagogical ogres, our teachers, were trained to know just which boy was experiencing the mother of all hard-ons and to humiliate him by dragging him from his seat to full exposure in front of his classmates. We vied to have the prettiest girlfriend—superficial, yes, but better than one of the loathsome gambits I discovered later at Yale, where once a year we competed to see who could invite the ugliest date for what was charmingly known (among us, not among our dates) as Pig Weekend. Girls were our grail and ribald talk about them our safest conversational gambit, but in an age when awkwardness around girls was regarded as normal, probably for others and certainly for me, the safest, least confusing friendships were with other boys. We all dated constantly, of course, but in truth I was happier hanging out with my pals.

I passed from one crush to another: first Gayle, then Sharon, then Rita and her twin, Renee, then Judy, and finally Ricky. The girls in my little harem were virgins, as was I, and so, I think, were my buddies. In matters of the heart I was a painfully slow learner. I was tall and awkward, having reached my full adult height of six feet by age sixteen, but I weighed little more than a feather. Eventually I layered some muscles onto my Ichabod Crane frame when Ricky's father, a psychiatrist who had been commissioner of mental health for Minnesota, told me that I would feel better about myself if I had a body worth noticing. Father Ralph, as I dared to call him, was ahead of the psychobabble curve in urging self-esteem, and he was pretty sure that I had none, at least insofar as my body was concerned. Ricky's mom was less interested in my body than in assuring that what passed for our courting never went beyond sitting in their closed-in porch and drinking Pepsi, listening to pop music on the radio. I had graduated from Granny Brudnoy's ginger ale to Mother Bea's cola drinks, but the doctor's younger daughter was as safe with me as with her cocker spaniel, Lancelot.

Dutifully willing to try anything to secure the doctor's approval of my campaign to capture his gorgeous daughter as my own true love, I joined a gym downtown, though it was nothing like today's posh health clubs with bethonged women and Nautilus machines and potted ferns. It was a smelly jock gym filled with grunting oafs constantly comparing their pecs and lats and glutes and abs. At age seventeen, putting muscles on a beanpole is easy, and in no time muscles wrapped themselves around my skeleton. While Ricky's dad gave his approval, Ricky herself cared nothing for my new physique and never let me go beyond first base with her. I wasn't alone in being a boy with no past and no present, sexually speaking. We got no diseases, our girlfriends didn't get pregnant, we boys usually just compared the agonies of our blue balls. It wasn't such a bad time, all things considered. In my fantasy imaginings of how things ought to be, I often wished that we lived in the age of the French libertines, when gentlemen would provide their young sons with courtesans to instruct them in the ways of the flesh. No such luck in Minneapolis, circa 1957.

In school I won the Norwegian Prize, just the ticket for a Jewish kid, but there was method in my madness. Harriet Apel, the Spanish teacher, doubled as the German teacher, and I didn't think that two classes a day, ten hours each week, with the formidable, sometimes terrifyingly demanding Miss Apel made much sense, so I took the only other available language. When my mother attended North High in the mid–1920s, the school offered Latin, Greek, French, Spanish, Norwegian, Danish, Swedish, and German, and in her day North boasted the greatest number of high school alumni who had won Pulitzer Prizes. By my time in high school, North was down to German and Spanish and the more or less useless Norwegian, the class into which Scandinavian grandparents shoved their granddaughters and grandsons. Norwegian was hardly my ancestral tongue, but a broad hint of my lifelong tendency to be something of a contrarian was doubtless at play. Plus, I loved my junior year Norwegian teacher, the redoubtable Miss Pauline Farseth, and her young successor, Mr. Lars Kindem. Lars wasn't a Mr. Scott exactly, but he was a genial young man and I immediately became his pet. So while most of my classmates were studying Norsk because their families insisted, I was studying it because I wanted to, and also because nobody else in my crowd would even dream of taking up such a thing. Valiant, generous, devoted Lars, expert hockey coach and true lover of the Norwegian language and culture, became another in the long series of adults who gave me freedom to explore and learn on my own whatever interested me.

I wasn't at the top of every teacher's hit parade, alas: my dark side couldn't contain itself in every class. One English teacher, who knew her stuff but tended to validate many of the stereotypes of the lavender-haired ladies who were continually shocked, *shocked,* by what came out of kids' mouths, had an understandable problem with me. I was good at English but contentious, given to snide remarks. I liked to put this dear, easily discombobulated woman on the spot, to carry an argument beyond any . . . well, reasonable point, and as I was with my pals, who could argue over nothing for years, so I was with her. My sotto voce snicker at her favorite expression, "poppycock," which I declared infallibly had "gone out with the dodo," wasn't quite as sotto as I thought. Now she had her long-awaited opportunity to drag me, almost by the ear, to the vice principal's office for suspension. What? Had I begun to take the behavior that made me a nuisance, a jerk, a horror at Hebrew school straight into public high school? This was a first, and as it happens, a one-time-only, experience—humiliation in high school for the erstwhile best little boy and for my mother, who had to come up to her alma mater and watch as her son was put on the rack and broken on the wheel and (the hyperbole was unstoppable) burned at the stake and beheaded on the block. My mother's errant son had to eat crow at North, and several cold meals of it were served by my infuriated mom at home. I never insulted this fragile lady again and even won her over when, under her tutelage, my sonnet commemorating Minnesota's centenary was singled out for praise. I am a published poet, sort of.

But Ruth Person, my tenth-grade English teacher—now there was a woman of my dreams! Miss Person was beautiful in a somewhat brittle way (she reminded me of Eve Arden's radio and TV character, Miss Brooks), and I hoped that she sensed that her ever-smiling student Dave harbored a shy passion for her. Miss Person's voice was captivating, her enunciation flawless, her perfume undoubtedly ordinary but to my innocent nose ambrosia. Plus she called us "people," not "boys and girls," as in "People, settle down!" I could never settle down in her presence; I was most definitely stirred up. I was barely fifteen when I landed in her class during her and my first year at North High. After years of tutelage at the hands of spinster ladies of a certain age and shapeless gentlemen, just being around this young woman, who I was convinced was hot stuff (whatever precisely that meant), was a kick and a half. This was no act for the benefit of my friends. I wasn't compensating for a secret gay yearning, though I was invariably hovering at the brink of some yearning or other. I truly wanted to be with Ruth Person. I wrote her name again and again on scraps of paper. I felt that a smile from Ruth Person—I never even thought of her name without Miss or Person attached to Ruth—was a triumphant validation of my worth.

In one assignment she asked us to write the first half of a story, which she then critiqued, after which we were to complete it with a surprise ending. I wrote about a lad who connived to get a girl into his room in order to, as he put it, "share" his "virginity" with her. The word "virginity," like "pregnancy," was not to be spoken, much less written, in American high schools of the era. Even *I Love Lucy* didn't dare use the p word in the six episodes when Lucy Ricardo was "in the family way." I feared that Ruth Person would expel me then and there for some unforgivable breach of student behavior. Miss Person gave me a B+ and noted that she eagerly awaited part two, in which this virginity matter would be resolved. I had her, I fondly believed! Did I communicate something to her, ever so subtly, or not so subtly, about my desire? Was the mere use of the word a clue that I was a virgin, that I wished I wasn't, and that I wanted her to be the agent of that desired change? You don't have to be a Freudian, nor did she, to see what I was up to. However, in part two of my story, the kid "sharing" his virginity turned out only to be showing his girl a rare stamp, the 1859 four-penny "virginity" variant of a Queen Victoria English stamp, a pure Brudnoy creation. The mother or grandmother of half the monarchs of Europe was many things, but hardly a virgin. I was aiming at three birds with one stone: I was showing off my philatelic savoir faire (thanks to Clara and Art's Stamp Shop), I was treading on dangerous territory by using a word that I didn't fully understand but knew was not in the standard lexicon of nice kids in the Age of Ike, and I was signaling, however indirectly, that I was enamored of my teacher. My yearning was never spoken and never reciprocated, though Miss Person gave me an A for my efforts.

In my junior year I applied to the American Field Service (AFS) summer abroad program, assuming that I would be sent either to Latin America, for my Spanish, or to Scandinavia, for my Norwegian, if selected. My application form required an essay, and I wrote of how, having come to love Vincent van Gogh after reading *Lust for Life,* I rearranged my bedroom to resemble Vincent's at Arles, though my mother flat-out refused when I started to take up the rug and paint the floor yellow. I wanted the AFS trip badly and set out to get it by standing out from the crowd. My application essay on Arles on the Mississippi, so to speak, did the trick and got the committee's attention. However, when I was selected as an AFS winner, I found that my destination was Japan.

My summer in rural Japan was another turning point in my life, both personally and, as it happened, professionally. The trip occasioned my first brush with national publicity, as the final 1957 issue of *Life* magazine was devoted to Americans abroad and included an article on none other than that long-ago best little boy in the world, now the know-it-all teenager from Minnesota, yours truly. *Life* was big stuff in those days, and for its pains in sending a first-rate photographer to spend a week with me, the magazine got several pictures, the most notable portraying the scrawny kid from the Midwest half naked in a wooden Japanese tub. There I was for all to see: Minnesota Jewish kid (I was erroneously depicted as religious) with Buddhist priest and his family in remote Fukui prefecture, Japan. I lived in a village so off the beaten path that it doesn't even exist anymore; at least, its name has disappeared from the map, as I found in 1993 when I made my return visit to Japan and tried to locate it. My Japanese "brother," Satoru Fujii, who became a priest like his father in the Jodo Shin sect, introduced me to his pals, and since Japanese kids travel in packs, I was never without piles of boys and girls practicing their English on me as I struggled with the few words of their language that I managed to learn. I found that despite my disinclination to practice the religion of my ancestors, the religious community of this Japanese village evoked my spiritual curiosity. Maybe because this particular sect, translated as "True Pure Land," required nothing by way of ritual other than the occasional repetition of one phrase—*Namu Amida Butsu,* "Blessed is the Amida Buddha"—and seemed indifferent to the apparently endless doctrines and prohibitions of Judaism, I found it congenial. Just as I had found a kind of tranquility when experiencing a high mass at the Basilica of Saint Mary on one of my voyages with Clara, the chanting, candles, and exquisite robes of the Jodo Shin priests entranced me.

Later, majoring in Japanese in college, I was disabused of the notion that Jodo Shin lacked a theology, but in my mid-teens I thought, This is more like it! A religion demanding nothing, really, other than kindness. I was impressed by the nearly daily appearance of local women who, on their knees, picked the grass and weeds in the grounds of the temple and their priest's house. In a short-lived burst of enthusiasm and family obligation (to my surrogate family), I volunteered to get up each morning at dawn and swing the huge wooden clapper to ring the temple bell. Rising once or twice with the rooster sufficed for that particular enthusiasm, but everything about the temple and our house, the former's simple elegance, the latter's huge size and lack of any but the most rudimentary modern conveniences, awakened in me a passion for learning.

In Japan I was more easygoing than I had ever been before,

comfortable with the kids who hung around me, developing a skill I hadn't needed before: communicating, really rather easily, with gestures and eye contact, sensing empathetically what, given the language barrier, I couldn't effortlessly understand in the standard way. Having once been a fairly picky eater—an egg fried for more than forty seconds was inedible, I insisted—I now tried everything put before me on the table. I went wherever I was asked to go, gave earnest if not particularly accurate or subtle lectures about America, and seemed almost overnight to blossom. I was Davichan ("chan" is an endearing diminutive), a giant by Japanese standards, thousands of miles away from our living room and the piano's constant reproach. I never had to listen to another biblical fairy tale; I had found a forum for demonstrating my adaptability and a context in which I was learning to adjust to new situations as if to adventure born. I took it all in and brought much of what I came to love in Japan back to Minnesota. My Japanese family may have learned a thing or two about America from me, but I undoubtedly learned enough from them to develop, then and there, a passion for Japanese language, things, and people that even after forty years is alive and well. From the moment I arrived until my final day, they enveloped me as if I had been with them all my years.

I came back to Minnesota with odd habits. My mother immediately put an end to my new custom of walking around the house without shoes, and she made no effort to find processed seaweed or unborn octopus for me to eat. But I also returned with a wild craving to learn more about the world, and, most important, I came back with a sense of my place in the world, not just that vibrant sense of my place in my family: I would be a scholar, I would spread understanding among the nations, I would heal the remaining wounds from the war, I would march to a new drummer, to the music of internationalism. Grandma Axilrod, knowledgeable far beyond her rudimentary formal education, always urged me to reach high, for the stars, she said, and never to assume that what I was willing to work for was unattainable. I dreamed big dreams, and those months in Japan confirmed my rather elevated estimate of my abilities.

I returned with another new and fleeting experience under my belt as well, one that I couldn't tell anyone. For the first time in my life, I had actually reached out to touch another boy, not in the split-second way a hand brushes over a pal's thigh while wrestling—was my broken wrist, courtesy of Jerry Segal, a heavenly signal that I shouldn't touch?—or just a prolonged gaze that holds someone a moment longer than expected, longer than a justifiable, inadvertent brush. This was different; this was intentional, and I knew it. A group of us were swimming in a municipal pool, and like almost every other recreation place in Japan, it was packed. It was there I spotted a stunningly handsome boy of my own age, to whom I was intensely attracted. I maneuvered my way into his path, turned my face to the side so that I would appear uninterested, distracted, and then as he passed by I moved my hand slowly so that it came up just below the waistband of his trunks, and I touched him. My heart was racing, with apprehension and desire and the expectation of what I was doing. I still remember how I got his midsection into my own path in the water and how the touch made me tremble. I was so excited by the one or two seconds of this new experience, I had to get out of the pool to calm down. I was literally shaking, and my friends asked me if I was sick. Yes, I was sick—with desire, unable to pretend that I hadn't done what I certainly had done, and jolted by one additional realization: I had never felt such a sensation, almost a spinning in my head, a flush across my skin, when I was making out with a girl as I had when surreptitiously touching this Japanese teenager. That was all that happened, but I couldn't pretend to myself that I was just imagining what it would be like to *be* him, as I had when admiring boys and men in photographs and on the movie screen. I wanted to be *with* this boy nymph in the pool, though that brief touch was the whole of the experience. I had crossed a barrier that had seemed proper and normal and right. I had reached out and touched someone of my own sex, and if the barrier between my fears and my desires wasn't leveled, it was at least penetrated. I was one month into my eighteenth year of life and I had done a forbidden thing. And I loved it.

Nine of us, four boys and five girls, made up that first AFS contingent to Japan. We spent more than a week with our group each way on the SS *President Cleveland,* a week together in Tokyo, and another ten days traveling around the country as a group. But the rest of the time we were away from one another, each with our own Japanese family. Still, close friendships developed, as they do among kids even in a short time. It was on this junket that I met Arthur Lederman and began a friendship that endures to this day. We hit it off immediately, in part, I suppose, because we were both from middle-class Jewish families but more, I'm pretty sure now, because we got some of the vibes, never explicitly acknowledged, of a shared sexual orientation. Art had a few same-sex experiences under his belt before our AFS summer, something I didn't find out about him until two years later, when we were both in college. We had no erotic interest in each other, not then, not ever, but something that discerned the commonality of our private yearnings and led us, figuratively speaking, into each other's arms was there and remains with us to this day. As the process of coming out in those days tended usually to be painfully slow—the pacing of an oncoming ice age seems an apt image for it—Art and I only quite gradually shared hints, then more explicit tales, of our emerging acceptance of our own homosexuality. I've never felt comfortable with the notion, fashionable in some gay circles, that one can always "tell," that homosexuals have a sixth sense and can invariably recognize our own, as if we had or have some secret handshake. We knew, but without, strictly speaking, knowing.

Art and I were and are soul brothers, but I yearned for another of our group, one Peter Martin, a stunning blond, a quintessential WASP, a sophisticate beyond his years. I tried to adopt his locutions and his pronunciations of words like "khaki," which to him rhymed with "top key" as opposed to my midwestern "hat tree." Peter was the only senior among us, prepping at St. Mark's and heading for Yale right after Japan, whereas the other eight of us had senior year to face first. We all intended to apply to Ivy League schools, and in the end Art chose Princeton and I chose Yale. I think the possibility is strong that I opted for New Haven in large part because I wanted to go where the boys (Yale was then all male) looked like Peter, though the real Peter Martin, once I entered the freshman class, hardly acknowledged my existence. One year's difference in our ages, like that between me and my cousins the real David Brudnoy and the godling in Wisconsin, appeared unbreachable. Still, on our steamship to Japan, during the couple of weeks when all nine of us were together before going off to our particular surrogate families, and on the return trip in sardine class on the *President Cleveland,* I couldn't take my eyes off this perfect model of young American manhood. I doubt that he even noticed. My tentative reaching out to that boy in the swimming pool was as far as I had gone toward actualizing anything resembling homosexual behavior. It was a part of me that developed at a glacial pace, tentative inch by tentative inch over many years. Arthur, whom I admired for his wit, charm, and brains, was just a few paces ahead of me.

I did my first professional writing in Japan, enthusiastic reflections of a precocious showoff, which were published in the *Asahi Evening News,* Japan's largest English-language daily, and in the *Minneapolis Star.* No mention, of course, no hint, nothing about physical attractions to boys my own age, filtered into my adolescent reflections about Japan; I neither understood my shadowy yearnings nor spoke of them to anybody. I was the foreign exchange student from Central Casting, and I rode on that summer for months to come, giving ill-informed but energetic lectures to Kiwanis Clubs and the like and experiencing my first bout of national publicity. Photocopiers weren't yet in common use then, and I remember my mother buying up dozens of copies of the magazine and distributing them to friends and relatives. I wondered if my disdainful, handsome cousin in Superior, Wisconsin, was sorry now that he had treated me so dismissively. The AFS summer in Japan broadened my aspirations, convinced me that I should try to go away to college and not follow my parents into the University of Minnesota, and turned me into a two-week celebrity when the magazine came out. I guess I never quite got over it.

During senior year my palship with Jerry and Sandy and Judd continued, and Ricky and I became officially girlfriend and boyfriend. For some reason Ricky didn't accompany the rest of our graduating class on our senior trip to Chicago, and like all opportunistic boys of that age, if I couldn't be with the one I (thought I) loved, I loved (or tried to love) the one I was with, in this case Judy. A boy who would later turn out to be homosexual was no less determined than his pals to try to live up to society's expectations. While I couldn't forget that brief interlude in the Japanese swimming pool, nor did I want to forget it, I hadn't the self-knowledge to absorb it into my self-image. After all, I had no good, incontrovertible reason to think that I was anything other than a normal boy who admired and wanted to emulate the attractive boys who surrounded me in school. Perfecting a persona that belies reality is not an unusual strategy for any kid who suspects he might be gay, but it was nothing less than a survival skill back then. So I made a half-hearted and of course unsuccessful attempt in Chicago to become a ladies' man *extraordinaire* with Judy, who was wholly of our era and was not about to be used as a learning tool by this groping, uneasy boy.

One incident during my senior year, however, makes me wonder whether I was giving off signals of yearning. I was taking a life drawing course at the Minneapolis Museum of Art one night each week, and one evening the model asked if I could give him a lift home. I had my father's car and of course said yes. I had been drawing this naked man for two hours, oblivious to the full implications of my interest in him, which was far greater than my interest in the female models. When he asked if I wanted to come up to his apartment and have a soft drink or something, I begged off. Have to get Dad's car back. Some other time. Thanks so much. Something told me this fellow was going to offer me more than a Coke, and if I didn't know precisely what, I knew somehow I wasn't ready. Our instructor had frequently adjusted the model's pose, both by verbal directions and by touching the young man's arms, torso, legs. I felt sure that I could rearrange his body parts with more sensitivity than the instructor did. Five months earlier I had chanced an illicit touch in a swimming pool, but when faced with a real man inviting an art student of no particular talent up to his apartment, I was paralyzed with fear.

It wasn't until the summer of 1958 that I finally had my first sexual experience, though not the one that I both feared and craved. My father, doing his yearly army reserve duty, was assigned to San Antonio, where we went for part of the summer. I had no recollection of my brief residence in Texas before my father went overseas, and I was happy to be given a tour of one of my childhood homes. But since I was about to head for Yale, three weeks after our return, I determined that the time had come to do *something* about getting or at least beginning a sex life. Since my mental censor prohibited me from acting on my real desires and I knew of only one thing to do about losing my virginity—the real thing, not a postage stamp—I randomly selected a cab company from the phone book one evening when my parents went to an officers' club dinner dance. When the driver arrived, I said with the most studied nonchalance (it couldn't have fooled him) that I wanted "a woman." I had read J. D. Salinger's *Catcher in the Rye;* I had become a habitué at the movies, including those where such a scene now and then was suggested, although never, to my memory, fully depicted; and that gutsy side of me, the one that had been unleashed for a few seconds in Japan, took hold and convinced me that I could do it. The driver, who was black, took me to a fairly delapidated house in a Negro neighborhood. I met the madam, stereotypically large of bosom and maternally comforting. She introduced me to her "favorite young lady, you'll just like her so much," a slight, bright-eyed, pretty girl who was probably younger than I. How I had the gumption to create this scene for myself, I don't know. We lived in an age before illegal drugs reached into the lives of white middle-class teenagers, and except for an occasional sip of Jewish ceremonial wine and some

53

saké when I was challenged to do so in Japan at one party, I had tasted no liquor. I hadn't the crutch of Dutch courage. I had nothing to embolden me, only something to propel me on: I wanted to enter Yale as a gentleman of the world. I assumed that a freshman class peopled with Peter Martins, suave preppies comfortable with episodes of carnality in their lives, would reject me decisively if I came on as a midwestern hick with all the baggage that that implied, and I probably had begun by then to sense that if I didn't do something with a woman quickly, those forbidden, enticing yearnings for men would consume me like the fires of Hell and something horrible would happen and ruin my life.

With my knees making a throbbing acquaintance with each other and my heart making noises in my chest that reminded me, ridiculously, of Edgar Allan Poe's classic story, I told my teenaged teacher in the ways of the flesh that I was very experienced in sex, this was routine for me. Then and there, in a ramshackle house, in a room lit by one candle, with the wind howling outside, the rain beating on the walls and roof, I began my irrevocable journey into real life. With all the finesse of an Irish wolfhound, I shoved, poked, and grunted while she groaned and moaned. She told me with practiced insincerity that I was *so* good, a real man, best she had ever met, oh how good I was. Five dollars later, I was a man, and felt more like one than when I had become a man in the tradition of my ancestral religion five years earlier. Handling a fountain pen as a bar mitzvah gift was less dicey than handling a prostitute, and although I was trembling during every minute of my ungainly entry into the world of the sexually experienced, I had done my part for all gawky virginal midwestern boys, and I felt much the better for it; at least, I felt better when I got back to our motel. In the morning my parents reported that they had had a real nice night at the officers' club dinner dance, and I chimed in that I had too.

I didn't tell Sandy or Jerry—or, God forbid, Judd—about my night of mad passion, so to speak, or talk of it to anyone until I told one of my Yale roommates about it a few years later. I had been visiting friends and we had gone down to West Virginia to a brothel, and I, boasting of how familiar and comfortable I was with ladies of the evening, masqueraded for another brief time as a sophisticate of the world. I knew that my roommate would be impressed with me, and he didn't seem surprised when I elaborated rather shamelessly on my adventures in the skin trade in San Antonio or in that West Virginia house of ill repute.

I wish that my sexual exploits in my late teens had been more alluring; I also wish that we had peace on earth and good will toward men. My few fumbling experiments with heterosexual love were mundane to the point of meaninglessness and less erotic, less stimulating, than the fantasies I increasingly permitted myself when thrown into the company of four thousand boys, many of them stunning, at Yale. But at the time, those experiences were milestones. I wondered if other boys could possibly be as indifferent as I to the presumed fabulousness of sex with girls, though the obvious corollary—that sex with some other type of person might be more the ticket—was too hot to handle. My denial was almost but not quite total. It certainly created a massive roadblock in my path toward crossing over into awareness, into the sexual life that nature intended for me. In academics I was swift, bold, and beyond merely competent; in my personal life I was a naif, a caricature of innocence, a barefoot boy with scarcely a clue. I required two more years to try what had clearly been my sexual orientation all my life.

Those ungainly moments of "passion" in San Antonio provided the highlight of my summer of 1958, and in a flash summer was behind me. I headed to New Haven, entering my college years with a brief stay, my second, in New York City. My first visit had been when I was thirteen and my parents gave me a bar mitzvah trip to Washington, Virginia, and New York. My father, who had had quite enough of visiting new places during his army stint, stayed home, and my mother and I took off for this exciting voyage. That my mother survived my inexhaustible dashing around the city, having to see every historical building, every noteworthy spot, still impresses me. We went to Broadway shows; our favorite was *The King and I,* with Yul Brynner, and though we talked about it primarily because of its spectacular set pieces and its beautiful score, I didn't mention that I had especially noticed the beauty of the actor playing the young crown prince; I think the juvenile performer in that production was Sal Mineo, before his brief, promising movie career and his murder, the rumors later had it, at the hands of a homosexual trick. Always the devoted mom, and not, I'm convinced, possessed of that vaunted second sense of mothers about a son who was even then teetering on the brink of a sexual revolution of his own, Doris Ferne Axilrod Brudnoy let her precocious son pick our entertainments. I was a boy with energy to spare and interest unbounded. I had done my duty to the family by shining on the altar of our synagogue, for which this journey to the East was my reward.

My second visit came in September 1958, just days before I took the train to New Haven to become "shoe," the Yaleism for cool—to wear the right Ivy clothes and learn to speak like Peter Martin. In Manhattan I checked into a YMCA, though I never witnessed any of those wild scenes reputed to be common in Ys across the land. In truth, I felt no passionate desire for anything but to become the best freshman Yalie on campus. College provided me with four uninterrupted years of stimulation. I found that I was as bright as the snotty preppies who dressed so wonderfully in their khakis and navy blue jackets emblazoned with their fancy school crests and their casually, even sloppily tied rep neckwear; they were the zitless of face and, like Fitzgerald's foils in *Gatsby,* uninterested in whom they might wound and what lives they might smash up. For the most part I found them lazy, possessed of a sense of entitlement, content to earn or at least accept their gentlemen's Cs and shine more on the playing fields and on weekends, when they imported their dates from the Seven Sisters, while I, the best male student in high school except for Judson Sheridan, became a grind. Adopting some of my classmates' affectations and vocabulary, I came close to looking and sounding the part, though I felt that I verged perilously close to being a fraud. Many of these boys seemed to me to have grown up too rich and too unbothered by worry, by self-doubt, to experience the kind of struggles that appeared, at least in the realm of sex, to be my constant companion.

I foolishly imagined that everybody else was truly experienced in sex and that the torments of youth had mercifully passed by them, like the touch of the Angel of Death sparing the chosen people while smiting the firstborn of Egypt. For someone who disavowed any attachment to biblical religion, I was deeply immersed in the imagery of the Old Testament. I learned what an "intellectual discussion" meant in the Ivy context, corresponding with my buddies and favorite girls and boasting of the rarefied atmosphere at places like the Elizabethan Club, to which I was occasionally invited for tea and impossibly precisely arranged little cucumber sandwiches. I went to lectures, acted as if I understood Arnold Toynbee's theories, cheered on the socialist Norman Thomas, and booed William F. Buckley, Jr., who later opened the world of national journalism to me. I tried to like Ravi Shankar's sitar concerts, and I went to every foreign movie playing in a dingy Yale basement for the delectation of would-be aesthetes. I joined Mory's—"to the tables down at Mory's, to the place where Louie dwells," as the Yale Glee Club song imprinted those lyrics on my wannabe mind. Mory's is a just passable eating club whose only requirement for membership is being or having been at Yale.

I shined in English, French, history, philosophy, and psychology, and while I was still lost in a fog in terms of my sexual orientation, my confidence in my academic abilities was from that point never challenged. I made new friends and visited Arthur Lederman at Princeton, and he visited me at Yale: two gay men who didn't know we were gay and in whose discussions the topic never arose. Like my friends, once in a while I dated girls from the fancy girls' schools whom we met at mixers designed for freshmen, but never the local girls at Albertus Magnus College, since they were "townies" and were beneath us masters of the universe. I railed against Yale prep snobbishness but was every inch the incipient snob myself. My mother, shrewder sometimes than I gave her credit for, remarked after my freshman year that "David was such a nice boy before he went east and turned into a Yalie!"

In my wretchedly battered dorm, "filthy" Farnum, on the Old Campus, the freshman preserve, I had two roommates: Fred Meine, who got ulcers within weeks and whom we visited in the hospital and gave blood to, and John Edmund (Jack) Lund II, who was possibly a fine lad, though more of a hick even than I; he believed that "pseudo" was pronounced "pih-swaydo," and this gaffe was the kiss of death in our ever-so-

sophisticated eyes. In the suite across the hall in our first-floor entry was a handsome oddity, Harry—of much money, we assumed—from San Francisco, who used to clean his electric shaver in the living room squatting naked over a waste bucket, a singular detail that, aside from his blond iciness and nearly complete disinclination to speak with the rest of us, is all that remains of old Harry in my memory. Harry's roommates included my two closest pals that first year and thereafter. One was the inimitable Boyd Murray, an athletic and fine-looking Presbyterian from Beaver, Pennsylvania, who in our sophomore and junior years, when we shared a bedroom, rarely let a morning go by without descending from his top bunk, puffing himself up and commanding me to marvel at his magnificence. I was flustered, of course, but Boyd was so totally insouciant and so confident of his 100 percent American maleness—you could be completely heterosexual in those days and make a joke like that with nobody thinking anything was out of place—that soon enough I was concocting witty insults to cast at my friend's only half-joking self-admiration. Harry's third roommate was my other best pal, Jon Paul Johnson, then known as JP, now as Paul, who was as much a bookish nerd as I and whose parents were our constant hosts in Darien, Connecticut. We kidded the first time I visited his home town that since *Gentlemen's Agreement,* a modern classic about anti-Semitism, had been set in Darien, maybe I should hide my nose as we drove into town.

We lived in the untroubled Era of Ike. We knew our place in the world would be secure because we were Yalies, ever so much superior to other, lesser Ivy Leaguers. Fred joined a fraternity, the Fence Club, and gradually drifted away, though we remained cordial. Boyd became a singer in the Augmented Seven, one cut below the august Whiffenpoofs, and he dated every beautiful girl on the East Coast, finally marrying his high school sweetheart, Brenda. Paul and I spent about an hour every evening getting burgers and shakes at a nearby bar and grill, George and Harry's, and in those ancient days of no meat on Fridays for Catholics, we often went out to have spaghetti at some New Haven restaurant. I had feared that leaving my Minneapolis friends would open up an impossible emptiness, but soon enough I was spending less time writing to my hometown pals than at the beginning of my freshman year, and Ricky, whom I fully expected (at least on some fanciful level) I would marry, occupied fewer moments of thought. Eventually she met and married another David—I couldn't resist kidding her about that: you'll never call him by the wrong name, I chided her—and my final efforts to get her not to do so and to wait for me were halfhearted and, of course, futile.

I was weaning myself of my boyhood home, living in my mind as well as my body in the East, hovering on the brink of a dramatic exploration, however tentative at first, of my sexual nature. On vacation in Minnesota, I was edgy, irritable, no longer interested in stamps or rocks or painting pictures, not much help around the house, though Clara and my grandmother and mother probably noticed few specific differences in my behavior and my father and I were, as always, cordial but not intimate. I joined a gym in Minneapolis to keep the body I had been working on at Yale in some kind of shape, and I began during the summer of 1960 to observe that some of the muscleheads at the gym were pleasing to look at. But I missed college, spent a great many hours studying the subjects I had decided to take in junior year, and spent many more hours just sunbathing on the back lawn of the suburban house to which my family had moved, idly thinking. I was aimless in my interior life, a dynamo in the world of academe, puzzled by the ineffable longing that was lingering tantalizingly around me.

In my sophomore year I bit the bullet and elected to major in Japanese. I had tried French as a freshman and loved it, but even with the passage of two years since my summer in Fukui prefecture in Japan, my interest hadn't waned. So I began three intensive years of Japanese at Yale, a major then regarded by most people as ridiculous and one that is undeniably among the hardest on earth. The boy contrarian evidently never quite got over the tendency to do the unexpected. Fred was the scientist, Boyd bathed himself in English and singing, in poker and girls, Paul headed into the thickets of history in preparation for law school, and I gave my life to Japanese, not insignificantly to the amusement of my roomies, confirming their suspicion that I was more than a little daft. When they ran out of other things to say, they teased me about my vastly popular major—we numbered four Japanese studies majors out of four thousand undergraduates—and said that I would end up no good if I didn't return to my senses and major in something practical. I even dated a Japanese graduate student a few times; I was a multiculturalist (of a very superficial sort) before it was fashionable, though Keiko must have sensed that I was dating her for learning, not yearning. I didn't put the data together and face the now obvious fact that I was looking for love in all the wrong places. A few years after college, two or three friends from those days said that they had tried to signal something to me of our shared sexuality, but the signals were way too subtle for me. In some areas, everything was too subtle for me.

Almost every teenager who moves beyond his comfortable high school years, facing either the dreaded thing, a job, or college, faces problems of adjustment. Sex is invariably a part of the transition, both sexual acts themselves and one's emotional reaction to them. For those who are uncertain about their sexuality, or certain but in denial, the world presents a picture of limitless options, enticing opportunities. At Yale I tried to be a scholar, a bon vivant, a do-gooder, and straight, meaning not becoming what I was convinced I was. I eagerly welcomed my pals' offers to help me learn to handle booze, and I even ventured to begin a sport. The proximate cause of my choosing the sport I did was entirely unaware of his influence on me during one of the weirdest occasions of my first freshman week.

We were all assembled at Payne Whitney, the gymnasium that looks from the outside like a medieval fortress, and required to strip to our birthday suits and line up to be measured for some semi-scientific (or quackish) notion of the moment that body types were somehow related to academic achievement. This may have been a spin-off of the somatotyping craze, but whatever its purpose, I couldn't have cared less. What I did care about was the humiliation of standing in this bare-ass line of one thousand eighteen-year-olds, feeling, as many others must have felt as well, inferior when contemplated in a throng containing many real beauties, many jocks, many terrific physical specimens. One of these guys started talking to me—I was eating him alive with my eyes—and casually let drop that he had fenced "at prep." Well, since part of the reason I had chosen Yale was because Peter Martin (and, I hoped, lots of Peter Martin–like fellows) was at Yale, maybe I should emulate this Apollo, this fencer, and take a stab at it.

I needed something to enhance my self-esteem, even though I had bulked up a bit owing to my weight-lifting regimen back home. I needed something that would be so indubitably Ivy League, so demonstrably a sport that no one at North High could do, that I convinced myself on the spot to become a fencer. The coach oohed about my left-handedness—I write with my right but do "athletic" things, if you'll pardon the expression, with my left—and painted seductive pictures of me as an Olympian fencer, gold medals being my reward for my unique skills and his brilliant coaching. My own fantasy was even wilder: I would enter the elevated fraternity of fencers, perhaps suffering one of those attractive scars on the face from some übermensch Hans or Dieter or, who knows, another Peter Martin. I truly had seen too many movies by then.

But this Technicolor wide-screen fantasy first had to slide by a couple of obstacles, not least among them the question of whether I really had the right stuff for the sport. All of us had to pass a number of tests at the gym during our freshman year or keep trying, three times a week, every week, and I came up against a wall: I couldn't pass the broad jump, try as I might. After a month, while I tried to learn fencing and also had to turn up for my thrice-weekly futile jumping, the gym instructor dispatched me to one of the school psychiatrists. I knew *something* was in my head, something driving me into overwhelming confusion about sex, but the *broad jump?* My dreams of a gold in fencing at the next Olympics vanished, and my fears that I'd flunk out of Yale if I did both the gym ordeal and fencing led me to drop the fencing. I never passed the broad jump, so the combination package I had envisioned during orientation week—trying to become a jock, trying to bloom as a scholar, trying to be like the naked freshman who fenced "at prep"—broke apart. I had to face the fact: I wouldn't be a jock, I would never look the Ivy League preppie part. I clung all the more to my books, and gradually eased myself into doing good by involvement in politics.

My strong liberal leanings, which had directed me into activities such as the Junior United Nations during high school, impelled me into similar activities at Yale; I even started working with a do-gooder club advised by the Reverend William Sloane Coffin, an ultra-liberal ahead of his time, and made one of my crusades the conversion to liberalism of any nonliberal who dared cross my path. My one bit of actual doing good instead of just prattling about it came when the first student march on Washington for civil rights was announced, during the early spring of 1959. I had joined the National Association for the Advancement of Colored People and found myself living up to an expectation, clearly implied, of my fair-minded mother. This may be apocryphal, and I wasn't old enough to recall the incident, but family lore has it that when we lived in Macon, Georgia, in 1943, my mother one day decided that she should sit in the back of the bus, with me in tow, with the Negroes, who were there not by choice but by regulation and segregationist custom.

Whether the tale of Doris Brudnoy and the Georgia bus is fact or fiction, I was raised in a household in which bigotry of any sort was avowedly rejected. The lesson I learned from my father, who simply never spoke disparagingly of any race or religion, and from my mother, who explicitly expressed her feelings about those bigotries, was that a decent person should believe in equality and work to help America achieve it. In the years just following the Supreme Court's *Brown* v. *Board of Education of Topeka, Kansas, et al.* ruling, and close upon Rosa Parks's refusal to move to the back of a bus, collegians, even at almost lily-white Yale (my freshman class had precisely one black member), were beginning to acknowledge some of the realities easily enough ignored by whites but never forgotten by black people. I wanted to do something real, not merely talk the talk of racial harmony—something that went beyond having had a few black friends in high school. By joining the

NAACP and trying to sign up my fellow Yalies for the organization, I made a start. I got a few boys to pay the dollar enrollment fee, and one day a kid came and signed up his pal, one Morgan. The next day Morgan, who was a sophomore, I think, came by, smilingly said that I could keep the goddamn dollar and give it to the goddamn organization if I wanted, but that he was of *the* Morgan family—the name didn't register, but later I learned of its distinguished southern provenance—and that his daddy would whup his hide if he found out that he had joined the goddamn NAACP.

With a bunch of Yalies and local black kids, I went to Washington by bus and, filled with righteous indignation about segregation and the generally woeful state of American race relations, marched alongside the thousands who came to be seen, to be heard, and, as Quakers put it, to witness. I carried the Yale banner with a black girl from New Haven, and we experienced cheers from some bystanders and jeers from others. We felt important and benevolent, our bodies on the line—this was a common delusion, that marching was almost as valiant as risking death at the hands of bigots in the heart of Dixie—and I was chock full of my sense of virtue. I easily found satisfaction in becoming somewhat more involved with political matters, more passionate in the expression of my views, but for reasons I still don't fully understand, I found myself increasingly turned off by demonstrations, marches, crowds, mob scenes. I discovered that I had a knack for explaining things in speeches, in my teaching, in the articles I later wrote by the thousands, and on radio and TV. Sometimes I've doubted my integrity in this regard, wondering if while I felt I was doing my part by writing and speaking my beliefs, I was really just lazy, somehow antisocial, more than willing to let others tromp around the streets carrying banners while I sat comfortably in front of a typewriter or microphone or camera.

I had been active in civic organizations during high school, but that pond was small and I was effortlessly one of its big frogs; at Yale, I was just one of many people who had the desire, and to some extent the skill, to put values into practice. My instinctive reticence had been chipped away at for years; I no longer needed to be the jokester and leader of the prank brigade in order to know that people would pay attention to what I had to say. Along with that sense of confidence, which is all to the good, came another ingredient, not unequivocally commendable—namely, a sense that I was above the crowd, that I marched to my own drummer and didn't need to march literally with others. Movements, no matter how virtuous their causes or how zealous their activists, frequently tear themselves apart, splinter into factions, betray the entirely human but not necessarily admirable tendency to substitute ego for energy. I have ego enough for two, or for three, but maybe I was just validating that old joke about not wanting to be a member of any group that would have me. I wish I had had a less ungainly, more convincing grasp of my own nature in this regard during those bright college years. Sex wasn't the only murky spot in my life.

The last night of our freshman year, Boyd and Paul and I decided to give ourselves an adventure, just the ticket for me and Boyd, always ready for anything, though Paul, less adventuresome—*saner,* we might say—had to be convinced. We met at eight and parted, each determined to find some new experience, then report back to our rooms at midnight. I wandered aimlessly, but my ambling brought me no adventures at all. Wearily heading back to our dorm, I came up to the New

Haven green and was about to cross the street when a little VW drove by me, circled back, pulled up beside me, and came to rest. A man leaned out the window and asked me if I wanted a blow job. I had no idea what a blow job was. "What do you mean?" I said, or something equally to the point. He explained, whereupon I said—I'm not making this up—"Why would anyone want to do *that?*"

Sophomore year was marked by a scandal that drew national attention. A local girl named Susie was given a telephone of her very own by her parents. Thus equipped with the pre-Internet device for "on-line" dating, Susie began calling Yale boys, whom she identified by our phonebook addresses: such and such Yale Station. This imaginative schoolgirl started an after-school extracurricular activity of stopping by the rooms of these lucky Yalies and giving them what the man in the Volkswagen had offered to give me. The term "blow job" was joined by another, "cocksucking," which I also didn't really understand. We tended to call each other cocksuckers, but that meant as much to most of us as "motherfucker," another term that didn't compute for me. You can take the boy out of Minnesota . . .

Predating Heidi Fleiss by three decades, Susie kept a diary of her doings, with names, dorm room numbers, and times, all featured soon enough in the *New Haven Register,* as her folks not only complained to the university but exposed her explicit notations to the masses' craving for details: "Dentist at 3:15, Billy Prepdoll at 4:30." The notoriety drove Susie and her hapless parents out of town, but not before the Yale radio station began playing songs like "Blow the Man Down" and something from Eddie Cantor, if memory serves, about the wonders of a girl named Susie. While Susie and her family slunk away, the ever-ready, ever-randy Yalies whom Susie had named in her diary were "asked" by the university to take a year's leave. The rich ones went to Europe for their grand tours; the others went wherever nonrich Yalies implicated in such bizarre scandals go. To the best of my knowledge, they all returned the next year, graduating one year later than their class, their lives none the worse for *l'affaire Susie*.

My mother, the village prude, was so offended by the Susie scandal that when Yale's president, A. Whitney Griswold, went to Minneapolis to give a speech, she boycotted it as her own way of expressing displeasure at the fleshpot that Yale obviously had become, or, she hinted, perhaps always had been. A fallout of the Susie episode was that our visiting rules, which had been liberal up to that point, including being able to invite girls into our rooms at any time (not that we had many to choose from, except on weekends), were curtailed. Years elapsed before this tragic event was forgotten, and then suddenly Yale admitted girls and the student dormitories became coed and the sexual revolution, for better or worse, charged across college campuses throughout the land. I only know that for me, the term for what Susie did to and for the boys, like the term used by the man in the VW, seemed like vocabulary from a strange planet. Would I ever come out of the closet? *Any* closet?

THREE

At Last, Love

School was study and do-gooding and parties and learning to drink. As a kind of vulgar centerpiece of our sophomore suite in Timothy Dwight College (colleges are the Yale equivalent of Harvard's houses), my roommates and I installed a bar that we had picked up for a few bucks and shellacked until it glistened. Facing this hick from the sticks now crawling into Yalie shoeness, or an approximation thereof, was amusing for my friends, instructive for me. They taught me to drink the cocktail of choice in those days, 7-Up and Seagram's Seven, and I began what I was sure was another stage in becoming a man, though I was prone to tossing my cookies most of the time. I kept trying to repeal the laws of nature, at least the law that says if you overindulge in booze on a more or less empty stomach and you're a complete neophyte in everything alcohol-related, your body rebels. When I wasn't studying or doing good, I could be found lingering hopefully along the sidelines of life, glancing at

69

handsome classmates, wishing that someone would drag me into the arena of action.

I went to New York on occasion with Paul or other friends and roamed through Greenwich Village, expecting to be struck by Sophistication Lightning. If not quite a poster boy for retroactive virginity, I was nonetheless going nowhere in my development as a sexual being. We went to folk music clubs, we ambled along the avenues, we ate on the cheap and stayed at the Biltmore Hotel on Forty-second Street, which then had a ten-dollar-per-night student rate. But nothing happened. My many weekends in New York didn't propel me into anything but a kind of tedium: the Village people seemed in their way as regimented as we Ivy guys, just wearing different uniforms. Back at school I learned that I could speak Japanese best when I was drinking or after I had drunk way too much, and that if I could down enough booze quickly enough, I could almost enjoy the dates I had with the girls we imported from the women's colleges. I could also suffer through the freezing afternoons watching football at the Yale Bowl best if I was tanked. These are not the confessions of an alcoholic, only a reference to the inescapable fact that one of the major ingredients in college life back then was alcohol, the more the better. I hadn't yet heard of marijuana or cocaine, and this was before LSD and Quaaludes or today's designer drugs as standard accompaniments to all-night parties. Save for drinking, we were babes in Ivyland.

Art and I saw each other when he came up to Yale or I went to Princeton when our schools were engaged in the ritual worship of the pigskin. Arthur and I hadn't yet talked about homosexual sex, but we had begun to make cruel remarks about those whom we took to be homosexual, whether primarily to appear cool or to distance ourselves from what was lurking in our own futures, I don't know. We double-dated in Princeton one weekend, and after the football game, as we were ambling back to Arthur's dining club, he began to rib my date, or maybe it was his, who was a descendant of Ralph Waldo Emerson. For some reason, though it was unmentioned in any biography of Emerson, we were convinced that the great Transcendentalist and scold had been a "queer," and we made much merriment out of that. Did we know then that we were resisting what was dawning on both of us? Having no understanding of our sexuality, we made sport of what we feared most. The girls were outraged, Arthur and I were ridiculous in our jibes, the weekend was a flop. Just trying to live up to the image of every college boy as a stud was chore enough. It's good training, I suppose, getting the hang of pretending to be interested in people in whom one isn't interested—sort of a preparation for faculty meetings or getting along swimmingly in business, or life for that matter, simply by learning to act interested in dates when the truth was hovering just offstage, waiting for somebody to put on the footlights and get this show on the road.

In the last days of my junior year I experienced a fit of unreasonable, idiotic fury when Boyd let a friend whom I happened to loathe use our suite while he finished his exams—but neglected to tell me about this before going home. All of a sudden here was this Neanderthal, this slob, and I was furious that my expected three days of quietude were ruined by his presence. When we all returned for senior year, I refused to speak to Boyd. I literally would not acknowledge him. A combination of pride and shame turned my vigil into an entire year of silence. Paul thought that I was going nuts, and Boyd, who tried to kid me out of my resolute silence, was first angry, then hurt, then accepting of whatever it was that had turned his jovial pal into a sphinx. The awkwardness, entirely manufactured and nurtured by me, was all-consuming. Our suite comprised two bedrooms, one shared by Boyd and Paul, the other mine alone, and our communal living room, in which on many nights the three of us sat as if in the tomb. I think that I had an unacknowledged yearning for Boyd and opted to cast this pal, who had never been anything but flawlessly collegial (and more, loving) toward me, out of my life rather than come to grips with my feelings. The silence while living in the same suite was improved only when Boyd married and moved with Brenda into a nearby apartment. Fred had moved to a single the previous year, thus leaving Paul, who by then had stopped trying to get me to see reason and stop acting like a fool, and me, each the possessor of a tiny bedroom and jointly of a living room in which we studied or at least opened books and moved our eyes across the pages.

Such was my self-punishment, a self-righteousness of biblical proportion, to abandon a true friend, who I am certain now loved me as a brother and who meant no harm to me or to anyone by letting a friend stay in our rooms. Part of coming out, I have learned the hard way, is accepting one's own desires and confronting them. Had I been more aware of the extent of my sexual orientation, which by then was impossible to deny but easy enough to shove into a corner of my mind, I might have been able to laugh off Boyd's act of kindness to his buddy and its irritating effect on me, kidded him about his macho posturing, and gotten a life.

Finally, in my senior year, I fell in love, or at least moved in that direction. But before that relationship changed my life and brought me at last to accept what I was and make the best of it, I had a brief interlude in New York, not quite like my San Antonio adventure, but a turning point, *the* turning point. A hooker in Texas was one thing, an accepted rite of passage for a young American male, but engaging in a homosexual encounter in Gotham was quite another: the act was illegal; people like that were pariahs. Maybe I would end up as another statistic in the city, which was just then experiencing a growth of seemingly inexplicable crimes—another body in a garbage can, young white male, no known motive.

On previous overnight trips to Manhattan, my friends and I invariably had stayed at the Biltmore, and often we passed nearby Bryant Park, just behind the New York Public Library. No one had said anything to me about that or any other park in the city, but I took careful notice of men ambling into Bryant, and out, and back in, and the thought dawned: maybe parks were places to meet a date? Perhaps this was an ideal place to get my first actual sexual act with a man over and done with. I was right, though the initial encounter was not the stuff of which romance novels are made. I stood by a pillar in the park while a tall, thin, grungy young man holding an artist's portfolio stood on its other side, and we sidled toward each other, a slow-motion inching of our way, finally touching hands, then having some trite conversation: Come here often? Wanna come up to my place? I mean my hotel? I mean my hotel room?

The initial encounter was ludicrous, but the actual sex was worse. I won't swear that my heart was in my throat or that my heart, wherever it was located then, was actually thumping wildly, but I was scared, and I was excited. When we got to my room, the young man deposited his portfolio in the corner and ripped off his clothes—he was skinny, all bones and angles and paleness—and I peeled off my own clothes, though more slowly. I was desperately anxious for the event to occur, but I wanted it to last. Whereupon my deliverer from virginity simply turned me over on my belly and did to this inexperienced

Yalie what that position implies. No lubricant, no caressing words, no foreplay, no riff on seductive rhetoric ("Oh, baby, you are so nice, let me show you the ways of the world"), nothing but a short, silent series of in-and-outs, and he was done. By "silent" I mean that he literally said nothing; I groaned, with pain and fear, and whimpered, with a sense almost of unbearable shame. How had I let myself sink to this? I hurt, I felt a fire (but not the fire of carnal bliss) in my loins, but I was too petrified by the realization of what I was doing to say anything, even while my brain was screaming at me to stop. I figured that if this was what homosexual sex amounted to, then it wasn't necessarily the thing for me, and in any case I wasn't going to let this cadaverous young man see my tears. Though he filled the role I had envisaged for him, albeit with none of the romance I expected, he was into his jeans and out the door in thirty seconds. I hobbled to the shower for the longest, most vigorous cleansing of my life, deeply upset by the act itself, by the rawness I felt and the mess I discovered on the sheets and on myself. I was joyful for a few minutes at the beginning, able for the first time in my life to caress a man, to feel his parts, his limbs, even his doltish face, but the prelude was so brief and the fucking itself so nasty, I needed many minutes to wash that episode off my body and out of my mind. Yet even hating what he and I had done, I still had quick flashes of a kind of pleasure because of the touching, and a bit of pride came into me simply because I had had the balls to pick him up in the first place. "Conflicted," I think, is the word for my combination of reactions. I knew what I didn't want to do again and also that I would certainly try some variation on the theme sometime, maybe soon. I felt soiled, abused, frightened, but I also felt a tingle, a wave almost of satisfaction that I had done what I set out to do and now I had the option to do it again and again.

74

Naturally I didn't tell a soul, just tried to block the experience from my mind, a futile task. However, I couldn't incorporate that passionless deflowering in the Biltmore into my self-image, even though I could no longer pretend to myself that my attraction to males was entirely an aesthetic appreciation, or twist reality around to wipe that slate clean, or simply rewind my life, as I would rewind a tape recorder, and start all over again. I had crossed a barrier, and all I could do was plow more energetically into my books, drive myself to a socially acceptable frenzy trying to master the Japanese language, and go on my nightly burger and milkshake run with Paul. I had left the closet, but I felt as if I stood in an isolation booth, like those then popular on TV quiz shows, completely alone but in full view of the world.

A few months after my evening at the Biltmore, I found myself on the train to New York again, alone. I wasn't planning another incident like that one, though the thought that maybe *something* might happen wasn't far from my thoughts, either. I was at the tail end of my junior year, nearly twenty-one, still looking for adventure in all the wrong places. More than once I've found that when you're not on the prowl, your chances of finding someone often improve, and that day was no exception. I heard a voice that attracted me even before I saw the young man's face—each word as if in some honeyed bell jar, phrasing things just so. I didn't look in his direction right away, which would have required turning around in my seat, but I kept listening to that voice, as of some ethereal being, soft, luxurious. Finally I approached the boy whose voice had already seduced me. We recognized our Yale connection and took to each other immediately. He was Stephen, he told me, Stephen Holden, a name that evoked Holden Caulfield in *Catcher in the Rye,* and though the parallel stopped with the name, a tingle of

75

expectation, not precisely delineated, struck me, and I wondered. But wondering is all I did during our brief encounter. We were soon gone for the summer, and only in the next year did we begin hanging around together. On the train I knew only that I had met a young man whom I wanted as a friend; nothing hinted to me that he was gay, nor to him that I was or was about to be. Stephen told me later that at that time he actually believed that he was the only one of his kind, as he put it, at Yale. I was a shade less unknowing than he, but I hadn't yet gotten any vibrations from any student—unlike the explicit invitation from the man in the Volkswagen—that gave me hope that one of my peers would lead me by the hand, gently and wisely, into the world I figured was intended for me.

In the summer after I met Stephen, I lived with Arthur in New York and dipped more confidently into the world of sex with men. I worked as a drone at Dancer-Fitzgerald-Sample, then the eighth largest advertising agency in the world, doing nothing more significant than media and market research and concluding once and for all that if this was business, I was right to plan a career in academe. The job, stupefyingly dull though it was, nonetheless gave me ample time to learn the ways of the world, which in its gay aspects meant that youth and good looks generally trumped any other attribute, though having money didn't hurt, either. I found the bars and streets where any personable young man could glance at somebody and within minutes have a "date." This was not an age of fear of random violence or of obsessed gay-bashers picking up homosexual men and slaughtering them for fun. However, this was the better part of a decade before the great turning point, the Stonewall (bar) riots, in which homosexuals resisted police arrest and harassment and fought back, gathering steam and inspiring the creation of the gay analogue to the black civil rights movement. Gay life was covert, and those who most vigorously disapproved were by and large ignorant of the whereabouts of gay men and, like Queen Victoria, couldn't even imagine that such a thing as a gay woman existed.

In the summer of 1961, Arthur and I lived just above Spanish Harlem, came and went at any time of the night, and felt no danger around us. Sexual encounters were as easily arranged as the daytime routine of the job. Nine to five I was the Ivy guy all spiffed up in a dull suit, rep tie, cordovan shoes, briefcase at hand, a clone among clones. At night my cloneness merely entailed a change of clothes, not really of attitude. I did my job efficiently; I came to do my cruising efficiently too. I abandoned the revulsion toward homosexual sex brought on by my brief interlude with the scarecrow from Bryant Park and discovered that at worst, most of the men I met were boring, not indifferent, and on many occasions I found myself in good company. One fellow, bearing one of those triple-barreled names with numbers following in its wake—II or III, I think— was so elegant that sex with him resembled a social occasion. We stayed friendly for years, this WASP princeling and I, as I did with a few others. I was beginning to integrate my lusts into my life, locating and cultivating attractive men of roughly my own age who had something to say before and even after sex, minds that didn't make me want to rush away. Poor Arthur was slaving away, often at night as well as day, as an elevated gofer at the American Field Service—his generous payback to the organization that had sponsored our summer in Japan— while I, with all my evenings free, was exploring, studying the wide variety of natives whose tribe I was entering, whose strange customs (gay courtship rituals were a tad odd; at least, to me they seemed so) I was becoming adept at. I had met Stephen and thought about him now and then, not knowing or

77

even suspecting his homosexuality, simply recalling his gorgeous face, but my summer regimen was playtime; the love stuff was several weeks ahead.

When I returned to New Haven after my summer as a Mad. Ave. ad man (that's how we styled ourselves), I happily discovered that Stephen lived in a room one flight above me and one entryway over, a mere twenty feet or so away but through impassable walls. We were near but distant, and only gradually, as we began sharing meals, did our friendship mature. Finally, the eons of avoiding physical contact with anyone other than the usual one-night stands of my coming-out summer in Manhattan came to an end. We came back from dinner to my room (Paul was in Darien with his fiancée) and I put on a record— Odetta, if memory serves. I sat next to Stephen on the couch. Our hands touched, but we said nothing at first, and then out poured our desire and our fears, our happy confessions of having both been attracted on that train the year before. It was not as if at that moment a dam broke and the floods cascaded, or however these things are sometimes phrased. But we were literally shivering with the excitement of the touch; we were both starved for it, for a person to stroke, for an end to the wanting, the waiting. When I think back on it, I recall that we really didn't do much—no reworking of the Biltmore Hotel episode for me, nothing like the genuine sexual encounters that Stephen had experienced with others. But we were wrapped in each other's arms in a room in an establishment bastion of heterosexual America, feet away from people who we thought might want to pummel us if they knew what we were up to. It was delicious: the excitement, the forbiddenness of it, the sense that we now had in each other an ally against the presumed hostility of those around us—we were on a roll in our babbling about what the moment meant.

From that evening till the school year ended, we were together as much as possible. Such was the climate of ignorance about such things in those days that our roommates thought nothing of it: just another Yale buddyhood. Still, to be certain, we would leave separately for the train station and sometimes sit in different cars on our way to New York so that other Yalies wouldn't see us heading off to Manhattan together too often. We rarely had a place to be alone together at Yale; on the occasional weekend when all our roommates were away from New Haven, we made the most of it, but we never spent the whole night together in our college dorm. We did little more than hold each other and listen to music, but this was a time when most of us at Yale locked our doors infrequently; even the presence of a girlfriend inside was signaled simply by hanging a necktie on the doorknob. One night my door burst open and a neighbor bounded in, looking for something in Paul's room. Stephen and I were sitting in the dark, save for a candle, listening to romantic music. This obvious giveaway to our doings didn't mean a thing to the other guy; for all he knew, we were *studying* in the dark. A naiveté of such scope is hard to imagine today; in the beginning of the 1960s it wasn't extraordinary.

I spent a weekend at Stephen's parents' home in New Vernon, New Jersey, and took to them immediately. They almost defined a kind of unaffected WASP civility; I liked them enormously. In his room, inches from his parents, we delved a bit deeper into a less than skillful sexual relationship. Stephen said that while he was "poetic," I was "political," meaning that he lived for emotions and I for facts. Neither of us lived as models of perfected sexual intimacies, but we did live for each other. Only one nasty lout at school seemed to intuit something of what was going on between us, and though he said nothing specific, he stared menacingly at us and whispered the occasional "fruit" as Stephen or I, or both of us, passed by. I took my quiet revenge on this fellow by sidling up to him and his parents when they came for a visit, oohing and ahing about what a terrific son they had and how we were just as tight as ski boots. His parents beamed, and the poor, furious simpleton had to smile and agree that we were indeed bosom buddies.

Stephen and I went from feeling that we were a band of two in defiance (secretly, of course) against the world to joining up with several homosexual grad students, whom we met more or less by accident. We partied with these guys and through them met others, including a few faculty members. We were doing little that was literally sexual, but I was still reluctant to accept my feelings for Stephen without a struggle. Even before I took the plunge and met that young man in Bryant Park or went on my merry spree of activity during my New York City summer, I felt torn about entering the world I both wanted and wanted to deny. Entering it fully would make my self-delusions impossible, but failure to enter into it, knocking on the door of sexuality but just softly enough to keep from being admitted, would be torment. I was a mess, trying to put all these muddled contradictions into some perspective.

In the middle of my junior year I began weekly visits to one of the Yale psychiatrists, but all I could bring myself to say to this kindly, patient man, who had no doubt heard this tale or one similar to it a thousand times in his career at Yale, was that my eyes were increasingly fixed on handsome Yalies, to which the doctor replied that I shouldn't do anything about it and maybe it would all pass in time. (That was the epitome of psychiatric theorizing about homosexuality at the time, at least at bastions of orthodoxy like Yale.) Then came buggery in the Biltmore and that train ride to New York when I met Stephen, and after three months of thinking about him over the summer, I now, at the beginning of my senior year, had a lover—a word that we began gingerly to use. I stopped going to see the shrink, in part, believe it or not, because I was convinced that *I* had failed *him.*

Stephen and I weren't notable achievers in bed, tending to what was then called the Princeton rub—I have no idea why that boys' school in New Jersey was saddled with the ridiculous term—which amounted to rubbing our bodies against each other until something erupted. None of this cocksucking for us, whatever cocksucking was—at least, not then. Stephen read his poems to me, I rambled on about the joys of studying odd languages, we exchanged glances when in company and found places to stay in Manhattan and went to foreign films and felt very adult, very *au courant,* very much men of the world. I met some of the people from his past, including his twin brother. Stephen actually *had* a past. While I was not his first lover, he insisted I was his best, which I sure hope meant a little more than what the working girl in San Antonio had told me three years before.

We were dear to each other, thoughtful, considerate to a fault, and while I was applying to graduate school, enjoying my evening burgers with Paul, and continuing my insane cold-shouldering of the blameless Boyd, Stephen was leading me into an acceptance of my sexual orientation. And for the first time in any relationship I had ever had, I was giving something valuable too: my devotion. I had been fortunate over the years in having good friends, supportive and loyal, but now at last I was able to add my body into the bargain, erasing the sole barrier that always had stood, and must now stand, between friends who were buddies and that rare friend who becomes what Stephen became to me. We were together sexually, together in our emotions. With Stephen I became a man in reality, not just chronologically.

The accepted view is that early sexual encounters these days come with less apprehension and less indecisiveness, owing to the varieties of support now available to youngsters inching their way out of the closet. Maybe, but I wonder. I know that in 1961 every step into that world of actualized sexuality was a giant one, every physical embrace a moment to remember. A young person's sexual orientation may well be, and I think probably is, indicated by genetic markers that science is only beginning to discern. Sexuality is certainly established early in childhood, if not in the womb, but the mind's acknowledgment and acceptance of that destiny is quite a different matter. It was for me, and for Stephen, and I would imagine for most, a dizzying voyage of discovery. I may have been more able than some boys to intellectualize what was happening in my life, and as a smart kid I naturally went off to the library and tried to read about myself or about people like me. But the relevant literature generally tended to describe homosexuality as a sickness, curable and in need of being cured, less a sin than an aberration, invariably a behavioral prescription for lifelong unhappiness. The most easily available books were enough to make you despise yourself.

American society, give or take a few exceptions—Walt Whitman could go on and on about his tenderly beloved wounded soldiers, and nobody quite got the point—portrayed the homosexual as a pervert and his behavior as loathsome. Save for specialists in sexology, who knew where to find alternate theories in scholarly literature, people easily came upon depictions of homosexuals that were vile. Stephen and I had a few friends who were gay, we could buck up each other's confidence by bold statements, but the environment in which we came out was not cordial to people like us. The dominant image of the ideal adult life was marriage: everything in our culture reinforces that, from the laws to the lowest detritus of pop culture. But since homosexuals cannot marry—just the current debate about it has taken on a revolting quality of hatred—they cannot enter into legally binding relationships. And since the male of our species, as of virtually all mammalian species, is biologically programmed to be a seed dispenser instead of a nester—in short, to perpetuate the species by promiscuity—the entire culture works against those possibilities for homosexuals that work so well to help heterosexual alliances bind into permanence. No wonder a society that disdains nonheterosexual behavior, that stigmatizes promiscuity in theory (though not necessarily in practice) as long as it's heterosexual, has erected a Catch-22 for gay people: you're despicable because you're promiscuous, but we certainly won't let you marry and have some social reinforcement for abandoning promiscuity.

In the early 1960s a young gay male had in a sense to invent himself, to draw boundaries and create behavioral patterns not out of a long and well-regarded tradition but out of the very act of coming to terms with his situation. We are none of us exact replicas of each other (however much, on an almost seasonal basis, the idealized look of the desirable gay man leads to flurries of imitation), but I've no doubt that many people are pretty similar to me, wanting, even perhaps needing, different experiences, different types of men for various parts of their lives. We are led by every signal along our way from infancy to the grave to apotheosize that one true love, but we are not allowed to solemnize that as heterosexuals can. We are betwixt and between, and even having, as I had, a Stephen to love couldn't be acknowledged beyond our small group of other outsiders. If the ppeal of variety, to put it politely, is powerful, the boundaries ut up by our culture almost propel us into promiscuity.

had experienced four fascinating years in New Haven; I had een on the dean's list seven out of my eight semesters, had graduated magna cum laude, and had been awarded a Woodrow Wilson fellowship, usable at any college, and a government fellowship to study "neglected" languages, to be used at Harvard only. But even after all the experiences that had certified my belongingness to myself and to others, I suspected that somehow I was a kind of imposter, someone who looked and sounded the part but really wasn't. Everything was coming to a close: Ricky had found her new David and she and I were just friends now, Stephen had his senior year yet to experience, and although I could have stayed in New Haven and used my Woodrow Wilson grant at the Yale Graduate School, I opted to go to Harvard. Granted, Harvard would add another feather to my academic cap, and even at age twenty-two I was beginning to think that if I was to have changes in my life, better to have them early, so now was the ideal time to move on. These rather amorphous and hardly conclusive arguments on behalf of going up to Cambridge instead of staying in New Haven seemed persuasive then, but I'm pretty sure now that I also sensed that Stephen and I had run our course—not as friends, which I knew we would be forever, but as lovers: I wanted new adventures, and Stephen probably wanted them too. With a callousness I had begun to recognize as one element in my being, I simply decided, announced the decision to Stephen, and that was that. Maybe he was relieved too. It's something we've never talked about. It's something we possibly were better off not talking about. I left. He stayed.

Once I decided, something about the prospect of either going back to Minnesota and then immediately returning to Yale for graduation or hanging around the college for several days between exams and the ceremonies unnerved me. I loved Yale, but I wanted to be done with it. And in my desire to cut the tie and move on to the next chapter in my life, I flat-out refused to give my mother and father the pleasure of seeing me participate in graduation. I was adamant about skipping the ceremonies, though I told my parents, with the snottiness that my mother had remarked on after I had been at Yale only one year, that *they* were perfectly free to go. I have occasionally awakened in the night from a bad dream about the wicked son who breaks his mother's heart; yes, this gets a bit purple. Still, it was I, not a creature in a dream, who denied his parents the chance to see their only child graduate from the university to which they had sent a rather substantial amount of money on behalf of that child's education. At best, I have tried to rationalize that selfish, even cruel behavior on my part as reflecting some desire, or need, to separate my family from what in my senior year I had become—a homosexual at Yale. But at worst—well, there is no limit to that particular worst. It was inexcusable, made all the worse by my forfeiture of three succeeding opportunities to remedy it: I went on to earn two master's degrees and a doctorate and proceeded to skip all three of those ceremonies as well. During my Yale graduation, I sat on the grass beside a Minneapolis lake while the ceremonies were carried on radio. Our speaker was President Kennedy, who said that day in June 1962 that now he had "the best of both worlds, a Harvard education and a Yale degree."

For graduation I got a car, my first, a little Buick Skylark convertible, a gift from my parents, who somehow forgave me in deed, if not in their expressions of annoyance, for cheating them of attendance. My parents, who were not poor by any means but were determined not to spoil me with things (they certainly spoiled me with their love), figured that I could live without a car during high school and college but deserved one as I headed off to graduate school. In those days a snazzy convertible cost about what a year of college cost—$2,800 or so—and the price was a bargain compared with subjecting themselves to a nonstop whine about how disadvantaged a carless David would be. With a car of my own I was suddenly liberated, and after having been home only a few days, I found my way into the gay scene. At a bar in downtown Minneapolis, the Gay Nineties (can you believe it?), I met a passable substitute for Stephen, a beautiful boy my age named Jim. I invited him home the next afternoon, and while my grandmother was upstairs doing whatever grandmothers do, Jim and I engaged in adolescent sexual groping in my downstairs room. Even the possible sudden return of my mother, who would as usual bound down the stairs to see what her darling was up to, didn't bring me to my senses. I wanted Jim then, there—to hell with discretion. Words having only the vaguest resemblance to reality in the vocabulary of horny young romantics, I swore eternal devotion to Jim, and he returned the oath of fealty. Stephen was in New Jersey and I was in Minnesota; what happened in Minnesota didn't violate what Stephen and I had, or so I told myself. The next night Jim and I drove to a well-known lovers' lane, where all of a sudden we were surrounded by cars filled with (I was convinced) rednecks and hooligans. This is the end, I thought. Jim insisted we just start kissing and pawing each other. They'll think I'm a girl, he said, and evidently they thought just that. We lived to laugh about it, but I almost swore off parks as the ideal locations for me to vent my sexual desires.

But I didn't learn that lesson well enough. Even while I was professing a kind of loyalty to Jim and believing that back east I would or at least might be loyal to Stephen, I was embarking on a path of experimentation. I had read too much Margaret Mead, about the polymorphous sexual practices of natives in the places she researched and the places she apparently imagined, and I became a kind of self-interested anthropologist of sex. I had read not quite enough of Voltaire, evidently, and took to heart his maxim "Once a philosopher, twice a pervert." I had been anally penetrated once, and that was it, forever. But what other intriguing things awaited me? My sole consideration, vis-à-vis my sex life, was enjoyment. One night I drove downtown to Loring Park, several beautiful acres just on the fringe of the business district, and picked up a short, wiry little fellow who seemed to be the soul of cordiality until we got to a deserted back street, whereupon he pulled out a pistol and claimed to hate people who were well hung, since he wasn't. Then he threatened to kill me. Even with my limited range of encounters, I could tell that he was neither particularly well hung nor extraordinarily bright. Fortunately, he bought my line about how his penis was just fine as it was, an ideal size, a splendid shape, complementary to his muscular, magnificent torso—boy, I sure wish I were built just like him! He calmed down, stopped whimpering, put his gun away, apologized, and asked me to let him off where we had met, and he was gone. So ended forever my adventures in parks. Unfortunately, that episode was not the last of my brushes with death owing to picking up the wrong person.

▢ ▢ ▢ ▢

In late June I left Minneapolis and Jim. I wrote him passionate letters but never heard a word back from him. I had been hired for the summer at Mt. Hermon School, a boys' prep school affiliated with the nearby Northfield School for Girls in an experiment that they called the Liberal Studies Program. My Yale years had disabused me of the myth that preppies were smarter than public school boys, but I was still captivated by the allure of these privileged bastions. Mt. Hermon is beautifully situated in the rolling hills of western Massachusetts. It is not in the first rank of what's called the "St. Grottlesex" schools—St. Mark's, Groton, Andover, Exeter—but it manifested a commendable belief in making boys into complete men. Each kid had to do physical work, at the school farm, primarily, and each was expected to participate in some sport, but none was demeaned if he wasn't an ideal jock. Chapel was compulsory, as were uniforms, and the dear lads were interchangeable in their politeness and generally WASP good looks. Prep school teachers, I learned, are a devoted lot, often impoverished unless they have inherited money, and for the faculty men at Mt. Hermon, the prospect of teaching a couple hundred public high schoolers who had been invited into the rarefied confines of a preparatory academy must have seemed rather like welcoming a boatload of illegal immigrants. At least one of the teachers spotted a kindred spirit my first day on campus and had me in his bed my first night. This was my first "older man," and I learned that night that I was desirable to people like him because I was young—it was as simple as that. Deriving only the most basic satisfaction from him, I also learned that if my sex partner wasn't roughly my age, bells didn't ring.

For me, the Mt. Hermon situation was ideal: I spent the summer at a junior version of Yale, I taught public school kids like myself (both sexes), I eased out of New Haven on my way to landing in Cambridge and Harvard, and I was trying out another possible vocation. In addition to my duties helping the senior teacher in our course, "The Asian Dilemma," I was a dorm counselor and was expected to sneak around at night with a flashlight and police the boys' rooms to make sure that they weren't still awake, reading or God knows what in their beds.

The boys came to me in my room to unburden themselves of deep secrets, which weren't significantly different from my own. I was, after all, twenty-two, and they were sixteen or seventeen, and in me they thought they were plugging into the wisdom of the ages. I told myself that if an older man like the Mt. Hermon English teacher who befriended me wanted me, fine, but I would never come on to a student, no matter how great the temptation. Still, I saw unmistakably why there are more than just a handful of gay Mr. Chipses out there in prep school land, teaching up a storm and pining away with desire for some handsome teenager.

All of the junior teachers were good sorts except for a couple of preppie snots who considered the rest of us below them. One of our cadre, Julie, a science major and one of the nicest, smartest girls I've known, bore the face of a Modigliani model—high color in her cheeks, almond eyes, sharp but appealing features—and she and I hit it off somewhat more intensely than was probably advisable. Nothing physical but something clearly emotional held us together, and most nights after the little darlings were presumably asleep, Julie and I and some of the other assistant teachers would drive down to the nearest roadhouse to drink and gossip. We were told by the school's headmaster that if we kept liquor in our rooms we would be cast out of Mt. Hermon heaven, like Satan paying for his disobedience to the Lord, and we took that to heart and did our drinking off-campus.

At the end of summer I went to Darien to usher at the wedding of my roommate Paul Johnson and his longtime sweetheart, Carole Maxwell. After the ceremony and reception, I returned to the Johnsons' house, where Julie called me and said that she had broken her engagement to the fellow she was to marry in a week. She didn't say then, nor did she ever say in so many words, that in addition to finding her fiancé less interesting than when she had become engaged, she was in love with me. We were of one mind about so many things, we had been almost an item at Mt. Hermon, and while I certainly didn't compare her to the boys and men who attracted me, I found her rare beauty compelling, her personality the most engaging of any girl I had ever met. Julie was at her grandmother's house in upstate New York and asked me to visit her on my way back to Minnesota. Of course I complied, and though Grandma naturally assigned me a room of my own for my stay, I thought that I wanted to sleep with Julie. I wanted more than just to touch her and kiss her and hold her. I was flattered by her attraction to me and mired in the transition from presumably "normal" to full acceptance of my homosexuality. Despite my wild nights in New York and back in Minneapolis and my romantic year with Stephen at Yale, I still felt that a regular heterosexual future might await me. We abided by the unstated but clear rules of Julie's grandmother, and we didn't go beyond a great deal of hugging. I know that Julie was the last woman I wanted to make love to, even though we didn't. But I am not sure that if we had been completely alone, with no impediment, stated or implied, I could have. The emotional, romantic instinct was vibrant, but the erotic desire was only vestigial.

90

□ □ □ □

After my visit to Julie's grandmother's house, I drove back to Minnesota. I stayed out of parks this time, tried to reconnect with Jim but failed, then drove back east to Cambridge, to Harvard. Julie moved to Cambridge too, as we had planned at Grandma's house, and this left me wondering about the prospects, however slim, that I could be for Julie what I felt I *should* be for Julie—a lover, perhaps a husband. I was excited by the idea of turning our summer's palship at Mt. Hermon into something much more, but I was worried too, afraid that I was leading her to thoughts about me that weren't very realistic, afraid once more that I was something of a fraud. I had become comfortable with, if not quite fully habituated to, my sexual orientation. Julie found a job with Dr. Watson, he of the double helix, and I settled in on Mellen Street to begin the program in East Asian studies, living with my Yale pal Karl Morris Nickel, who was enrolled in the art history department at Harvard. Since I was now the recipient of that federal grant to study neglected languages, Morris liked to joke that I was neglecting languages with great facility, but actually I was a devoted little grind and threw myself into my studies, and into dating Julie and hanging out with the Johnsons, who had also come to Cambridge.

I was finally at the world's greatest university, as it calls itself, studying advanced Japanese, learning about Asian art, history, and politics (some of it redundant after similar courses at Yale), and auditing courses in European and American history—trying to have it all, to learn everything I could, heading along a conventional career path straight to a professorship at some idyllic ivy-covered college. I spent no time looking for love—I told myself that I hadn't the time for that sort of thing—but I had Julie as my regular date, the Johnsons and Morris, and new friends too. I was coming into my own as a serious man, eyes on the prize. And then one night an event occurred that, like my time in Japan, changed my life yet again. His name was Paul Venable Turner, and he was Morris's classmate at the Fogg Museum, Harvard's center for art history studies. Paul came by to pick Morris up for an art department party and it was lust at first sight. I *knew* that I had to get to know this man; I *knew* that this stunning Paul Turner would return with Morris after their party, and I *knew* that I would be waiting with the proverbial bells on. I showered and dressed in what passed with me for a becoming outfit; I shaved till my skin squealed. I was ready for it, whatever "it" was going to be. I am only occasionally intuitive, but I had no doubt at all that evening that Paul Turner would be back at the end of the evening, with our mutual pal Morris Nickel unwittingly playing Cupid.

Paul did indeed return with Morris, and I began a lifelong friendship with the man who I *knew* was my destiny. Morris soon moved out of our Mellen Street apartment, reluctant to hang around with me too much since I was now living a life that he didn't approve of, at least then. After I tried out a few would-be roommates, all of whom seemed wrong for the part, Paul decided that we might just as well go the whole route. He moved in and we grew close, fast. We learned to cook—my early experiments with Morris hadn't been encouraging, but practice of course makes adequate, if not quite perfect. Paul was devoted to his studies, and to me; I, however, was the apex of a triangle entirely of my own making. I loved Julie—I know that that feeling was quite genuine. I even took her to Minneapolis for a long weekend, which was awkward for my parents, who were upset that she wasn't Jewish, riled that I had more or less decided to bring her without discussing the matter with them, and worried that appearances (their son and a girl in the same house for several days) would be scandalous. And I loved and was erotically in love with Paul, who very liberally tolerated the situation but hinted once in a while that I was both playing with fire and not playing fair with Julie. She was a woman of extraordinary intelligence, but she had been sheltered in her Christian Science upbringing and was not then, in her early twenties, capable of reading between the lines. Could she possibly have missed what was in the air between Paul and me? If she didn't miss it, why did she put up with it? We have seen each other recently and corresponded, and she's been as loving and supportive as I could have wished. I haven't had the guts, however, simply to ask her what she made of the Paul–Julie–David triad during the better part of an entire academic year.

For my part, I simply wanted Julie, on one level, and I wanted Paul, on another, and I had what I wanted for a considerable time. I sometimes think that without intending it, I was being cruel to a woman who deserved much better than I was giving her, and possibly I've repressed some episodes that might demonstrate that the arrangement worked less smoothly than I remember. The three of us went out together often; we painted Paul's and my apartment one weekend and trooped off to dinner afterward, paint-spattered and eager to drink vast quantities of wine. We were, I grant, an odd threesome, and that I felt now and again like a heel didn't mean that I stopped being one. I dated and loved Julie, I loved and was in love with and slept with Paul.

So it went with the three of us during those heady times in the seemingly bright new era ushered in by our bright young president, John Fitzgerald Kennedy. Paul and I did everything together—two bright, competitive young scholars living together and loving each other. Though we were both academic grinds, we immersed ourselves in as many of the opportunities that Cambridge offered as we found time for. We entertained our friends and they broadened our horizons; we criticized each other's papers and boasted of our accomplishments; we were scintillating (we liked to think that of ourselves), and we were up for anything. We hadn't a penny to spare, but we were charming, knowing, the inheritors of western civilization and destined to make our marks on it. If we were in fact somewhat less marvelous than we liked to think, we entertained our friends with our charades and our mimicries and (we thought) our superior wit. We were, in Paul Venable Turner's favorite word, fabulous.

He knew more than anybody I had met, he was more intense than any of my friends, and I was completely in love with him, so much so that I became undone by the merest scowl from him. I assumed that I had done something wrong if he showed even a tiny disinclination to talk when I wanted to interrupt our studies and chat. We had violently abusive arguments, verbal swordplay that took ages to heal. I was often incorrigibly dependent on him. I wanted him every minute of the day, except of course when *I* wanted to study. How Paul put up with me I'll never quite know. That Julie, whom I continued to date and who was truly the only young woman in my life, and Paul and Carole Johnson never realized or pretended not to realize what Paul and I were to each other amazes me still. I don't know how I kept all those balls in the air.

My need for Paul was all-consuming, and I was incapable then of coming to grips with my insecurities. I felt that I was funny-looking; I knew that Paul was beautiful. I felt that I was vastly inferior to him in intelligence, a plodder, not a long-distance runner with ideas; I was a person prone to wistfulness, who merely brought out sadness in this terrific man, this fabulous Paul. I couldn't take my eyes off him and felt abandoned, or nearly, when his eyes remained fixed on his books. We were at Harvard for study, to become great in our fields, but I wanted our study of each other to transcend all else.

In his consideration and wisdom, Paul concluded many years later—or at least told me his thoughts years later—that we were both too much the star, at least in our own minds, to work out an enduring relationship. As a japanologist and neophyte sinologist, I tended to see our problem as too much yang, not enough yin, at least in one of us, though Paul has always rejected that kitschy verbiage. Had one of us been passive or less demanding, the relationship might have worked for a much longer time. But we were both the center of attention in our own imaginings, and our connectedness was hampered by our individual need to be in control of things. I thought then that I was trying to defer to him whenever possible, but that too is a form of controlling behavior; maybe a psychologist would say that I was exhibiting passive-aggressive behavior, though I've never quite understood the concept. I adored Paul, he loved me, but in the final analysis we couldn't live together.

Paul urged me to consider moving to Boston while he remained in Cambridge during our second year at Harvard, then led me to a dozen or so of the godforsaken dungeons available on Beacon Hill and eventually found 69 West Cedar Street for me. He was right about that tiny apartment on the hill: it had charm, it was a block from the subway stop to Harvard, and it helped create a mental as well as a physical separation between me and Cambridge, which I identified with Paul. I didn't know exactly how I would function at Harvard while not living with him, and in an inchoate way I guess I was stumbling about trying to discover how or make the accommodation needed to continue my studies and resist becoming depressed about my separation from Paul. But that Boston apartment was filled with

Paul: he constructed a bookcase for me, nestled in an alcove in the tiny twelve-by-ten-foot bedroom-living room; he found an old desk, stripped it of its layers of guck, and finished it for me. He jerry-built a shower in my tub: the apartment was a tribute to Paul's ingenuity. I wasn't going to have a very easy time divorcing myself from him, no matter how much he tried to convince me that we would be better friends at a distance.

I was beginning to feel apprehensive about remaining at Harvard for several years more; Harvard was Paul. And I didn't want simply to run away. Maybe, I thought, I can find a cause, a validation for leaving Harvard, in something useful to others, not just something career-oriented like my graduate work. I briefly toyed with the idea of becoming a teacher of deaf children, but nothing came of that idea. Reluctantly, and with a definite sense that my second year at Harvard wouldn't be particularly gratifying, I went ahead with my work in East Asian studies.

Paul helped me move into my new apartment, though not before we spent a few final weekends together in Provincetown, at the tip of Cape Cod. We slept on the beach and made the most of the last days of summer. We knew that our affair was over but also that however much sense it made to go our separate ways romantically, we both would lose something. A chapter in our lives ended.

In my second year at Harvard I found out how easily a decent-looking young man, or maybe just a young man, period, could find sex partners. Living in Boston, I was near the center of that sort of thing and found comfort, if not romance, with a string of people my own age, though I pined for Paul and found myself thinking of getting back somehow with Stephen—a Paul before Paul—who had graduated from Yale and was immersing himself in publishing in New York City. Julie and I finally drifted apart; she moved away from Cambridge. And my studies, now of Korean as well as other aspects of East Asian culture, began to bore me. Or maybe I was unable to remain the happy camper living across the river from Paul, who was invariably considerate and kind to me but had found a new love of his own.

I decided that eighteen uninterrupted years as a student were maybe one or two too many, and I applied for prep school teaching jobs. One boasted of the Christian climate of its campus—just the thing to make me pass on the opportunity. I applied for a job at a Catholic women's college just north of New York City, Manhattanville College of the Sacred Heart, since I figured that teaching young women would be completely safe for me, a dose of abstinence. I also responded to an invitation from the Woodrow Wilson Foundation to enter a new program that sent northern grad students, largely but not exclusively white, to southern black colleges. When Texas Southern University offered me a job teaching history and directing its honors program, I decided that Houston was far enough from Cambridge to give me something to think about besides Paul, and that after six years in the Ivy League, spending time in the southland helping (as I saw it) my black brothers and sisters would be good for me and maybe good for them as well.

My last night in Boston brought Paul and me together for a final dinner and more than a perfunctory expression of our mutual affection. One of the guys I had met at Mt. Hermon School two years earlier was moving to Boston, and I arranged for him to take my apartment, asking only that if and when he decided to vacate, he would let me know first, so that if I wanted to come back to that place, which was so filled with

97

Paul, I could. As I left Paul and my tiny apartment and my life at Harvard and drove off to Texas, ready for whatever Houston would bring, I was tearful for miles and found myself listening at night to Boston radio station WBZ—an omen, perhaps, that one day I would wind up on that powerful station, whose signal, on 1030 AM, reaches parts of thirty-eight states once the sun goes down. WBZ accompanied me most of the way, as I clutched at the familiar sounds of Boston with its distaste for terminal *r*'s and *g*'s and the much parodied broad *a*'s of the Kennedys. What awaited me in Houston I could hardly imagine. I knew only that I would be miles from Paul, from the Ivy orbit, from the agonies of yet another East Asian language, and, sadly, from the Johnsons and Morris and Julie and a life that I had enjoyed but knew I had to put behind me.

Everybody my age remembers where he was when President Kennedy was murdered. I was in Korean class, and a messenger brought the news to us. Professor Edward Wagner paused for a moment and then directed us back to our Korean lesson, appropriately, I know, but painfully. I left class that late November day in 1963 and went to Paul's room in the grad dorm he had moved into, and we hugged and cried for the loss of our beautiful young president. I think that a plausible interpretation of our tears would also include a recognition of our own loss: we couldn't live together successfully, and we couldn't ever live entirely without each other, at least in memory and affection.

My mother, who said years earlier that I had been ruined by the temptations at Yale, never knew the half of it, but when I visited my parents briefly before that long, sad drive to Houston, she was good enough to sense my mood and be gentle with me. My parents always urged me to do what I thought best, and if I felt that my obligation now was to become a part of the new era of racial change in America, so be it. My dad had occasionally said that when we lived in Macon and San Antonio before he went away to the war, he and my mother had seen clearly how wretched the lot of blacks was. Possibly some of my social activism in college, in graduate school, and in Texas the next two years derived from a mother and father who exuded a passion for justice. I am a quick study in some areas, if not in the long process of recognizing, accepting, and functioning in the sexuality that nature intended for me, but I absorbed many things, primarily values, from my father, mother, and grandmothers.

I thought of the president's death nine months later as I drove from Boston to Houston, worried about the challenge, miserable because of my separation from Paul, despairing that death, which was so cruel as to have taken JFK from us, was so arbitrary, so sudden, inescapable. A person of exceedingly conservative temperament, I was never happy about changes and wanted then, as I do now, for things to remain as they are. They couldn't, and the drive to Houston awakened the inescapable knowledge that change is the real permanence.

FOUR

To Dixieland

Cruelties, those committed against yourself as well as those inflicted on others, are difficult to forget or forgive. Few people manage to avoid being cruel at some time, and while I've not been a particularly cruel person, I have keen memories of the times I have smashed into the lives of others. For instance, I still vividly recall a day when I had been arguing with the daughter of one of the city's Orthodox rabbis, and in a rage—over what issue I have no recollection—I grabbed a book, excerpts from the Torah, from her hand, and I flung it down on the sidewalk. In all the memories of my childhood that remain with me still, I have none other in which I was beastly (or even just bullying) to a girl. She bravely held back her tears, reached down for the book, brushed the dirt off its cover, returned it to the side of her hip, and walked away, never to speak to me again.

Why that incident stays with me I don't know, but I reimagine it in my mind's eye whenever some similar act of intolerance or disdain comes before me. Now and again a group of AIDS activists will make news by jeering at newly ordained seminarians or tossing condoms at priests in their churches. I find myself infuriated, not at their passionate concern for what matters to them and certainly matters as well to me but at their cruelty in offending the most deeply held sentiments of the people whom they taunt and the faith they mock. I still shudder to think that my first deliberate act of cruelty was that desecration of my schoolmate's book of sacred writings. Likewise, I still recall the less calculated but unquestionably hurtful way I shut Boyd Murray out of my life. I went far beyond a fit of pique; like some Old Testament prophet issuing jeremiads to the disobedient Hebrews or like God inflicting torments on his rebellious people, I cast him out of my life, banished him from the golden rays of my being, deprived him of my friendship and me of his, a double stupidity on my part and a cruelty I cannot forget.

However, it wasn't until my arrival in Houston that I committed my third act of cruelty, the one that affected the most people and to this day causes me a certain amount of shame. I found a decent apartment and entered immediately into my duties in the classroom and as the new director of the honors program at Texas Southern University. Upon taking possession of the honors program, its office, and its records, I just went through the college grades of all the students in the program and, without so much as an interview or a discussion with my senior colleagues, dropped from the program those students whose grades weren't up to my sense of what acceptable grades were. I didn't ask anybody about the students' attitudes or ambitions or the circumstances that might have contributed to their low grades. I simply assumed that as the director of the honors program, the twenty-four-year-old wizard of knowledge that I was should certainly take the responsibilities seriously, which meant that I should retain some of the kids in the program and cast out the others. I was so blind to the meaning of my action, so oblivious to the fallacy of regarding grades as everything in an academic environment, that I never even felt the urge to rationalize my action to myself. Those kids were dropped from the honors program and that was that. Worse, I never gave the matter a second thought until years later, when I was teaching in Boston. I had been looking at the academic records of all my students and discovered—no big surprise to anybody else but clearly a revelation to me—that some were late bloomers. Suddenly it dawned on me that I had assumed bad grades to be a kind of life sentence of inadequacy, that the Texas Southern University kids who weren't "good enough" by my arbitrary criteria could just be tossed aside without a thought.

Of course I know that the girl whose book of Bible excerpts I tossed on the sidewalk survived and is probably the mother of seven wonderful Orthodox children, and those TSU kids who didn't meet my rigid standards for remaining in the honors program went on to their own lives and most likely have done well. It is not merely the scope of the cruelty, like my overreaction to Boyd Murray, but the indifference with which I could commit those acts that haunts me. These sorts of ill-considered doings have a life of their own. In my case, I developed a reputation for being a hard-ass or some such, a reputation for toughness, which would be laudable if the toughness were tempered by compassion and wisdom but which by itself is not such a good thing.

Thankfully, other memories from my two years in Texas ameliorate my shameful expulsion of some of the students from the honors program. For one thing, I met Patricia Kennedy, an English and speech teacher who has been a part of my life ever since. Our friendship was not destined, however, at least not at first. She resented me instantly for having replaced her close friend, whose job I was taking. Somehow we got through the first few weeks of her distrust and my probably near-total bumbling. Recently divorced, Pat had four small children, who soon became more or less my stepkids as I, callow but energetic, took on an avuncular role. I found them fun to be with, and their mother gradually fit me into her life as I fit her into mine. I became a passable substitute for their father, "Daddy Brudnoy" to the youngest and buddy to their mom.

We even gave the old college try to turning our friendship into something more intense, but Pat, a navy veteran, had enough experience to recognize a homosexual when she met one. We ended one evening in bed together, but I was useless: my efforts weren't significant enough to qualify even as passable, and Pat, as I learned not long after, had been told by a friend that he had seen me at a gay bar. Pat probably had enough men crowding into her romantic life, and she found me unthreatening in that department, a welcome change. We came to love each other greatly, and I think that I had a small role in raising her kids. We worked closely in the honors program at TSU, she teaching honors speech and English and I history and philosophy, and when I returned to Boston two years later, she came along, bringing her children, John, Regina, and the twins, Carol and Charles. She found a teaching job and moved into a big old house in nearby Brookline, and we've been together, though living a mile or two apart, ever since. In Texas and in Boston we compared notes on our romantic involvements, or wannabe romances, and settled into growing comfortably middle-aged together. A cliché of the homosexual world is the gay man with his female beard, and I suppose we fit the bill, at least to acquaintances and the passing world. But beneath the surface we have been much more to each other than conveniences. I've often wondered if even married people are as supportive and understanding of each other as we are.

Houston provided me with my first full-time teaching experience as well as a life so filled with work and play that wistful memories of Paul Turner faded. Unlike Boston—it is more than just a ditty to recall that in olde Boston, land of the bean and the cod, the Lowells spoke only to the Cabots, and the Cabots spoke only to God—the city was accepting of newcomers. I became wrapped up in the honors program, sometimes even going into the office on weekends and working from morning to sundown; I became so entwined in the program and with the kids that I learned what dedication means in regard to the teaching profession. My salary, $7,200 per annum, seemed like a fortune to me then, though my father advised me that reality would dawn on me soon enough. But I wasn't working for the salary alone; I was working for the joy of it. I felt that I was making a difference, and perhaps in 1964, a time of extraordinary changes in race relations in America, I was. Texas Southern University itself was the outgrowth of an incident that occurred shortly after World War II, when the state of Texas set up a separate law school for one black student, whom the authorities wanted to keep out of the University of Texas. Over time the law school flourished, and the undergraduate college flourished soon thereafter, supported by state funding and insuring that blacks wouldn't clamor to be admitted to white schools. TSU was known as a "predominantly Negro university," the way Hadassah is a predominantly Jewish organization. In short, it was an all-black college, with a mainly but not entirely black faculty.

At Yale and Harvard I felt that the professors more or less

floated through our lives, neither helping us nor smothering us. But at TSU I felt that my students' futures reflected on me, that I was living not just for myself but in some small way for others, really for the first time in my life. We loved the kids, and many of them loved Pat and our associate honors program director, Bruce Robinson, and his wife, Sylvia. We were a team of equals, harmoniously working toward the same end. Bruce and I were committed to integration and believed that a black school like TSU should be a transition, not an end point for bright black students. We learned soon enough that discussions about merging TSU with the University of Houston, another state institution, which was a mere two miles down the road, weren't so pleasing to our black faculty colleagues. After all, in the 1960s they would likely have lost out if a small college was folded into a larger and predominantly white university. Today perhaps such a merger would provide chairmanships for some of the black professors; then, certainly my colleagues would have become subordinates. For Bruce and me, and in my second year at TSU for Bill Alexander, another black colleague, who became the associate director of our program, questions of status, of who would wind up heading academic departments and who would take second place, were absent.

Our students were mainly first-generation collegians, some of them from all-black towns in Louisiana and Texas, all of them from all-black high schools, each of them aware that this experience at college would be crucial to his or her future. They took their collegiate years seriously, as did we. These were the hope-filled years. The Civil Rights Act of 1964, passed by a Congress prodded into action by Lyndon Johnson and grieving still over the death of Johnson's predecessor (whose programmatic commitment to civil rights was not notable, whatever JFK's private thoughts), was a landmark that gave

105

the entire nation a jolt. It was an exciting time for students and teachers alike, especially for those of us on black campuses, where history was being made. I've had thirty years of an interesting life since those days, and much of that life has been of value, but I've never felt as needed and as entwined in the future of others as when I worked at TSU.

During my two years at TSU I peered more deeply into the realities of racism than I ever had before. Bruce and I attended a conference with others like us, well-meaning young scholars teaching at several of the predominantly Negro colleges courtesy of the Woodrow Wilson Foundation. The conference was in Atlanta, at an airport hotel, and Bruce, forgetting where he was (we both forgot), went off to get a haircut. He returned to report that the barber had refused to touch his head, obliging my friend and colleague to take a bus into town to find a black barber. On my father's recommendation, I called one of his old army buddies and was invited to dinner, along with my friend. But when the man asked what had brought me to Atlanta, he immediately figured out that Bruce was black and without missing a beat managed to "remember" another engagement. In the space of an hour at an airport hotel in Atlanta, the city "too busy to hate," as its slogan has it nowadays, I witnessed two petty examples of what my black students and my friends Bruce and Sylvia Robinson experienced throughout their lives.

I learned that things I had taken for granted couldn't be taken as such in the Houston of the mid-1960s, even with the sudden changes in federal law in 1964 and 1965. I joined a health club, which I soon learned wouldn't enroll Bill because of his race. Supper clubs, where you could drink hard liquor, then banned in public establishments, were like virtually all social environments in Houston: segregated. And one night after a party at my apartment with TSU colleagues, I discovered the neatly painted slogans "KKK" and "Nigger lover!" on my windows. I have to assume that the culprit was a neighbor, somebody who lived in my building, someone who had seen Negroes entering the building and did the brave deed while the party was going on, just on the other side of the windows. I felt mortified—furious, actually—but as my guests left, they seemed, if not quite indifferent to the incident, then certainly not surprised by it. I complained to the building manager, who expressed some rhetorical concern but said, simply and wisely, that the presence of black visitors as guests instead of as servants in our part of town was bound to draw attention. If I couldn't stand that degree of hostility, as a white person tangentially affected by it, maybe I was in the wrong line of work, or in the wrong town. I often had black friends in to visit and never again experienced anything like that, but I was more attuned after that event to the little things, to the nomenclature of racism—the frequent omission of an honorific when referring to a black person, the more distanced and less ingratiating manner of shop clerks when waiting on black customers, the assumption by ticket takers and such, when black friends and I were out for an evening, that I was in charge, that I was the one to be addressed, that I, by virtue of my color, was the decisive one in our party.

I also found within my first week in Houston that the gay bar scene in the city was, if not quite segregated, then segmented. The first bar I found was overwhelmingly black, and my first thought was that I might encounter one of my students and there would go my private life. I stayed away from predominantly black gay bars after my first visit, but in my second year at TSU I crossed a different line. One of my more interesting students in the first year, Lenny, popped in to visit me late one afternoon. He was now enrolled in one of the graduate programs at TSU, and I was happy that he cared enough to come by to tell me how things were going. It turned out that he had an agenda beyond merely giving me a progress report on his academic doing, and he was quite blunt about it. "I admired you last year as my teacher, and I admired you as a man. I still do. I'd like to know you better. Much better." We went out for a couple of beers, and by eight we were in my apartment, enjoying the most passionate and affectionate encounter I had had since my life with Paul Turner had ended. Lenny was magnificent to behold and remarkably intuitive about what would please me. It was an idyllic night in every way. I had a code of behavior that seemed not so much a deprivation of pleasure but simple good sense: never sleep with any student. It was and is a good rule and one I've maintained in ensuing years, but Lenny's straight-out approach to me in my office, not to mention his tenderness beneath his awesome physique and almost stereotypical machismo, led me to be directed by desire where reason would have said no.

At TSU my academic interests were shifting. Suddenly I couldn't bear the prospect of returning to Harvard, which I had left on an informal leave, to continue my study of East Asian languages. Suddenly I found that my interests were in American, especially Negro, history, though in my first year I didn't do anything to cut my ties with Harvard. I subscribed to *The Journal of Negro History* and began wide reading in the field, and I thought that maybe my destiny in academics would be teaching black history. I was convinced that whites owed a commitment to blacks that went beyond mere tolerance and into affirmative action. Then the term meant something far less politicized than it does today; it meant just that whites should be willing to do more than preach, pontificate, and point fingers. If my student march for civil rights carrying the Yale banner in 1959 had suggested an involvement beyond the merely rhetorical, my teaching at TSU and my desire to speak out on race matters, to coordinate with black friends and colleagues to create a better, more integrated America, spoke of that involvement unequivocally. I had come to TSU with the assumption that the blacks I would be teaching needed me not just as a teacher but as someone who would demonstrate by my actions that I meant what I said.

I found that I was challenged and gratified every day of my time at Texas Southern by the eagerness of my students to learn and to make their futures bright and productive. That was the delightful thing. But I soon saw that white liberal condescension—the belief that unless whites "did" things for blacks, blacks wouldn't succeed—amounted to nothing more than another stereotype, not cruel like avowed racism but cruel in its premises and perhaps counterproductive in its inevitable results. I came to think, although in a hazy and not fully developed form, that liberal assumptions, which amounted really to patronization, weren't necessarily the most useful and were certainly not the most valid assumptions. In any case, I had a reason for being alive: to teach, to act as a mentor, to stand in body and soul for a more harmonious America. I felt good about myself.

My social life was splendid. Patricia and her kids became my surrogate family. My body responded quickly to gym workouts, and both at the gym and elsewhere I met young men who helped me fill in the blank spaces in my life. In those days before AIDS, nothing seemed impossible or dangerous or unhealthy. I had the sense that whatever I wanted was within my grasp, that whomever I wanted I could have, and that I could successfully function as a college teacher, program administrator, and man about town—a gay blade, though the expression didn't come to mind then. My energy seemed limitless, and on an ordinary day I would be at the college by seven in the morning, teaching and administering the honors program until late in the day, then at the gym for a strenuous workout—and sometimes a quickie in the steam room—and then, as often as not, I would pop by one of the bars and once in a while find the true lust du jour.

On weekends, when I wasn't working alone at my desk at the college, I was often with Patricia and her children, and she and I would go to the shore in Galveston, to dinner, for drives in the country, and to her first love, the theater. The Alley Theatre, a fine enough actors' stage then and a superlative company now, had us in attendance for virtually every production, and the great and near-great museums had me on their invitation lists as soon as I made a phone call. I met a wonderfully talented painter, Richard Stout, and his fiancée, Anne Winkler, and they adopted Patricia and me into their orbit and invited us into Richard's fascinatingly quirky house on Bonnie Brae, a short street more inviting than its cutesy name. I never before or after felt more physically adept, stronger, more desirable to others and worthy of being desired. My grandmother Axilrod had invariably said that a man without a cause is not fully human, and I felt in Houston that I validated her view. My cause was my job. My reward was the sense of well-being arising from a job I believed well done. The frosting on my life's cake was the social (and the carnal), and I believe that for the first time I was completely comfortable in any company, proud of what I was doing and satisfied with what I was becoming. I had more friends than I had time for and more duties at TSU than I had talent for, but nothing was out of reach, nothing was out of the question. Ask and it was mine; wish to do it and it was done.

110

❑ ❑ ❑ ❑

At Christmas during my first year at TSU, in 1964, Paul Turner came down from Boston and we drove into Mexico, visiting small villages as well as the capital. Paul painted some watercolors of our trip (I have them framed on my walls to this day), and we actually got through two weeks without a tiff. The only alarming moment was when somehow we lost each other at Teotihuacán, the great pyramid just outside Mexico City. I was on one level looking for him; he was below me on the next, looking for me. A childish terror of abandonment suddenly hit me; all at once I was back in Boston on my last night, setting off for Houston in my car, weeping as if tears were raindrops in a downpour, awakened instantly to what was missing from my life, namely my soulmate. He insisted later that he knew we would find each other eventually, which of course we did, but the difference between our two reactions—mine near-panic, his calmness and certainty that we weren't so much lost as misplaced—summed up a great deal of our relationship.

Late in the spring of 1965, I decided to visit Europe for the first time. With my princely $7,200 salary, I felt flush with money, and I figured that twenty-five was getting a bit long in the tooth for making one's first tour of the Old World. So off I went, leaving my apartment and car with a pal, my deepest affections with Patricia, and my promise with Richard and Anne that I would be home in time for their wedding in September. I flew to New York to visit with Arthur Lederman for a few days, and it was as if we were both back in the summer of 1961, when we had shared a sublet above Spanish Harlem. Now Arthur introduced me to a gay bathhouse, and somebody there introduced me to amyl nitrite, "poppers," which chipped off another little corner of my sexual innocence in a matter of seconds. My late blooming as a drinker was matched by a pro-

111

found innocence regarding other drugs. I had never had marijuana at that point, certainly nothing more serious, and the rush of the poppers amounted to a wholly unexpected thrill, an instant, woozy high. Years later, in seeking to explain AIDS, some people speculated that the inhalation of amyl nitrite somehow created a fertile field for the syndrome to do its worst. Nothing has been proved about that theory, but I know this: for a minute or two, a popper-inhaling person is a more adventurous soul than ordinarily, and this near-virgin as far as drugs were concerned took to the new high instantly. Arthur led me into the bathhouse scene, another patron gave me poppers, and I steamed off to Europe on the *Queen Elizabeth* (the original, not the *QE2)* one small step closer to full sexual adulthood.

Europe became the matrix for my conception of myself as fully autonomous. Unlike in Japan, where I had been shepherded around by local factotums of the American Field Service, in Europe I was primarily on my own, after a brief stay in London with a graduate student friend from Yale and visits with my great-uncle and his wife, the relatives with whom my mother had stayed in Los Angeles when she had had her "episode" during the war. Off then to the continent for my own bargain-basement grand tour. I wanted to see everything—each castle, all the museums, every one of the notable parks and avenues, the totality of the culture that I had more or less taken for granted before. I also wanted to sample the sex scenes where possible, and everywhere that was of course possible. The pattern of my life in Houston—hard days at work and then the frequent hard day's night, as the Beatles put it—transferred easily to the Old World. Europe for a young American on the go was one delight after another, and with energy to spare and a compulsive's intention to let nothing be unseen if I had time to see it, I was the ideal traveler by day, and if not exactly the ideal then certainly a successful visitor to the darker side by night. I sought the completion of my evolution from recently "out" adventurer to sophisticate, to become the architect of my desire and the builder of experiences of almost every kind. All the sights received their fair share of my appreciation, I was able to forget about work and push Paul Turner out of mind, and I more or less slept my way through the Old World, considering a country a failure, or my visit to it a fizzle, if I didn't carry back from it at least a memory or two of what that country's young men were like.

My bizarre Harvard friend Armen, who presented himself as an exiled Albanian prince (a claim none of his pals in Cambridge chose to investigate), showed me Madrid, where he was then living and engaging in what he liked to say were adventures; he presented me one night with a human surprise, Felipe, for the evening, a thoughtful gift indeed. I saw my first bullfight (didn't cotton to it), drank my first sangrias by the side of a fancy private pool (liked the pool, got drunk on the alcohol), and rather quickly developed a fondness for the handsome men of Madrid. For three months I thought not a thing about my previous academic specialties, nor anything of what I had begun in Houston and would return to: my possible emergence as a scholar in black studies. At Yale I had read Henry Adams's *Mont-Saint-Michel and Chartres,* and I carried a copy with me in France, attempting to understand something of what had inspired the great cathedrals, the peasants' subordination of their own material well-being to serving God by constructing his temples. I saw no contradiction in merging the interested observer of European culture with the eager sampler of the carnal pleasures of European males.

In Holland I met a Danish soldier on vacation from his duties in NATO in Paris. Gunnar aroused in me that I-can't-resist impulse and introduced me to sadomasochism, S & M (or as I came to call it, M & M). He wanted to be spanked and abused, and I tried to oblige, but I was terrible at playing the sadist and had no desire to play the masochist. Still, I was easing into a view that if I had a good chance of not dying in the act, I would give a try, at least once, to anything. Literature, of course, among its other benefits, is supposed to function as vicarious education, but my reading in sexual matters was insignificant, and I had to learn what I could by experience. I did things that nobody in his right mind would do today. I followed a young German home from a bar one night in Munich and had sex standing up in his family's bathroom while his parents and his sister, *kleine* Hilda, slept in the next rooms. I let a complete stranger take me to Dachau, a heart-rending experience, and then let him have his way with me outside the walls of the concentration camp as my payment, so to speak, for my educational trip of the afternoon. I slept with a Swedish military cadet in a park in Stockholm and had a picnic on the grounds of the royal palace in Oslo, where, with a theology student from Bergen, I finally found a use for my high-school Norwegian. I experienced the baths in Amsterdam, Vienna, Copenhagen, and London, this within weeks of my first experience in such a place. I rode a motorcycle clutching onto a wild, sexy creature at three A.M. in Copenhagen's suburbs. I slept with an English godling—he was as beautiful and epicene as Jim, the boy I had met and pledged eternal devotion to in Minneapolis three summers before—who lived in Beirut with a jealous Arab who would "fry me," as he put it, if he found that my new friend was "cuttin' out" on him in our *pensione* in Rome. I sunbathed on a raft in the Tiber, then gawked at the Sistine Chapel, then returned to our hotel for more fun and

games with my Beirut-dwelling limey. I cruised and got a Swiss
Guard at the Vatican simply by doing something straight out of
a movie: I wrote the name and address of my hotel on a card,
indicated in pidgin Italian that I would wait for him in the little
street-level café of the hotel, and did so. Venice simply took my
breath away: I had never seen anything so gorgeous as the
Grand Canal at sunrise. I remembered *Death in Venice,* the
Thomas Mann novel that Paul Turner had turned me on to,
and I imagined myself now and then as Aschenbach, not necessarily with a winsome Polish Tadzio but with any number of
prospective delights. And early in my continental excursion, on
the train from Madrid to Italy, I met a young American student, straight, whom I was immediately drawn to and whom I
kept running into in various cities along the way. We spent a
few days together in San Remo, on the Italian side of the
border and cheaper than the posh spots on the French Riviera,
and we picked up girls and double-dated in Vienna and Copenhagen and elsewhere. As I had done in my senior year at
Yale, I lived two lives, having ordinary straight dates when this
fellow and I were palling around, gay encounters when I was
on my own. The pattern was not unique. Most gay men of my
generation perfected its rudiments early on: be or at least act in
public as if you were what most people were and expected that
others were, and go on your sexual quests out of sight. Not
precisely a prescription for better living through honesty, but
for most of us it was the best, sometimes the only, pattern of
behavior that we could imagine.

In three months in the summer of 1965 I saw the great
sights, did it all for pennies, and experienced a veritable diversity of European locals as a celebration of my entrance into my
second quarter-century of life. I found that giving out Kennedy
half-dollars was the entrée into cordial relations with people

everywhere, much as, I suppose, nylons must have done the trick for GIs in postwar Europe. And cheaper, too. I was much like hundreds of thousands of young American visitors every year in those days, rich by European standards, although hardly by our own, attractive enough to draw the occasional glance and the occasional date, and fearless enough in those more innocent days to go where my yearning directed me. I completed my European jaunt where I had begun it, in London, reporting to my no doubt bored great-uncle and -aunt about my reactions to the Continent. I felt that this was indeed a glorious world, where a young man could spend a mere $800 and experience an unforgettable summer in Europe.

At Heathrow Airport, waiting for my plane to America, I picked up a book called *The Virtue of Selfishness,* a collection of essays by the irascible, brilliant creator of what she called objectivism, Ayn Rand. Had fatigue from my ten weeks of nonstop tourism and nonstop sexual experimentation unhinged me? Whatever it was, I was hooked by Rand's reasoning, especially by her contrarian insistence that "altruism"—putting strangers ahead of one's self and one's loved ones—was in fact a vice, not a virtue; that affirming one's right to live and to do what made life worth living was a positive good; that much, perhaps all, of the philosophy and ideology of the liberal worldview was flawed. Well, it was a heady little book of essays to dip into on a flight back to the States, an eye-opener. Years later a man named Jerome Tuccille wrote a book entitled *It Usually Begins with Ayn Rand,* meaning that for many people the first knockout chink in the customary liberal armor was delivered by Rand.

When I returned to TSU, I began to read all of her novels and essays and even took the unexpected step of devoting my

entire spring semester honors philosophy seminar to her works
and to something by each of her enemies, as a fair counter-
weight. Result: eighteen black objectivists, aged twenty or
twenty-one, and one twenty-five-year-old professor entering
into a long, still-vibrant period of rejecting the liberal verities.
Bill Buckley, whom I had booed at Yale when he debated
Norman Thomas, now became regular reading fare for me, and
Barry Goldwater, whose candidacy for president the previous
year had filled me with foreboding, suddenly began to shimmer
in a new light. I read Russell Kirk on conservatism, reread
Edmund Burke on the revolution in France, and offered myself
up as a latter-day Descartes, determined to set aside all previous
beliefs and let my brain lead me into more reasoned thoughts.
"I doubted liberalism, therefore I am" became my motto, and
as if I had been waiting all my life for a new take on politics and
culture and life in general, suddenly I discovered myself, first in
Rand, then in others along the fringes of objectivism, and in
libertarianism and conservatism. Just as I had in only a few
months broken through my sexual reticence in the summer of
1961, coming out of my closet not in name but in action, so I
experienced a new birth of thought. It was without any doubt
whatsoever from that day in the London airport to this that I
can chart a path never imagined by me or my New Deal parents, or by my pal Paul Johnson at Yale, a Democrat and liberal
to the core, a path that was yet another turning point. I had
drunk the last of the wine of reflexive or knee-jerk liberalism
and was headed for a new adventure in ideas.

First things first, however, as romantic lightning struck for
the third time. It happened early in October, shortly after
Richard and Anne's wedding, during one of their dinner parties at their ramshackle, art-filled house. By that point I should
have been more self-aware. There is a certain type that gets me

every time: an aura, an inviting, distinctive voice, a look of innocence and youth, litheness of body—"no fems, no fats," as the gay personal ads routinely require—a sparkle in the eyes, and I'm wasting my time resisting when the occasion dawns. That night the occasion dawned in the person of one Andrew Belschner. I concocted an inane little game, reading Andrew's palm and predicting great things for him, when the greatest thing that could possibly have happened was a quick remove to his or my place and the immediate ripping off of his clothes. My prediction of an immediately brighter future for him became reality when the ripping began as soon as we could politely leave the dinner party. Whether the others noticed our early and simultaneous departure, I don't know, and I didn't care. The stars were properly aligned, I was flush with a brand-new Randian sense of entitlement to what I wanted so long as I was prepared to take it, and I was very prepared to have Andrew to myself then and there. And I did.

What to say of Andy? That he, like Paul (and like Rand's famous character Howard Roark in *The Fountainhead*), was becoming an architect; that he, like Stephen, was of a poetic nature; and that he, like both Stephen and Paul, was irresistible to me: a tight, compact body to die for, a precise profile, a voice with a hint of rural Texas in it overlaid with a slightly throaty, comparatively high-pitched, near-singing quality. Andy would say "yes" as if it had six notes, elevating from the mid-range to a whispery high note, then settling down to somewhere in between. I loved to listen to him on any topic, just to hear that voice, those impossibly arousing cadences, that amazing laugh that appeared to pick up resonance as it lost volume. There are many fish in the sea, but only so many people who catch one's bait, and despite my growing appetite for sex, easily satisfied in Europe and in Houston the year before, once I met Andy I was a changed man: I had a lover, for only the third time, and in reality for the last time.

We had a splendid year together. We even took Evelyn Wood Reading Dynamics together, because Andy wanted to find something that we could do together and I was determined, having read that JFK and some others had learned to read *War and Peace* in fifteen minutes, to maximize my time. Soon Patricia and Andrew and I were almost constantly together after work hours, as Pat and I were pretty much inseparable at the college as well. This was not an exact analogue to the Julie-Paul-David rigmarole in Cambridge, though on one occasion our togetherness went a bit too far. I was on a brief vacation in the east, and while I was there Andrew and Patricia slept together, which I learned about from Pat during an otherwise uneventful phone call. I was floored by this, but the two of them rationalized their fling as somehow "consolidating" their affection for me. (Oh. Right.) I hadn't the vaguest idea what this "consolidating affection" thing meant, but I determined— adulthood was dawning—that I wasn't going to turn this into another Boyd Murray incident and slice off two more friends from my circle, certainly not my lover and my beloved friend. After all, even though I wanted to believe in sexual fidelity, I wasn't always exactly up to the task myself.

On one occasion, while I was sitting on my balcony, a young man passed by; we glanced at each other and then did more than glance. Maybe this was some kind of payback for Pat and Andy's "betrayal" of me. Maybe not. In any event, I confessed my moment of extracurricular passion to Andy, who brushed it off as nothing to worry about. That was that. Even after all these years, I've no grand theory about sexual fidelity, but maybe more out of necessity than conviction I've come to maintain that sex is a kind of plumbing function and can be good or bad, depending, but love transcends plumbing, and sexual exclusivity needn't be confused with romantic and emotional fidelity. Really high-flung philosophy, not so? I have been generally a good friend, and I have my skills in bed, but I've not invariably been the most sexually faithful lover or the most consistent in giving the same consideration to those I have loved as I have expected from those who love me. I do know that my relationships with Stephen, Paul, and Andrew were the closest I've come to true romantic love in my long sojourn in the gay world. Those men were the most noble in their character, the most considerate in their willingness to put up with me—no easy task—and the memories of all three of them endure unsullied by regret, save only by the inescapable regret that we can't go home again and what we had then we can no longer have.

Two years in Houston suddenly seemed enough to me, and I was determined to return to graduate student life in the Northeast. I had come fully to terms with my yearnings for Paul Turner and felt that I could live near him without becoming a specter haunting the Cambridge landscape. Andrew and I were enjoying a fine friendship, a love relationship that was far more supportive than neurotic. While we were not losing interest in each other, exactly, neither of us made the desire for me to stay in Houston explicit. Nor did either of us say anything to dissuade me; it was as if we were enjoying the better part of a year as best pals and lovers but the time to let go had come. I have mentioned the pattern of my life, with its intense bursts of academic or professional energy accompanied by an easy-going promiscuity. But consider: I had left New Haven, which meant leaving Stephen, after our year together; I had been prevailed upon by Paul to leave Cambridge and move across the river to Boston, then to leave the East entirely and settle in Houston;

and now, recapitulating aspects of both these previous leavetakings, I was on my way back to Boston. These three men are the ones who got under my skin for a long period of time. I loved them passionately and love them to this day. Still, in each case, after finding true love and embedding myself fully in the relationship, I went away, leaving my past behind me. Even with the perspective of thirty years, I still can't figure out why I acted as I did.

I accepted a teaching position at Northeastern University in Boston, where I had taught briefly in the summer of 1964 before moving to Texas. Andrew and I never really talked about my decision to move, and I said nothing of my wish that he would come to Boston too, maybe because I didn't quite wish it; nor did he say anything about that, maybe because he didn't quite wish it either. We took the year together as a lovely interlude, a nearly friction-free affair, and we let it end. With Patricia, however, my life continued. Pat moved to Boston just ahead of me, arranged for the return of my Beacon Hill apartment to me, and introduced me to Boston as if she, not I, had long lived there.

I didn't weep driving back from Houston, though when night fell and I found WBZ on my car radio, I had the reverse reaction to that of my drive to Houston two years earlier: a definite sense of coming home. I was ready to see Paul again, without, I hoped, the thick layer of regret that had followed me to Houston. I was determined to become an American historian and to learn more about the black experience in America. I had discovered myself by then as a sexual being, and I was comfortable with what and who I was, though still presenting a straight image to much of the outside world. I had begun to find myself a niche in the world of political philosophy, delving

121

into conservative, libertarian, and Randian ideas and abandoning the liberal verities one by one. I was coming into my own as a kind of hybrid, a blend of academic, activist, libertarian-conservative, and hedonist. These elements sometimes were in competition, sometimes jarred each other uncomfortably, occasionally melded into a consistent, albeit unusual, whole. The David who was emerging and jelling was entirely unaware of how and in what directions those elements would shape my future. I had learned that I could love another man and that other men—worthy, brilliantly talented men—loved me. I had developed a strength that surprised me, one that proved useful—essential, even—when thirty years later I faced the greatest crisis of my life, AIDS. I could take risks and accept the likelihood of failing in some of them without collapsing into despair and fear that a failure must mean an unvarying series of failures to follow. I could say yes to a love affair and goodbye, without tears, to it as well. It was a glorious time and I was happily in it and of it.

F I V E

An Embarrassment
of Riches

Asian studies were now behind me, and although I continued to do translations now and then for *Monumenta Nipponica,* a Tokyo-based scholarly journal, and reviewed books once in a while in the Asia field, I made the decision to switch to American studies with a concentration in Negro history. My Asian majors at Yale and Harvard, with informal minors in American and European history, gave me sufficient room to handle two areas in teaching, which I did at Northeastern University beginning in the fall of 1966. Northeastern had begun as an adjunct to the YMCA in downtown Boston in the late nineteenth century and had become one of the largest private universities in America and a pioneer of the co-op program, now found in many colleges throughout the nation. Co-op provides students with a five-year program combining studies with hands-on work in government or in private companies reflecting each student's interests. The student body was primarily white, though more diverse each year, and I felt right at home after my two years at Texas Southern, whose students, like those at Northeastern, were primarily first-generation collegians. These were not youngsters whose other choices included Harvard or Yale, but just as I had realized rather quickly that many of my classmates at the Ivy colleges were far from the academic stars they may have considered themselves to be, so I came to see that students at "lesser" institutions often included some terrifically bright young men and women.

I was back on home turf, inching closer to my almost certain return to graduate studies in a year or two. I had a built-in friendship clique at the university of people I had met during the summer of 1964, before I moved to Texas. I also returned to my physical exercise routine, this time joining the Y—it was literally next door to the university—and forcing myself to appear, along with Dick Fletcher, an old friend, at an exercise class three mornings each week at seven o'clock. To deny that I liked routine and felt comfortable with sameness, with repetition, would be pointless. I was compulsive about my work and faithful in attending those masochistic early-morning workout sessions, which seemed essential to keep me in the market for desirable sex partners, whom I met in bars or at parties, on the streets or through professional organizations, anywhere and everywhere.

Paul Turner and I saw each other occasionally, but the embers, although not quite extinguished, had begun to die. Stephen Holden lived in Manhattan and we kept in touch, as I did with Andy Belschner, still in Houston at that point and blossoming in his architectural career. My three great loves of the past were becoming sweet memories, and while I made some halfhearted attempts to find a replacement—a "meaningful relationship," as a Northeastern University friend phrased it—I concerned myself primarily with my career. I had a goal: to excel in academic work and somehow to live less in the ivory tower than in the actual world. My two years at TSU had showed me that one can combine teaching and activism, and now, in my mid-twenties, I believed that I had my priorities straight. This meant, among other things, letting the erotic life function primarily on the basis of an occasional one-night stand, letting a love relationship come, if it came, by happenstance. I had not so much retired from the arena where one battles for affection and emerges with a trophy, a lover, as concluded that I needed less of the total involvement just then than I had before. I wasn't aiming for monasticism or celibacy, but I was now entering the second quarter-century of my life and I was all too apparently aging. The gay world is not so much a complete antithesis to the straight world as a hyper version of it: superficiality was then and is now a powerful ingredient; youth and looks are esteemed, maybe no more than in the straight world but more forthrightly. Twenty-six wasn't retirement time, but I was already getting a bit old to function successfully in the bars. The competition was younger, ever younger, bolder—my generation was shy by comparison—and more insistent on immediate gratification. I had my share, but mine was a narrower slice of the pie than it had been.

Woody Allen's witticism that bisexuality doubles your chances of a date on Saturday night applied to others, not to me. Even so, I had one last sexual experience with a woman. A former student, a young man who had impressed me greatly with his wit, his intelligence, and his common sense, evidently decided in talking about me with his wife (whom I had met and liked a great deal) that I needed a woman, at least once in a while. When I came home one night, I found my former student's wife sitting on my doorstep. Since she and her husband lived only a block away, I assumed that she had locked herself out and was waiting for me to take her in until her husband returned home. When she apprised me of her mission, I was floored. Or almost. They knew about my sexual orientation, though we didn't talk about it, so why this invitation to the dance, as it were, of heterosexual sex? I learned that she and her husband had cooked up the idea as a way of bringing out another side of me. I still let my mind roam into a more conventional scenario for my life: if not quite white picket fence, two children, a girl for you and a boy for me, plus Rover, the standard American ideal occasionally attracted me, at least in theory. Of course, for me to have pursued this avenue, I would have had to enjoy sex with women; in those days I had no tolerance, not even much understanding, of marriages of convenience between gay men and straight women, marriages that sometimes worked beautifully, that often produced children and a happy all-American life, if not quite life*style*. Now you could fill a big city phone book with the names of such couples; those in the public eye specialize in such alliances. I was too self-righteous then, too insufferably idealistic about these things, so the notion of marrying a woman seemed ridiculous for me unless I enjoyed sex with women. So I thought, why not give it another try? I did my best, which wasn't much, and she went home, having been polite during the moment of "passion" and made the usual noises.

She and her husband were not the evangelical sort and never said before that evening or after it that they felt I was deficient for being homosexual, but even with the best of friends, sophisticates, moderns, something often lingers that says you are best if heterosexual, all right if bisexual, and not so fortunate if homosexual. I played into that mentality myself, at least rhetorically, simply by gradually easing friends into a full knowledge of the way I was (and am) by first offhandedly letting them assume that I was comfortable sexually both with women and with men. I was acting a lie, but a gentle lie, or so I told myself. I thought that I had moved beyond the best-of-both-worlds illusion with this young couple, but maybe I had not. My farewell to sex with women was painless but also lacking in passion, lacking that erotic thrill that sex with men often provided. My final sexual encounter with a woman was simply a brief return to an earlier phase of my life. It had no sequel. Likewise, I never repeated my sole impropriety at TSU, taking a student home to bed, and I managed to keep my mind on the job. Not a shred, not so much as a strand, of the hair shirt of guilt attached to what I did in my private life when I acted on my urges, but I hadn't the desire or the temperament to make a public declaration of my personal being. Some people got the message, however mutedly I conveyed it; some didn't. It was truly all the same to me.

I had no revolutionary tendencies per se, though I admired the activists who began after 1969 to speak out, sometimes to shout out their sexual sense of themselves. My one day of marching, for civil rights in Washington in 1959, remained a unique experience: I wasn't comfortable then in the limelight, though I was trying to get over that residual shyness by beginning to speak out and occasionally to write about gay-related matters, although always from a detached point of view. I even testified before a state senate committee on a proposed gay rights bill, though the distinguished members of the legislature—the General Court, as it's called in Massachusetts—chatted with each other while the other do-gooders and I made our case. I spoke once at a Homophile Association meeting held at Boston University, meeting for the first time a brilliant Harvard graduate student, John E. Boswell, who went on to chair the history department at Yale and to write remarkable books about religion and homosexuality. I was *of* the movement but not deeply *in* it, a scholar making a reasonable case for acceptance and for changes in the law but not coming out in any significant way. Serious academics who spoke out from within the homosexual environment were rare; Martin Duberman comes to mind, but few other names do. The late 1960s were days of discretion in the sexual battlefield, and the antiwar movement took front place among people prone to activism.

Ayn Rand's writings and conservative and libertarian thought along a broad spectrum continued to engage me and eventually led me to speak out on political matters in general. I functioned as an adviser to the Northeastern University Students for a Democratic Society (SDS), a leftist organization, while I was beginning to challenge the ethos of the left. When a Northeastern history department colleague, Bob Feer, and I designed the university's first course in American Negro history, he taking the period up to the Civil War, I to the present, we disagreed not only on emphases but also on how to relate to the black students. Bob said that he tended to grade the black kids more leniently than the whites; didn't I agree? I told him that during my two years at a black college, where all my students were black, I hadn't developed a sense that condescension to those young people served their needs in any way. Soon thereafter, beginning in the Nixon administration, "affirmative action" of a new kind entered our lives and our lexicon, with a meaning far less benign in practice than the rhetoric made it seem, and within a decade or so it became a major bone of contention in America. I saw such programs as useful for outreach but harmful both to their intended beneficiaries and to the society at large, condescending to those favored by the quotas and set-asides, derisive to those who weren't in on the special favors. These ideas were merely germinating; each step

128

along the way to a coherent political philosophy was a struggle between my new beliefs and the inherited New Deal mentality of my family and the Ivy-influenced liberalism of my college and Harvard years. What struck me then as a kind of bifurcation of my thoughts, a tender heart qualified by a hard head, never resolved itself until years later, when I shucked virtually the entirety of my left-liberal beliefs and cast my lot with the right.

One night in 1967, Patricia, who had been moving in her own rightward direction, and I attended a lecture by Ayn Rand, who was viciously unsparing of anybody who criticized her, as she saw it from ignorance. We encountered for the first time her disciple Nathaniel Branden, then as blisteringly unsympathetic as Rand was herself. The audience comprised Rand groupies, pilgrims like Patricia and me, and scoffers, and the scoffers of course made nuisances of themselves but didn't disrupt the speech, as college protestors against the Vietnam War increasingly did in the next few years. I felt embarrassed watching this brilliant woman and her young acolyte sneering at those who hadn't yet received the full Randian gospel, and I felt that embarrassment particularly because I recalled how evangelical I had been at Yale, trying to shame my classmates into joining the NAACP, trying to inflict my superior wisdom on the deficient, puny intellects of those who had dwelled in darkness and hadn't yet seen the great light that I did. But sitting in that hotel banquet room, we observed the cruelty, the disdain, the arrogance of the admittedly remarkable Ayn Rand and of her designated intellectual heir, the young man who had changed his Jewish-sounding name (as the Jewish Alice Rosenbaum had changed hers to Ayn Rand) into the all too revealing Nathaniel Branden, which, if you fiddle with the letters, turns into the anagram Nathaniel Ben Rand *(ben* is "son" in Hebrew). That scene reverberated in my brain for a very long time. I felt that it was all too weird: here was a woman proclaiming her total devotion to reason, shrieking like a peasant in the market, believing that she could convert the not-yet-Objectivist heathens by bullying them. I wondered, and Pat wondered too, whether we were hanging around with lunatics, banshees, that night. Years later, Branden split from Rand, announcing that they had been lovers but that he had given up that relationship, although she insisted that it continue. Nathaniel Branden became a new man in later years, a thoughtful, kindly psychotherapist who is now enemy number one to the faithful remnant of the Randian movement.

I can't pin it down to a definitive date, but within weeks of this lecture I began to realize that I might be biting off more than I could chew, much less swallow and digest. I wanted to have it all: snippets of Randian Objectivism but without the rudeness and almost sadistic glee in savaging the as-yet-unsaved; large dollops of the sort of conservatism I had begun to cotton to in the pages of *National Review;* and the instinctive compassion that seemed to me then to reflect the best of liberalism. A generous evaluation of me, favored by some friends, was that I was a Gemini and so was naturally drawn to multiple value systems; a less generous but probably more accurate take on the matter was that I was intellectually a mess, philosophically in the midst of a transition, ideologically a hybrid. New friends on the right found me conflicted; old friends on the left found me impossibly inattentive to the verities that they held dear and that I had for many years espoused.

I felt comfortable nesting with conservatives on economic matters and in their opposition to communism; I felt more comfortable with liberals on social matters—at least then I did, before much of liberalism simply flung itself into the oncoming path of the New Left and gave up the ghost. There was libertarianism, the political movement and even a political party, but many of the libertarians I met, like the Randian Objectivists, seemed bloodless, icy, intensely "rational," no doubt, but also dead to compassion. I just had to muddle through these contradictions and polarities and come up with something that made sense to me. So when I'm labeled a conservative in the newspapers, I can hardly object; likewise with libertarian, though when people on the furthest fringes of the right, those who make Attila seem like Mary Poppins, brand me a liberal, I think they're going too far.

In the last few years of my twenties and the first of my thirties I constructed, piece by piece, something at least resembling an integrated theory of politics and—boldly going where few men had successfully gone—of life. It is a political philosophy that adheres to Jefferson on government—that government which governs least, governs best—but doesn't collapse into the swamps of anarchism. It is a political philosophy that admires the humanitarian Lincoln but not the Lincoln who tossed the Constitution aside when he felt that he ought to possess extraordinary powers. It is a philosophy that doesn't doubt Franklin Roosevelt's good intentions but considers his New Deal creation of huge government a platform for ruination, which Lyndon Johnson's Great Society marched merrily upon, since which the country has been going to hell in the proverbial handbasket. In life, I believe we are all the makers of our own destiny, save only those who are born with exceedingly bad luck—incapacitating handicaps, feeble intelligence, crummy, abusive parents, and the like—or exceptionally favored by inherited wealth. If twelve-step programs do some good, fine, but surely the person joining the program is the author of his own

131

success, if success there is. We diminish our individuality when we console ourselves for our miseries by blaming others; it is unacceptable behavior for men and women who struggle to make their own lives meaningful and productive. The victim game—"all my woes are the fault of somebody else, anybody except me"—sets my teeth on edge.

I found a philosophy that cherishes the charitable urge and the charitable deed, an urge that rises within a person and must be voluntary to be charitable, else it is government taxation and redistribution of somebody's hard-earned money to someone else. My libertarianism doesn't equate with libertinism, however much I have in earlier decades been quite the libertine. Rather, my philosophy emphasizes freedom: to make our own potty choices, to succeed or fail on our own terms, to construct our lives on our own terms. Even back in the heady days of my college liberalism, I became convinced that individuals can do most of what needs doing without big government guiding us. I respect the flag, but I think that we enter into major lunacy when we ponder adding an amendment to our Constitution forbidding dimwits from acting disrespectfully to that piece of cloth, however significant its meaning is to most of us. This isn't a book about politics or philosophy; it's about a life—mine—and these thoughts are among the ingredients that made and continue to make me thrive and act.

I made a fateful choice in the spring of 1968. My intention was to return to graduate school but not to Asian studies, and I was accepted at Yale, Princeton, Brown, and Brandeis, the only non–Ivy League university on my list of possibilities. Ideally, considering their reputations, especially Yale's, in the history field, I should have opted for any except Brandeis, but I decided that I had had enough of moving and enough of the Ivy

League. My lack of any coherent religious sense never changed, but I felt increasingly comfortable with my ethnic heritage. I had come to see that every religion was and is saddled with bizarre legends and preposterous miracle tales, but some were also graced by inspiring values and worthy ethics, mine among them. The Jewish university Brandeis it was, then, and my entrance into that university in Waltham, Massachusetts, in September 1968 coincided with my first publication in *National Review,* a satiric poem about Hubert Humphrey, long my Minnesota family's *beau ideal* and now the Democratic candidate for president. That was followed two weeks later by a cover story on black power, my first published piece challenging, more or less root and branch, one of the major totems of contemporary liberalism.

Being an avowed conservative on a resolutely liberal campus didn't endear me to my fellow graduate students or to some of the professors, though I found that even at Brandeis a coterie of right-of-center professors functioned, almost under the table, and for every three Brandeisians who regarded me as beyond the pale, there was one who secretly cheered me on. I was older by four years than most of my graduate program classmates, maybe one of the few homosexuals (however closeted) among them, and I had already established a life in the adult world in Boston, so that I kept to my academic knitting at Brandeis and didn't try to enter the social world of my fellow students. The road not taken always remains a mystery. Just how different my life would have been if I had returned to Yale or removed myself to Providence and Brown, or made it an Ivy Big Three grand slam—Yale, Harvard, Princeton—by setting up shop in New Jersey, I'll never know. The choice of Brandeis, however fortuitous it turned out to be, with close supervision by splendid professors, was made more because I wanted to retain my sense of place in Boston than because I thought that the youngish college in suburban Boston was superior to the Ivies. When I look back at my life to this point, I can't escape the obvious conclusion that temperamental conservatism, even more than philosophical conservatism, has determined much of what I chose to do or was led to choose. I did not choose my sexual orientation, and I doubt very much that I can be said to have chosen my political orientation either. Sometimes I think that the one more or less necessitates the other, that one's worldview—the Germans have the impressive word *Weltanschauung* for it—arises out of emotions deeply embedded in one's being as much as or perhaps more than from an intellectual exercise of weighing and balancing various options. When the revelation of my AIDS went national, so to speak, and I was chastised by some gay activists for being both gay and conservative, I tried (futilely) to convince most people that I could see no obvious or even probable reason to believe that people chose either their sexuality or their politics, that temperament is the villain (or the hero) in each person's development.

I believe in equal rights for all but not in special favors for anyone; in a society that would neither discriminate against homosexuals nor turn them into an affirmative action class; in a society in which nobody was held back because of inherited wealth or lack of wealth or because of any other artificial impediment to developing his or her own values and achieving something worthy. If I understand traditional Jewish ethics correctly, I can say that the worth of each person and the relationship of each person to God, if there is a God, is personal, that each individual is capable of perceiving what is right and acting upon that perception, and that considerate, loving behavior to others is the profoundest service to the Lord.

The late 1960s provided me with an intellectual environment

to nail home my academic aspirations, to pursue and finish a doctorate and go forth and multiply the stock of educated young people who would sit at my feet and imbibe wisdom. And I also found myself growing more comfortable with my dual nature, tiptoeing into position to integrate my erotic life into my public life, not yet in a declaration to all the world of my orientation but within my own being, leading to a less fractured existence. I had taught full-time for four years, two in Houston, two in Boston. I was twenty-eight, healthy, strong, bright, optimistic, determined, energetic; I was a plausible adult version of the best little boy in the world. I was ready to make my mark on academe and maybe, just maybe, to make a dent in the world.

Just as I entered Brandeis's master's degree program in the history of American civilization, in 1968, and then the doctoral program in history, in 1969, America was propelled into the throes of the most contentious years imaginable, certainly the most troubled of the century except the decade of the Depression, when my parents were roughly the age I was in the late 1960s. The war was turning into a catastrophe and dividing people along lines almost as impassable as those in the argument over slavery more than a century before. In the aftermath of the murder of Martin Luther King, Jr., came riots, a burst of enthusiasm among some blacks for the separatist solution, and a not entirely welcome realization by some whites of how much remained to be done; the murder of then senator Robert Kennedy occasioned a burst of cynicism and a hardening of the lines dividing Americans on a wide range of subjects. The presidential campaign of Richard Nixon was in part a practical validation of the so-called southern strategy, which—*mutatis mutandis*—less than a decade after Barry Goldwater's crushing defeat in 1964, became a revivified conservative movement whose spin-offs are known to everybody. A cheap slogan among some young people was "Don't trust anyone over thirty." I was thirty on June 5, 1970. I was writing in almost every issue of *National Review* and on almost every topic of public interest, then writing in other conservative journals and beginning to hover about as a kind of junior mentor at the fringes of the newly created Young Americans for Freedom, sponsored by William F. Buckley, Jr., whom by then I admired tremendously and reaching by my writings into virtually every leading campus in the land. I was moving further away from liberalism and at the same time observing my tendency, however contradictory to my temperamental conservatism, to try new things.

Shortly after I returned to Boston in 1966, I revisited Provincetown, the gay-friendly resort at the outermost tip of Cape Cod where Paul and I had spent some weekends before I moved to Texas. There I met a professor of French at Queensborough Community College in New York, Robert Stovall Davis, who, as we grew into a friendship, became a brother in all but name. We visited each other frequently and found that being together was easy: no sexual longing for each other, no competing with each other for anything, and no doubt of each other's intelligence, integrity, or ironic sense of things. For nineteen years, until his death in 1985, we had a relationship as adult pals, increasingly aware that our salad days were over (speaking, that is, of the sexual wars) and that there was more to life than cruising, much more.

This is not to say that either Bob or I had become a monk. In the summer of 1970, as I was midway into my graduate program at Brandeis and teaching part-time at Northeastern, Bob rented a cottage in Provincetown and invited me to share it on weekends. I would finish my last class of the week on a Thursday, scoot down to P-town as quickly as my car would take me, and we'd have a fine time. But during my drive down to the Cape on the first planned long weekend, I began to concoct a scenario in my mind: Bob would have illegal drugs at this cottage, I would be angry and would insist that we keep the place drug-free, I had deputized myself the Pleasure Policeman. I had it all worked out, and by the time I arrived at Bob's cottage I was in a doozy of a state of mind. I had long resisted the drug culture, as it came to be known, and at Harvard had turned down an invitation to be a human guinea pig for Dr. Timothy Leary and Dr. Richard Alpert, whose offices were about 150 yards down the street from my apartment. What was this thing called lysergic acid diethylamide (LSD) that my pal Ned was ranting and raving about? I had wanted nothing of drugs when I was in school or in Houston, and I certainly didn't want to become familiar with them now.

How quickly an ideology crumbles when confronted by a more enticing reality. Bob offered me a drink and told me in his faint southern drawl, the measured cadences of a University of Virginia graduate, that he had recently made a lovely discovery among his friends in Manhattan. This new enticement in Bob's life was mescaline, which he said was a harmless little ole drug that gave its users, those who "dropped" it, a kind of delicious high, far better than marijuana, which didn't do much for me in any case. Before you could say "road to Damascus," the antidrug Bruds had eagerly accepted Bob's offer of a mescaline tab. I sat reading a book for my Northeastern course on Chinese history, stuck in a chapter called "Squeezing and Slicing the Melon," a reference to dividing China up among the imperial powers in the late nineteenth century. As the drug took hold, I began to fixate on the silliness of that title. Then, without any provocation, I announced my intention to walk on the waters of Provincetown Bay to the other shore. I waded into the water, fully dressed, whereupon Bob waded out to intercept me and tried gently to convince me that I would discover many delights in mescaline but not the ability to walk on water. Thus began a summer, in fact a decade, of use (did somebody say abuse?) of psychedelic drugs.

Something emerged from me that had never been let out before: a tendency to lavish affection on people. I must have been a tedious friend that summer, declaring my feelings to anyone who would listen. One friend, Conrad Harding, whom I had met through my exercise partner, Dick Fletcher, reminded me that I had gone from being the guy who fulminated against *Easy Rider* because its characters smoked grass to being a mescaline maven. Bob told me that mescaline was natural, from plants, thereby safer—we didn't say "environmentally friendly" in those days—than LSD, whose effects, I was told, were similar. I read Aldous Huxley's *The Doors of Perception* and took his effusive encomia about this "natural" drug to heart. I began to have a really good time, and the allure of this was powerful.

But I wasn't hampered in my career aspirations by my heavy use first of mescaline and then, almost inevitably, of LSD. I was energetic in my scholarly activities, keen and on target in the articles I was writing at a furious pace for conservative journals, teaching part-time while preparing to research and write my Ph.D. dissertation, going without sufficient rest many nights, exercising and keeping fit, and, of course, sleeping with the occasional lovely who caught my eye and who wanted me too. A charming older man, an antiques dealer who lived in a glorious apartment on a better street on Beacon Hill and who had a telephone in every room, which I regarded as sinful extravagance but pretty slick as well, used to ask me to come over just, he said, to warm his bed. I liked him enormously but resisted his request that I move in with him as his lover. Yet here I was, stretching my ability to express affection as I never had before—the direct result of whatever it was that so deliciously came upon me when I started experimenting with psychedelic drugs the summer before.

I became a champion of hallucinogenic drugs in 1970 and remained one for the better part of the decade. I even lectured one day to eight hundred boys at Dartmouth while tripping on acid, and received a standing ovation; I went to family parties in Minneapolis on LSD and no one had a clue: I was capable of carrying on a public speaking engagement or a family event without conveying to anyone (I think, though at Dartmouth, who knows?) that I was tripping my brains out. It wasn't until I attended a party on the sixth-floor roof of a former Northeastern student's apartment building that I had serious occasion to take sobering stock of my drug use. My chairman, Ray Robinson, was there, as well as the fellow whose wife was delivered to me at my front door, virtually everybody whom I cared about at that university was there, while I was tripping on acid all by my lonesome. Suddenly, and without warning, I leapt up on the ledge of the roof and slowly began to walk, to parade, around it; for at least a couple of minutes, I was high enough above the street to risk certain death if I fell. I never had a bad time on LSD or mescaline, but my judgment was so impaired that only sheer luck or, as my religious friends would say, God's grace kept me from toppling down to be squished on the street below.

That episode on the roof was the only incredibly awful thing that I did to myself while on LSD or mescaline. But it was one experience during several years in which I believed myself invulnerable to mere human considerations and needs, a mentality that came back to haunt me in 1994, when I worked myself nearly to the brink of death by denying that I was sick and needed the ordinary amount of sleep and food and medical attention. This was a young man in his early thirties who was having it all: an academic career of some distinction, a sex life that was notable for its immediate gratifications, and a life in the drug world that exemplified virtually everything that my intellect told me was foolish. Not that that stopped me.

In my second year at Brandeis, I made a series of research trips to read and analyze the papers written by my dissertation topic, a quirky libertarian named Theodore Schroeder, whose works in the early twentieth century helped inspire the creation of the American Civil Liberties Union. The bulk of Schroeder's papers are housed in the library of Southern Illinois University in Carbondale, a flat, not particularly inviting city that had little to recommend it except pizza parlors and churches seemingly on every corner. One night I took a bus to a nearby city to see *Woodstock,* the movie of the renowned concert extravaganza the previous year. I was tripping on acid and enjoyed the music hugely. Then I hitchhiked back to Carbondale on the back of a biker's cycle, the first time I had ridden one since my travels to Copenhagen in 1965. The pattern of taking stupid risks is clear, I think. On acid I might walk on a ledge six floors above the ground or accept a ride from a tattooed biker or God knows what.

But I think I had found a partial way to reconcile the contradictions of my life. I was teaching successfully, becoming popular in the classroom, becoming justly proud of my ability to convey my love of history to young people. My dissertation was coming along nicely, and although I entered my doctoral program later than most of my classmates, I finished it more quickly than any of them: two years from start to finish. I was

becoming a small-gauge star in the conservative journalistic fir-
mament, writing for *NR* and other journals and lecturing
widely. I even flirted with the idea of jumping into politics.

In early 1970, some of the powers in Republican and conservative circles in Massachusetts, among them Laurie McCarty
and Alan MacKay, invited me to breakfast at the Ritz and
proposed that I run as the GOP candidate for Senate that year
against Senator Ted Kennedy, who had, it was thought, been
wounded politically by the Chappaquiddick incident. I was
suddenly known in the state as a conservative comer, though
this was even before I had begun to appear on television.
Though the prospects of winning were slim, the opportunity to
delineate a conservative option to the liberal Ted Kennedy
would be instructive to the voters and helpful to the Republican party, of which, by the way, I wasn't a registered member.
But, I asked, what about the gay thing, as I put it? Oh, they
insisted, that could only help: how, after all, could a supposedly
liberal Democrat express or incite hostility to a homosexual
when liberals are presumably beyond such bigotry? I considered
the offer of the nomination, which these worthies insisted
could be delivered on, since no other credible candidate had
then emerged to challenge the senator. When I ran this by my
dissertation adviser, the Pulitzer prize-winning historian Leonard Levy, I was told simply to weigh the alternatives: finishing
my doctorate and getting on with my academic career or wasting a year in a hopeless, expensive, probably humiliating race
against the last remaining brother of the family that my state
had come almost to worship. Common sense won out, and the
Congress of the United States has had to suffer without Senator
Brudnoy in the chamber.

With the Republican candidacy for the Senate race a rejected option, I was asked to become chairman of the newly

formed Conservative Party of Massachusetts. As a history teacher I had often instructed my students that American politics had always been fierce, even vicious, that third parties were almost always repositories of crackpots and wild-eyed dreamers, and that such congeries rarely won anything but disdain. An exception had come before us in 1970, when Bill Buckley's brother, Jim, received the New York Conservative Party endorsement for the Senate and, running between a liberal Republican and a liberal Democrat, triumphed. I had been asked by a neighbor of Bill and Patricia Buckley, Tony Dolan (known in our circles as *our* folk singer), to work on some position papers for Jim Buckley, which I did. So the idea of forming a third party in Massachusetts and possibly doing here what the Buckley campaign had done in New York was attractive. My chairmanship was short, ineffective, and illustrative of precisely what I had taught my students: the leadership cadre was a den of vipers, internecine squabbles were brutal and largely pointless, and even with Patricia Kennedy installed (by Chairman Brudnoy) as our paid executive director and a few good folks as part of my faction, the thing crashed on the perhaps unavoidable rocks of ideological dispute and evanesced into insignificance.

By then I had finished my graduate studies and was beginning to teach full-time. My only other flirtation with elective office came when House Speaker Thomas P. (Tip) O'Neill retired from Congress in 1986. The field to succeed Tip was filled with liberal Democrats, and when I consulted on this with Arthur Finklestein, a renowned conservative strategist and campaign wizard, we determined that a conservative Democrat—I had gone so far as to register, finally, as a Democrat instead of an independent—might just squeeze through a crowded field in the primary and then face the hapless Republican. That fantasy went away in an instant when the late Bobby Kennedy's son Joseph P. Kennedy II entered the Democratic field. Joe Kennedy crushed the other Democrats, easily won, and again and again has won reelection to the seat once held by his uncle, JFK. The gods were not disposed to see David Brudnoy elected to anything. Just as well.

By the end of 1971 I was beginning to appear on television in Boston at the public TV station, WGBH, as the token conservative. I learned later from a producer at the station that Vice President Spiro Agnew's criticism of the liberal bias in the media had sufficiently alarmed the station's honchos that they thought they should throw a bone to the right. I was that bone and did rather well in a weekly commentary slot. The host of the show eventually stopped speaking to me entirely; the presence of a nonliberal on the hallowed ground of WGBH-TV was apparently offensive to our liberal prattlers about diversity and fair-mindedness.

My first appearance on the *Louis Lyons News and Commentary Show* made heads spin at WGBH. I came out against censorship of pornography, a perfectly understandable position, I thought, especially since my Ph.D. dissertation was the tale of a crusader against censorship. *Oh dear God,* they must have thought, *he's a liberal!* No, I was libertarian in my conservatism—not that they made such distinctions among people who were too primitive to know that a virtuous person could embrace only liberalism—and since I had been brought on board as their token conservative, what, oh what could they do? Not to worry: the next commentary was pro capital punishment. And so it went, the seemingly conflicting sides of my political philosophy—conflicting in their eyes, not really very much in mine—got their communication sounding board, the distinguished programming of WGBH. I was now seen instead of just read; there was a face to go along with the name of that guy whose articles had begun appearing everywhere along the rightward spectrum. And I got a huge kick out of it, as I had the first time I saw somebody on a plane reading an article of mine in *National Review*. It was a trip and has always remained one. I find it very hard even imagining that I went through shy periods when I was younger. The more cameras, microphones, and reporters, the better, if you ask me.

I became a fixture on television as of 1971 and on radio as of 1975, in Boston primarily but also for a time on the *CBS Morning News* on television. I put together a life that satisfied me—more than satisfied me; it delighted me. I was doing something worth doing, teaching and conveying interesting thoughts in the broadcast and print media, taking a measure of pleasure from my sexual urges, earning the affection of worthwhile friends, and having my own private joke: becoming an acid-tripper and living to write about it. I never did intravenous drugs and can't pretend that I contracted HIV from needles. I tired of acid—and feared, too, the quality of the stuff that began to flood the market in the 1980s, which was often contaminated and dangerous beyond the drug itself—and that part of my life gradually came to a halt. If we develop our philosophies and our life habits because of our temperaments, then the strongly libertarian side of my conservatism surely derives to a great degree from my risk-taking nature. I think I am cowardly or at least not notably brave in physical ways: I've never been any good with my fists. I haven't a sadistic bone in my body, as I learned with my masochistic, melancholy Dane on holiday in Holland. I weep at movies about nice people bullied by oafs. I am a sucker for tales of woe. But I look back on a pretty eventful life and conclude, unavoidably, that I am a thrill-seeker, pushing the limits of the acceptable, pushing at the envelope of what will pass muster, and expressing the bolder side of my nature by speaking truth on radio, never trying to please the thought police of political correctness, and becoming the same man in private as in public.

Perhaps turning thirty affected me more than was sensible. Maybe my drug excesses reflected some kind of asinine craving to deny my passage into the generation we were being told not to trust. Doubtful, but maybe so, since everything else that I was doing reflected a maturing man's understanding of what adulthood is about. I also experienced the deaths of loved ones during the first few years of the 1970s. My grandmother Axilrod suffered many illnesses and finally died, heartbroken even after all those years by what had happened to her son, my uncle Arnold, but nonetheless always positive toward her children and grandchildren. She was no longer my algebra tutor but always my champion in the family. The book editor and my mentor at *National Review,* Frank Meyer, who helped me see a way to reconcile traditional conservatism with programmatic libertarianism, died while I was on a research trip for my dissertation. Clara Leahy, my childhood ally against the "real" adults, retired and went to live with relatives in Iowa, disappearing from my life. I've kept my stamp collection and think of her every time I glance at it.

Not long after I earned my doctorate in June 1971, my mother suffered a heart attack. We had been estranged—I guess that's the fashionable word for it—for some years, not owing to any significant issue between us but just because we both had grown increasingly stubborn. We weren't not speaking; we were speaking all too often and often too bitingly, though we had no ideological, philosophical, theological, or any other kind of significant disagreements. I invariably got headaches during my stays in Minneapolis, but rarely at other times. Usually I would get a cold just before flying to the Midwest, and it would magically vanish as soon as I got back to Boston. My sex life was never discussed, and despite what is often said about mothers always knowing, I doubt that my mother knew. I was just thirty-one when I received my doctorate, not an extraordinary age at which to remain a bachelor. My father was twenty-seven when my parents married. Maybe because my distancing myself from my mother was so deeply rooted in things I couldn't objectify—friends would ask me what was wrong, and I had nothing concrete to tell them—that distancing, of all the behaviors that I regret, remains the most embedded in a level below my consciousness. I had done my part, as a fairly standard middle-class American Jewish boy should, excelling in school, becoming a professional, beginning to take my place as a responsible adult member of the Boston community.

Fortunately, when I visited my mother in the hospital, we made peace. Nothing specific was said. In fact, we said little, just sat together, she in a wheelchair in the hospital solarium, me next to her, holding her hand. It was a visit that appeared to change everything, as stunningly moving for both of us as were a few of the visits I received from dear friends in my own near-death experience. Less was said than one might have expected, but more was expressed, through simple touch. The doctors said that she would recover, that this was a narrow miss, and she appeared to get better and was soon home. Shortly afterward, in December 1972, I was visiting friends from *National Review* in rural Connecticut. For the first time, I had told my parents where I was going to be that weekend—a minor instance of the new, more considerate David, who had previously just gone where he wanted to go, not bothering to let his folks know where he was for days on end. Within an hour of my arrival at my friends' home, my Aunt Kathie called to tell me that my mother had died peacefully while sitting with my father and watching television. While my friends called to find out the bus schedule back to Boston, I spilled out my memories of Doris Ferne Axilrod Brudnoy and realized, as always too late, how much I had loved her and how stupidly I had often behaved toward her.

As I sat on the bus back to Boston that night, quietly crying, I spotted a handsome young soldier and found myself attracted to him at the same time I was unburdening myself of my sadness. We talked for two hours, and he was a paragon of kindness. When the bus came into the terminal in downtown Boston, I gave him a book that I had taken with me to my friends' home to read along the way and told him that I had at last left childhood behind. I felt old suddenly, infinitely grateful that my mother and I had parted in Minneapolis on good terms, and at the same time I was fantasizing something erotic about that soldier. This incident reminded me of a crucial incident in Camus' *L'Etranger,* whose protagonist went to sleep with his girlfriend immediately after his mother's funeral and was later tried for murder and chastised by the prosecution for having defiled his mother's memory. I didn't have sex with that soldier or with anybody else, but I wanted to. I wanted a human touch beyond the hugs of the friends whom I had been visiting, beyond the warm handshake from my seatmate on the bus, that handsome soldier boy; I wanted some validation of my life in tactile form. I've since learned that sexual arousal is often intense while one grieves over the death of a loved one, though at the time I felt extraordinarily guilty for those thoughts. I walked the few blocks from the bus station to my apartment. I packed for the trip to Minneapolis, which I arranged first thing the next morning. I thought of my mother, and of the young soldier on the bus. That night I masturbated and I wept.

Mother's funeral took place on a typically freezing Minnesota December day. I shuddered both from the cold and from my sadness. I seem to recall giggling for an instant, standing at the gravesite without an overcoat—another of my habitual stupidities, the disdaining of warm clothing, which my mother had often criticized me about. The day was so bitingly cold and windy that I actually flashed back to one of her typical responses when she saw me without an overcoat: "You'll die of the cold! Dress right," she would say. For her funeral I finally had on a black suit, no mere sports jacket like I had worn to my cousin's wedding, enraging my mother. I was again the best little boy in the world, but destined, it seemed for one frozen half-hour at a cemetery in Minneapolis, to join my mother in the grave within days. I lived, of course, and one doesn't get colds from the cold outdoors, but my last thought as we left the cemetery was *She's right: I really should dress more sensibly.* Later, at my parents' home, I wrote an article about my mother, which was published in the papers that were then carrying the syndicated column I had just begun. Often I have found in writing a path for walking out of the paralysis of grief, and though my article about her wasn't very good, it was genuine, my last tribute to the woman who had given me the totally enveloping certainty of being loved. Years passed before I could stop myself from crying when some memory of her came to mind. Television shows about families in trouble would unleash my tears—they still do—and whether that's in large part or in small a reflection of my guilt for not having been the best son in the world, I don't know.

A few weeks later I was in Manhattan for New Year's Eve and the weekend, staying with Bob Davis, when my father called to tell me that his mother, Granny Brudnoy, had died. He insisted that I not come home, because the funeral was the next day and he felt that I had been through enough when my mother died. My father thought of my well-being; he always did, while I as often as not thought mainly, perhaps only, of myself. Now they were all gone, all but my father, and along with them some of that sense of invulnerability, of the permanence of things and the enduring existence of those one loves.

SIX

The Good Citizen

Doctor Brudnoy: it sounded nice, and I deserved it. Some graduate students take up permanent residence in grad school ghettoes while working for their degree and can't wean themselves of the pleasures and the routine, coccooned life of the eternal student. Not me. I got my dissertation done by working literally day and night and confining my socializing to a few close friends and my sexual adventures to the occasional evening. In these days of computers, many students understandably consider the most advanced technology of that era, the electric typewriter, a residue of the Dark Ages. I didn't even have that, though after typing 535 pages of my dissertation on my clunky, though reliable, German-crafted Voss manual, when each page had to be flawless (meaning no errors, no whiting out, no erasures), I treated myself to an electric machine. Talk about putting the cart of pleasure after the horse of labor! My first electronic typewriter landed in my life in the mid-1980s and my Mac, at last, in 1995. I am not one to rush things.

But what precisely could I, one of a trillion Ph.D.'s in history hanging around the Boston area—the Hub of the Universe, the Athens of America—do? My chairmanship of the Conservative Party, from 1971 into the next year, paid nothing. I located a teaching job in Guam, but a glance at the map convinced me that life on Guam meant life literally *on* Guam, half an ocean away from anything else. I might have found a job in the cornfields of Kansas, and I almost had one at Claremont College, gorgeously situated not far from Los Angeles. My dissertation adviser, Len Levy, had me out to visit for several days so that we could go over the last drafts of my dissertation, and as chairman of the history department at the Claremont Graduate School, he invited his colleagues from the affiliated Claremont College to meet me and consider me for a junior professorship. But I screwed up, simply by expressing my honest opinions about some of the extreme views then coming into play among American feminists. The final vote, I learned, was three against, two for. The deciding vote, Len told me, came from a woman who thought my views were too conservative.

My résumé made the rounds of a hundred or so schools in New England, joining those of well-educated young Ph.D.'s vying for a handful of jobs teaching history. In the next few years I wandered, like some mendicant scholar in the Middle Ages, from school to school, taking a one-year appointment here, a fill-in assignment for a professor on sabbatical there, anything to get my foot in the door of some inviting college. If there is such a thing as a natural teacher, then I'm one of them. I had little patience for faculty meetings or college politics, but I was the boy who can't say no, so I did whatever I was asked: advised some of the conservative groups at Boston College; speedily became a fixture at Merrimack, the lovely little Augustinian college just north of Boston; turned into a kind of *émi-*

nence (almost) *grise* at the University of Rhode Island among students who turned out to be fans of my articles in conservative journals; and began to conduct seminars on conservative topics at the Institute of Politics at the John F. Kennedy School of Government at Harvard. What I liked best was the interaction with students.

No one but my former student from Northeastern ever attempted to enhance my social life with the gift of a wife, but one of my favorite students at Boston College enlarged my appreciation of contemporary noise by treating me to a Rolling Stones concert, with Stevie Wonder thrown in as the opening act, at the Boston Garden. I took her to drinks and dinner; she provided the joints, which we smoked (at least I tried to inhale) right there in the upper row of the Garden. I wasn't quite that pathetic stereotype the thirtyish professor trying to clutch my fading youth by acting like one of the vibrant youths in my classes. But I came close, and in those heady days of flower power and peace signs and the fracturing of the previous walls of decorum between teachers and students, I fit right in. My record collection grew beyond Mozart and other demigods of the classical tradition, my hair curled below my neck, my glasses were like Granny's, my trousers were belled, my shirts occasionally came with ruffles. I resisted the Nehru jacket, but just barely. In London on my second trip I shopped in Carnaby Street but wound up having a suit made at a much snazzier store, Blade's, patronized as well by John Lennon, whom I almost knocked over in my rush to gush before him when he picked up his suit. I sported a droopy mustache and wore sandals and (God help me) love beads, and though I kept my acid habit to myself when with the boys and girls of the right, I was unapologetic about favoring drug legalization. In conservative circles I was regularly identified as the hippie. As the fellow

152

who preached the conservative faith but looked like a leftie, I was manifesting one of those seeming inconsistencies so puzzling to observers, like my later reputation as the conservative who is gay, and eventually the conservative homosexual with AIDS.

I loved teaching, but except for the one at Merrimack College, which would have happily kept me if I had been willing to accept a rather killing teaching schedule, none of the part-time positions I found were destined to grow into full jobs. It was the need for a job, not a wish to leave the groves of academe, that led me into television. Had I not left Northeastern University to go to Brandeis—had I taken an academic leave and thereby been able to reclaim my job when I finished my dissertation—I would have realized my dream: a tenure-track position at a good university. I doubt that I would have responded with interest to the call from one of the Young Americans for Freedom's local honchos, a good pal, Dan Rea, telling me that WGBH was looking for a conservative who could put sentences together into paragraphs and appear on a news and commentary show, where in due course I criticized Richard Nixon from the *right* rather than from the approved direction, to port. The host was furious and barely acknowledged me once I had said that Nixon's opening to Red China was a betrayal. Nonetheless, I was *on* TV, and that made all the difference. Now I was becoming a fixture around town, employed at thirty-five dollars per commentary once each week, and I was able to use that forum, watched more by the Harvard elites than by hoi polloi, to push libertarian ideas like drug decriminalization. And no, I didn't do a WGBH commentary while tripping on LSD.

A nice win-win synergy developed by accident: I quickly became something of a "character" in Boston owing to those commentaries, which, combined with my writing in *National Review* and elsewhere, led to my being the man people called to speak, to write, to lecture, to turn up for TV or radio shows if they wanted a conservative; and WGBH-TV got its own mileage out of me, trumpeting me as an example of how broadminded the station was: see, there's *our* conservative! I got some mileage of my own about pornography and other subjects from the focus of my dissertation, Theodore Schroeder. I cannibalized the dissertation, publishing chapters in scholarly journals while propounding Schroederian ideas in my public TV and popular magazine pieces. Since my search for a full-time academic position was proving futile, I became less dutiful about hunting for that ideal college job.

One thing leads inevitably to the next, and in 1973, two years after I had begun at the PBS channel, I was asked by the CBS affiliate, then WNAC-TV, to become a commentator for them. I happily accepted, keeping my fingers in at WGBH while working twice weekly, on the eleven o'clock news, on WNAC. As I moved by necessity further away from my dream of full-time employment at a decent college, I moved by the same necessity, and by the fun of the job, into what had never drawn me before, work in a broadcast medium. When I was asked in 1975 to fill in for a friend who hosted a talk program on WHDH-AM, I loved that three weeks' experience, and when my friend moved to another radio station early the next year, I was hired by WHDH for a ten-to-midnight job that soon became eight-to-midnight. My news director at WNAC, Mel Bernstein, required no persuading to shift my duties from the eleven o'clock to the six o'clock news. Suddenly I was commentator, then film critic, then critic-at-large for a major TV station and host of an instantly successful radio talk program. I even served a brief stint as a point-counterpoint commentator on the *CBS Morning News,* debating the issues with Susan Cheever; our segment lasted until Richard Salant, the president of CBS, decided to scrap the entire series of these mini debates, thus ending my national TV exposure until twenty years later, when news of my disease coupled with my unexpected politics shoved me back into the national spotlight.

Now I was everywhere in the Boston media, recognized, sometimes even respected (often by those on the fringes of the liberal left and the conservative right), and despised, which validated Oscar Wilde's aperçu that the only thing worse than being talked about is not being talked about. I liked it. More, I loved it. (It did nothing for my sex life, however, since I was even more prone than before all this attention to assume that a friendly glance my way was not in any way an overture.) The radio program took off and has remained at or near the top of the ratings heap from its beginning till the present. I was working nightly on the CBS television affiliate, writing constantly, and thoroughly enjoying my life. By 1977 I gave up sending out those résumés to colleges. My destiny, I felt pretty certain by then, was probably in TV and radio and print journalism; the halls of ivy would have to survive without me on their faculties. But I kept one foot dipped into academe, directing seminars at the Institute of Politics and spreading the libertarian and conservative gospel to students, among them Bill Kristol, now editor of the *Weekly Standard;* Steven Chapman, a syndicated columnist; and others who have made more than a negligible dent on the public consciousness. I doubt that I am even slightly responsible for their successes, though in the right mood I'll claim otherwise. I was writing constantly for *NR,* at one point going to New York every other week to write editorials. Sometimes I had as many as three articles in one issue, and a colleague developed the acronym Andy Drubdovi for me so that it wouldn't look as if I had written the whole magazine some weeks.

I did reports from the academic battlefield for *National Review,* travel pieces from Europe and the Caribbean, book reviews, and eventually film criticism. I even tossed off the occasional humor piece, including a mock rock review about Danny Candle and the Wick-Dippers and their latest disc. Nobody at *NR* seemed to get the joke, but I was perfecting my parodic style and enjoying all the layers of the routine: sounding serious about nonsense and making up nonsense to sound serious about. My articles appeared throughout the full range of conservative and libertarian publications. I was called on to give speeches across the land, which I did without the assistance of LSD or mescaline. I appeared on Bill Buckley's *Firing Line* with Professor C. Eric Lincoln on the subject of the Black Muslims, as the Nation of Islam was then commonly called, and I was a participant in a made-for-TV documentary about the evils of Red China, as we called it then. I began writing for *Boston* magazine on movies and restaurants, on film and then on politics for the *Boston Herald,* on travel for the *Boston Globe,* and on anything whatsoever for the *Alternative,* now the *American Spectator.* If someone wants an article or a speech or a colloquium participant or a debater or a college lecturer, call Brudnoy: has opinions, will travel.

I was finally making a livable income and in 1976, prodded by two buddies, traded apartment living for a condominium in the Back Bay. My infatuation with hallucinogenic drugs attenuated in the late 1970s, and as I aged, my appeal to the kinds of men who appealed to me also attenuated, which made my social life more casual and less sexual. My drug use was limited almost entirely to alcohol, leading some friends to tell me that I was becoming an alcoholic, though of course I denied that.

No, I just enjoyed three or four martinis before dinner and a half-bottle of wine with supper, every day . . . and in such ways do we humor ourselves. Gradually I accepted the fact that my drinking was getting out of hand—I have a series of photos taken of me sleeping it off on the couches of assorted friends across New England, and I'm not so attractive in a drunken stupor—and I tapered off. Friends recommended AA, but in a preview of coming attractions which is spooky now that I think of how I nearly died by refusing to seek help in 1994, I said that I didn't need anybody's damn twelve-step program and could control my drinking all on my own. "I'm dysfunctional, you're dysfunctional" was years away; this boy was totally in control of his life, didn't you know?

I've often shuddered thinking back to the 1970s, wondering how I actually survived. I had no recognition of the effect my alcohol intake was having on me until one night on radio we did a program specifically designed to find out. It was the day before the beginning of the July Fourth weekend in 1977, and our aim was to educate our listeners about the effects of a significant bout of drinking, with me as the guinea pig. With a representative of the governor's Highway Safety Bureau and a cop in attendance, your genial host started in with straight shots of gin, ounce after ounce, periodically taking the Breathalyzer test, which supposedly determines how much booze is in the blood. I began babbling, singing, telling lousy jokes, and slurring my words, sloshing out the words rather than speaking them. By the time I was taken off the air and left to whimper in the corner while the police officer took over the show, I had tested at .29 on the Breathalyzer; .30 is comatose. A close miss, but not sufficient to get me to put my drinking excesses in check. Once I nearly went careening off the road and into a house when going to visit a friend in Truro, but I managed to turn the wheel somehow and drove merrily on my way. On another occasion I had so much to drink while doing a radio show on restaurants that my usual carefulness about my language sailed away into the ozone and I referred to the proprietors of a snooty restaurant as pigs. A $600,000 lawsuit and appeals right up to the highest court in the state later made the case a landmark. You can look it up: *Pritzker* v. *David Brudnoy and WHDH Radio.* Any restaurant critic who wants to use the word "pig" can cite the case and probably be vindicated, as I was. But I don't recommend it. My delusional sense of invulnerability should have caught up with me by then, but I continued to sail along on a high-altitude flight via LSD or mescaline, or to yuk it up after way too many cocktails. I was happy, joyfully warm to one and all, and utterly unable to judge how far I was going.

On one occasion I went into a blind rage when a heckler approached me as some buddies and I were walking into the Napoleon Club, a venerable old gay club. "Fruit," "fag," and "cocksucker" were among this charmer's more cordial epithets, to which I, already a few sheets to the wind, responded with something brilliant like "Takes one to know one." I was livid, unleashing a heavy load of barely repressed resentment at the world at large. Why do people think that homosexuals are punching bags? Why does American society regard gay-bashing as a minor affair, if an affair to remember at all? Why couldn't primitives like my name-calling antagonist learn to walk upright? Suddenly, after I had matched him insult for insult—Breeder! Cretin! Cro-Magnon Man! Redneck!—he was on me, punching away and yelping. *In vino veritas* and all that, and this fellow found himself encountering that rarest of creatures, a physically aggressive Bruds. I punched back, kicked, flailed at him, and—I'm not making this up—he fled. I was shaking with fury. I began to pound the brick façade of the bar, stomping up and down, uncontrollable even by my friends, none of whom had ever seen me physically out of control, much less in a blue rage.

But it wasn't until about 1980, when I turned forty, that I finally took control of my drinking and stopped denying what friends were telling me. At last I swore off all illegal drugs and became a polite social wine-drinker only on weekends, if then. I was the city's leading radio talk host, one of the most respected television arts critics, something of a big cheese in national conservative and libertarian circles, and happy as a clam sans sauce. I didn't need drugs or booze to give me courage, and I think that I was becoming a more thoughtful man. It was a long journey, probably only partially accomplished, but it had me pointed in the right direction. I was, God help us, middle-aged, and though I didn't look the part, I felt it.

I knew everybody and could have anybody on the program by, in essence, summons. Orson Welles came by, as did Buckminster Fuller, and George Bush in (fruitless) pursuit of the Republican presidential nomination in 1980, and Billy Friedkin, one of my favorite movie directors. Governor Michael Dukakis, who confused me with my producer (who was dressed like an adult, whereas I was in jeans), became a regular guest, a guest host, and a friend. His wife, Kitty, became a part-time cohost on my weekly TV show, *Nightscene,* or *Nightmare,* as the crew called it, until her husband's defeat in the 1978 Democratic primary, whereupon the TV powers decided that WNAC no longer needed her contribution. We remained friends—I had nothing to do either with hiring or with firing her—and I've taken more than a few lessons in courage from Kitty's frankness in describing her own troubled life and addictions in a much maligned but chillingly honest book. I was learning about the reality of the broadcast business: you're of use only if somebody else wants you, and it isn't what you did for us the day before yesterday, it's today that counts.

Over the years I interviewed Barbara Bush and Jimmy and Rosalyn Carter; assorted presidential wannabes, such as Steve Forbes, Pat Buchanan, Dick Lugar, Arlen Specter, Bob Dole, Lyndon Larouche, Harold Stassen, Newt Gingrich, and Colin Powell; evangelist Pat Robertson; novelists like Anne Rice, Robin Cook, P. D. James, and Robert Parker; Gennifer Flowers; Janet Pilgrim, the first *Playboy* centerfold star; porn actresses and actors; athletes such as Bruce Jenner, Greg Louganis, and Bobby Orr; singers like Tony Bennett and Dennis Day and Betty Buckley; Cabinet secretaries such as Donald Regan and Dick Thornburgh; movie and television luminaries, including Jerry Lewis, Sid Caesar, Imogene Coca, Lauren Bacall, Ruth Gordon, Arnold Schwarzenegger, Rob Lowe, Vanessa Redgrave, and hundreds more. I've interviewed countless senators, governors, mayors, scholars, inventors, crackpots, dreamers, and visionaries. I've happily locked horns with David Duke and other race-baiters and spoken with ex-Nazis, ex-cons, ex-nuns, ex-priests, ex-Marines like Oliver North, and Generation Xers by the barrel. The list goes on. It used to be said that if one sat long enough at an outdoor table at the Café des Deux Magots in Paris, eventually everybody worth knowing would pass by. Twenty years hosting talk radio in a major city is like a broadcast version of that choice spot in the City of Lights. If a non-liberal talk host could make it in liberal Cambridge and Boston in the 1970s and 1980s, ain't America grand?

But the real meat and potatoes of my show have always come from the callers, who of course are only a tiny fraction of listeners—maybe one out of five hundred listeners ever picks up the phone and calls—but who are the necessary second part

160

of the duet. The programs with big-name guests can be wonderful, but my favorite shows are the ones where the callers open up, whether they are anxious, furious, or joy-filled. It's the level of involvement that makes the programs come alive. I'll never forget one young fellow from Michigan who called to tell me that his girlfriend had been raped and he was determined to kill the bastard who did it. I truly had never heard a caller in such a state of pained agitation. I didn't know what to do except to keep this young man on the air with me for the better part of a half-hour, trying to talk him into going to the police instead of taking matters into his own hands. I asked my producer to put on only those calls that might help. A regular caller, a terrific lady from Connecticut, Gabrielle, a newcomer to America from France, offered the most soothing, intelligent advice, reinforcing my own, and a retired police officer from Cape Cod called to explain how our young man could use the police and depend on them for support. Our collective efforts calmed him sufficiently to act rationally. My young friend from the Midwest has called occasionally over the years to report on his life; he didn't kill the man who raped his girlfriend, he has a job, and he has started a family, all of which provided me with more than just a momentary sense of accomplishment.

The years raced on, as I did, on radio from WHDH to WRKO in 1981 to WBZ in 1986, and on television from WNAC (later WNEV, finally WHDH) to WCVB, the ABC affiliate, where the town's eight-hundred-pound journalistic gorilla, Mike Barnicle of the *Boston Globe,* and I did point-counterpoint for two years, then to WBZ, my radio station's sister channel, for a similar shtick with first *Boston Herald* star columnist Margery Eagan and then our arts critic, Joyce Kulhawik. My departure from WNAC in 1983 was not my choice. RKO General lost its television license and so lost the station, and the new owners turned the news operation over to people whose idea of a good time was celebrating by cracking open the bubbly when they told somebody to clear out his desk and leave the building immediately. I was permitted to run out my contract, though I was humiliated by being demoted from the six o'clock to the noon news.

I felt diminished by this and spent a great many Wednesday mornings discussing the matter, and everything else that was lurking in my mind, with a psychiatrist. My self-confidence, bolstered by my achievements, was fragile, a sometime thing. I felt I had been made a lesser person by wretched management types who have left shambles in their wake at every station they've been given access to. I loved the limelight, the influence as a critic, the sheer fun of being known—a good definition of celebrity: being known for being known. What began as a few months of therapy to handle my sense that maybe I really wasn't good enough to be doing what I had done (I thought successfully) on TV for ten years stretched on well beyond the proximate reason for my visits to the good Dr. Avery Weisman. Despite my successes on radio, on TV, and in the pages of magazines and newspapers, I felt small and insufficient. My visits to the shrink enabled me to weather that period as well as to discuss matters close to the bone, including the fact that I had everything except a lover.

Friends concluded, fairly enough, that since I seemed to prefer noncommital one-night stands to anything more involving, who was I kidding when I bemoaned my solitary life? In 1966 I left Houston, parting from Andrew, the last of the three great gay loves of my life. Never since then have I been "in love," the sort of spillover into romanticized and idealized yearning, for more than a few weeks. I absented myself deliberately from the places where somebody of my age, interests, and position in the community could meet similar sorts. Did I even want that part of life anymore? Clearly, I had segmented my life into two parts, the public persona and the private man, which I think I'm now moving to reconcile. It was the second segmenting, however, that of my affections (for a very few) and my lusts (for men who are now the age that my lovers and I were when we were in love), that I hadn't and haven't found a way to fuse. I haven't much expectation of living out a scene from *South Pacific*, which is to say that I doubt that I'm about to meet a stranger across a crowded room.

Still, in the early 1980s I was living well. I traveled to at least one interesting country each year, often to some Third World country that gave me fodder for my travel articles and for my radio discussions about the comparative wonders of America. I became a habitué of San Juan, Puerto Rico, and later of Santo Domingo, two places where I could maintain my anonymity and give vent, in compact bursts of activity, to my desire for male company. I encountered many prominent media figures from New England and the national TV world in those backwaters, and realized that I wasn't alone in enjoying public attention but wanting a portion of my life removed from the glare. I didn't deny my sexuality, but I made no big deal of it on radio or TV or in print, though I did quit the *American Spectator* when that monthly magazine, now rivaling *National Review* for circulation, began to make sneering references, obsessively, to gay people. I made waves in conservative and libertarian publications, I taught the occasional college course, and I remained a major player in the local broadcast media world.

My loss of a front-line position on television in 1983 was my only serious career setback. The loss of two close friends in the 1980s, however, gave me a much greater jolt. Bob Davis, who introduced me to mescaline in 1970 and with whom I had spent nearly twenty years of shared weekends in New York or Boston, plus a summer in Provincetown, died in 1985, officially listed as the victim of a heart attack, but I suspected that he died at the hand of one of his occasional pickups. Bob and I shared many interests and helped each other accept the reality of middle age. He had a quiet but forcefully expressed dislike of cant, and while he could rise to the occasional insincere compliment, he wasn't very good at flattery. He was a severe, shrewd critic of my writing and a wry evaluator of my choices in bed partners, and though he didn't turn sufficiently away from alcohol, he was able to carry on, while quite drunk, as if he were merely languid. I admired his savoir faire but worried about his inability to shake off the vapors, as he uniquely described his seeming lack of interest in career achievement; I loved his wit, his subtle mastery of the *mot juste,* and mourned his loss. I find myself sometimes hearing a faint southern accent in a crowded room and involuntarily turning around as if I expect to see my friend, even a decade after his death.

My second great loss, the greatest to date of a friend, occurred in 1989, seventeen years after Blitz and I met at a conservative conference in Indiana sponsored by the *American Spectator.* Our friendship developed during the next few years, as Blitz worked on his graduate degree at Harvard and I taught and began to work on television. We both played the game of pretending to be straight, each of us assuming that the other was a standard-issue heterosexual who wouldn't be very well disposed to homosexuals. This charade ended in 1973, when, falling into an atypical reverie for a young man whom I met in Provincetown—I learned yet again that intergenerational love affairs are rarities and that they are usually short-lived and ended by the younger partner—I decided to tell Blitz what was going on in my life. This was the first in a series of hundreds and hundreds of endless telephone conversations. Our friendship did not depend on similar habits or on our tastes in men. Blitz, short, balding, with piercing blue eyes and a gymnast's body, affectionate beyond anything I was capable of, had more younger men than he had time for clamoring for him. I sometimes gawked in amazement at his success rate with his harem of worshipers. We were united by our libertarian-conservative ideas, by a love of good dining and good theater and books and selected films. I introduced him to Provincetown and to Puerto Rico, and except for his visits to me in Boston and my very rare visits to him in Washington or New Orleans, and one trip to Haiti—he hated it; the boys didn't instantly court him—we never traveled together. I smoked pipes and did a great deal of dope in the 1970s and drank heavily. Blitz neither drank nor smoked, and he regarded me as drug addict. Was this a friendship made in heaven? On occasion it seemed so.

Blitz always encouraged me in my writing and was as good an editor as I have ever had, tougher even than Bill Buckley and the others at *National Review,* invariably right about emphases and verbiage, toning down my excesses and helping me build up my strong points. He was the best friend anyone could ever hope for, selfless in his willingness to take time and expend energy to help a pal. It can also be said that he was remarkably attractive to remarkably attractive people, and as I lived through his various affairs, often with people who I was convinced didn't deserve him, I saw clearly how a lover like Blitz, however neurotic and compulsive and given to bizarre eccentricities he was, could hold the total loyalty and affection of those whom he chose to love.

His odd habits were legendary. He would pack twelve pairs of jeans for a twelve-day trip to San Juan, insisting that he couldn't wear an "unclean" pair, but then he would do laundry every other day or so, so that when he returned home, his suitcase had eleven pairs of clean jeans and the remaining pair was on him. He insisted on getting extra towels in hotels, "just in case," as he put it, so he wound up with fifty or sixty towels in his closet. He traveled with a dozen bars of soap, with a dozen T-shirts and a dozen long-sleeved white or blue shirts, and with a half-dozen pairs of sneakers and a dozen pairs of socks and briefs—all of which he washed repeatedly, "just in case." In restaurants he would invariably find our table somehow deficient—it was too near the door or too far from the window; too near the canned music, which he always insisted be turned down; too close to a light fixture or too far away—and the waiter was always either too much the hoverer or not attentive enough. If we ever went to a restaurant where he expressed no complaint and made no demand for some change, I don't recall the experience. On airplanes he would demand a change of seat, sometimes more than once, and once he actually delayed a plane's departure by a few minutes, standing in the doorway and trying to negotiate a better seat assignment while flight attendants indulged him. He either wanted none of something on the menu or two orders of something else. Tomato juice without ice was his drink of choice, and if it came with ice he sent it back. He liked to try a little piece of whatever a companion ordered and insisted that we all try his food too, but he had no taste for the kind of restaurants—Chinese, for instance, or Indian—where that sort of sharing is common. In short, for Blitz the world was a place in which things didn't quite fit, except his true place as the friend of all friends.

No matter what our planned time was for meeting to go someplace for dinner or to a speech or whatever, he was late. If I pushed up the time from, say, six-thirty to six, hoping that he would arrive at six-thirty, he would turn up at seven. There was no winning with Blitz, no way to contend with his neuroses except by giving in to them, and on my better days I did just that, though on most days I railed against his weirdnesses and his lateness, to no avail. If he was rained on, he had to return to his rooms to change his jeans and shirt, because he was convinced that the world would find him repulsive if he wasn't immaculately dressed. Blitz's sense of himself defined the oddest of insecurities, since from a friend's point of view he had everything, but from his own perspective he was nothing.

We had both known people who died of AIDS, but we were living in a haze of hope and denial and couldn't imagine—even Blitz, whose sexual preferences were risky, as I thought mine were not—that *we* could be infected. Blitz and his doctor published a serious article attempting to attribute AIDS not to sexual behavior per se but to previously acquired deficiency owing to drug abuse. He was drawn to the theory, propounded first by Dr. Peter Duesberg, a retrovirus specialist, that HIV was not *the* cause nor perhaps even *a* cause of AIDS. With his brilliant mind and exquisitely clear and elegant prose, he could make a believer out of almost anybody. But his belief that he would not fall victim to HIV proved false, and by 1986 he knew that he was HIV-positive.

As his condition began to decline in the late 1980s, Blitz became, quite understandably, obsessive about his health, sometimes devoting entire days to filling out insurance forms, reading about the latest AIDS research, and visiting doctors, sometimes two or three for the same condition, though for long stretches he refused to take the AIDS-related medications that his specialist prescribed. When I was diagnosed with HIV, he introduced me to his principal doctor in Washington, who was the cowriter of his first piece on AIDS, and convinced me,

as a well-recognized public figure in Boston, to have my treatment and diagnosis confined to Washington, avoiding any
AIDS clinic in Boston. He was right about that, and I did as he
urged. Blitz's concern for my well-being was unending in its
duration and fathomless in its scope.

I began to fail him, he believed, when I, fully employed and
unable to get away to visit him, preferred that he visit me. I was
"selfish" in not visiting him as often as he visited me, he said,
and maybe I was, though I rationalized my failure to do so as
the result of my lack of freedom. He said that I was always
perfectly correct in behavior, meaning that I wrote the correct
thank-you notes and said the right things to people and met all
my deadlines and fulfilled all my obligations—I was the good
citizen but not the ideal friend. To Blitz, "good citizen" was a
damning criticism, and when he broke off contact and then
suffered an attack of *Pneumocystis carinii* pneumonia (PCP), he
told me nothing about it. His family and a former lover who
was his roommate took care of Blitz, who forbade them to tell
me of his condition. Then, in a final act of self-abnegation, he
became resistant to medical advice and wound up a second
time in the hospital with PCP, which killed him.

I came back from the gym one Saturday morning in early
November 1989 to find a phone message from Blitz's roommate. As soon as I heard his voice, I knew. I called back, talked
with the roommate and with Blitz's father, and was told not to
come for the funeral, because it would be private and immediate, but please come visit in a week or so. I said I would. I sat
stunned by my telephone. I buried my head in my lap and wept
for an hour, then ambled around the house looking at things
that Blitz had given me and pictures of us on vacation.

A week later I delivered a tribute to Blitz on the radio and
published a piece about him in the *Boston Herald*. My tribute

detailed my friendship with him, lauded his academic and journalistic achievements, described the last troubling years of our
friendship, and concluded: "As Mrs. Loman says of her husband Willy in *Death of a Salesman,* 'attention must be paid;
attention must be paid to this man.' We pass into life and out of
life so fast; attention often amounts to a small obituary notice
and then to the dark encompassing shroud of forgetting. I
could not let Blitz leave without commemorating his life, the
premature cutting off of which has deprived America of one of
its most brilliant men, and his loving family and friends of a
remarkable, loving, loyal brother."

Having always felt like an adopted son around Blitz's parents
and having assumed by their words and actions that they fully
accepted Blitz's lovers and friends, I always thought of them as
accepting of their son's homosexuality and then, when he died,
as surely willing to acknowledge that he had died of AIDS. But
I was jolted out of that comforting illusion when, after they
heard of my radio tribute and read my newspaper profile,
which I sent to them immediately upon publication, they accused me of having betrayed them and Blitz. Should I never
have said in public how dear he was to me? Or told the truth
about his wonderful mind and loyal friendship? Or was it simply that I said he had died of AIDS-related diseases? Blitz's
father wrote to me and banished me forever from the golden
light of his family. I hoped that grief had caused him to mistake
my intentions and misread my tribute to his son and that time
would change his mind. But even seven years later, even as my
own medical condition has received so much attention, Blitz's
parents have never said another word to me.

Blitz was with me through seventeen years of my life, my
advocate in every endeavor that drew my interest, a wise counselor, devoted to me. I thought during all those years that I was

as good a friend to Blitz as he was to me, but he saw me near the end as deficient, as imperfect, as merely the good citizen. Blitz's parents banished me, perhaps with as much belief in the correctness of their behavior as I felt when I banished Boyd Murray from my friendship. With Blitz's death, and with my certain knowledge that I too would die of this disease, the Age of AIDS had begun in earnest for me.

SEVEN

Denial

Health we take for granted when we're young. Apart from summer hay fever, my boyhood was unexceptional but for one episode, which I dutifully recorded at age fourteen in a school project that I titled, rather grandiosely, "Genesis: The Story of My Life." This junior autobiography was written shortly before my uncle Arnold was tried for murder, and it reflected a near-total optimism. In chapter one, "Birth to Kindergarten," the cheerful Davy wrote: "In December of 1944, this fun [the joys of being four years old] ceased temporarily for me. I had had bad tonsils and they had caused a mastoid condition in my ear, giving me many caraches and much pain. I remember the day the doctor decided to send me to the hospital as if it were yesterday. I was sitting in the big chair in the living room and the doctor had just finished examining me. He was talking very softly to my mother and I don't think I was supposed to hear. But I did. . . . I was in the hospital six weeks and during that time had my tonsils out. Luckily, I did not need a mastoid operation and I have had no ear trouble since." I think that my fourteen-year-old self had already begun the process of self-censorship. The matter was more serious than my little autobiography indicated: I had been growing increasingly deaf, and the hospitalization contended successfully with that, but my family simply repressed the whole matter, as did I. There are patterns in everybody's life, and in mine denial figures heavily.

I had the usual childhood diseases—chicken pox, measles, mumps, strep throat, flu, and the like—and maybe in some measure owing to my mother's paranoia, I escaped infantile paralysis during the great polio scare of the late 1940s. She kept me inside, playing in the basement (literally), for one entire summer, lest I contract the disease, which was then thought incurable and in the fullness of its wrath. In general I was healthy, and except for two hernia operations in the late 1980s, I was never hospitalized again after that long period for the mastoid infection.

The seemingly sudden appearance of a new scourge in 1980, briefly referred to as GRID, gay-related immune deficiency, and then as AIDS, acquired immunity deficiency syndrome, made little impression on me for several years. A few friends and acquaintances contracted AIDS somehow—we knew nothing for the first few years about the pathogen now generally thought to be the villain in the disease, human immunodeficiency virus (HIV)—but I couldn't figure out any reason why they, and not most of the other people I knew, were getting and dying from this thing. Theories flew around, attributing AIDS to heavy use of amyl nitrite, or to insufficiently diagnosed and treated syphilis, or to experiments by (take your pick) the U.S. government, Jewish doctors aiming to infect black babies (a favorite of one Steve Cokely, an aide for a time to Chicago mayor Harold Washington), mad scientists in a communist laboratory operating within our very midst, and on into the wildest reaches of the paranoid mentality. Theories abound to this day, and when my own AIDS became common knowledge, I was deluged by pamphlets and earnest letters and bizarre books explaining why AIDS is caused by anything imaginable except HIV. The prominent virus specialist Dr. Peter Duesberg, whom Blitz recommended to me as a radio guest, insists to this day that HIV is harmless and that AIDS is caused by something else, as yet unknown. Other researchers have recently begun to theorize that HIV may be necessary but not sufficient to cause AIDS—that some other pathogen is required, though if it exists, this sneaky virus or bacterium or parasite or whatever has not been discovered.

The common wisdom never quite settled on a single cause of AIDS, but until the blood supply was found to be contaminated to some extent by HIV, which accounted for AIDS cases in many people who had had blood transfusions, and until transmission from unclean needles shared by intravenous drug users was found to be a major cause of HIV infection and thence of AIDS, the major entry route for HIV was thought to be passive anal sex. Like many people, I wanted to believe that AIDS couldn't touch me, since I was neither an IV drug user, with or without shared needles, nor a recipient of blood transfusions, nor a practitioner of anal sex, passively or actively, unless that experience with the young man I met in Bryant Park in 1961 could have infected me and led to symptoms nearly thirty-five years later. Getting "it," as some people came to call AIDS, was not to be my fate, or so I chose to believe. I fell for the fairly standard view in the mid-1980s that oral sex is either the rarest of ways to become infected or no way at all. Even now, some presumably informed people dismiss oral sex as a transmission route for HIV, and the now extensive documentation shows that oral sex is an *unusual* way to become infected. Unusual doesn't mean impossible, as those of us in the "unusual" category have learned to our sorrow. Denial is sometimes just one variation on a theme of madness.

When Blitz told me that he was HIV-positive, I was jolted and alarmed, though not really surprised, because I knew quite a lot about his sexual practices. But I resisted getting tested for a few years, believing that I didn't fall into the high-risk categories that the medical profession and the increasingly interested media referred to. When the psychiatrist I had been seeing for several years insisted that I get an AIDS test, I did it, but I thought the whole thing was ridiculous: what had I done to contract HIV? A week later, Dr. Martin Hirsch, Massachusetts General Hospital's leading AIDS physician, informed me of the bad news, which stunned me. How could this have happened? I didn't try to convince myself that the test was inaccurate, but of course that is almost everybody's first panicked, confused thought when told that an HIV antibody test is positive. Except for having the flu, I was fine and looked healthy, and I believed that to look healthy was to be healthy.

Dr. Hirsch suggested that I enter a double-blind research study at Mass. General that was experimenting with a newly developed drug, or rather an old drug that was being tried out on people with AIDS, AZT. I was willing to do so until Blitz convinced me that I would be better off not appearing frequently at Mass. General's AIDS center, since I was so well known in Boston. Despite the signs throughout the hospital to "respect patient confidentiality," people gossip, and somebody, Blitz insisted, would probably report Brudnoy sightings to the town's then-powerful gossip columnist, a woman who repeatedly slammed me in her column. She wouldn't have written point-blank that I had AIDS; rather, it would be something like

"What's darling Doody Brudsy [her term] doing sneaking into Mass. General's AIDS clinic the last few weeks? Maybe a research trip for a radio show, Eye say!" I had seen the national hysteria and derision when well known people like Rock Hudson and Liberace were revealed to have AIDS. Roy Cohn, the McCarthy-era attorney who had gone on to be a power in Republican circles, denied to the end that he had AIDS, but he did, and everyone knew, and a great many people laughed about it. Given my political views and my frequent criticism of the sort of people who believe that it's always somebody else's obligation to take care of them, I would be an easy target. A youngster who had contracted HIV through blood transfusion, Ryan White, had been literally kicked out of school, and he and his mother had fled their home town because of the fury, ignorance, and cruelty of his neighbors. I didn't expect anything like that, but in the late 1980s the era of understanding about AIDS was barely a sunbeam on the horizon. So I took Blitz's advice and had Dr. Caceres, in Washington, D.C., examine me two or three times each year and arrange for CD4 cell counts and HIV antigen and antibody tests, which immediately give away a patient's HIV status to any informed person looking for evidence.

My longtime Boston physician, George Cohen, took blood samples every two or three weeks, and I submitted the results to Dr. Caceres. My privacy was maintained at the cost of lots of travel time and money; I didn't submit any bills for AIDS-related tests to my insurance. The pattern that the doctors and I worked out, which eventually included getting AZT and some other drugs in Boston under a pseudonym, with a friend making what we called the drug runs, provided me with good monitoring and with complete anonymity in Boston.

It all sounds ridiculous to me now, too cloak-and-dagger,

but even less than a decade ago, a diagnosis of HIV or AIDS was like a diagnosis of leprosy in early modern times. I took to heart the advice about practicing "safe" or "safer" sex, and when (increasingly infrequently) I had sex with someone, I was almost obsessive about using condoms. I knew that the chances were as good as not that some of the people I met were HIV-positive, though nobody told me anything. Maybe these guys didn't know that they were infected, if they were, or were like me, wanting to keep that part of their lives private. But as soon as I fully accepted that I was infected, I found that my desire for anonymous or, better put, casual sex waned. It didn't disappear, but between my HIV status and my age—I was in my late forties in the years after I was infected—I naturally tended to be less driven to have sex with the proper (or improper) stranger.

Perhaps one day, when HIV-positive people aren't frequently tossed out of their jobs or their apartments or in some cases banished from their families, Americans won't feel the need to live this kind of big lie. That time still hasn't come; witness current arguments about legislation to protect people with AIDS from job or housing discrimination, and current maneuvers by many insurance companies to avoid having to cover patients who are HIV-positive. I had written and spoken on radio and television about homosexuality and in recent years about AIDS, and the reactions in most cases were so hostile to the former and so hysterical and terrified about the latter that I believed strongly that coming out as an AIDS patient wouldn't be easy. It might have changed—ruined?—every facet of my public life.

When I finally began to come to grips with the severity of my condition, I arranged for a kind of informal support group of three friends in Boston to be aware of my diagnosis, along with Blitz, who served as a kind of reality test for my health. I chose my neighbor, Bob Cord, a friend whom I had met when I taught at Northeastern University in the mid-1960s; my WBZ Radio colleague Peter Meade; and my closest pal, Ward Cromer, who turned out to be the man for all seasons.

Once in a while I regretted inflicting this information on Bob, who is the most solicitous of men, since with the best will in the world but against my strong desire, he tended to bring up my health when we were together. Bob believed, I guess, that talking about it somehow made a difference. All it did was make me irritable. I wasn't then in denial about my condition, but I was in the business of getting on with my life and was determined not to become a hypochondriac. I don't fault Bob's concern in the least, or doubt that he loves me like a brother, but sometimes I avoided him just to spare myself another round of questions and earnest concerns about my health. He is as reliable and honest as any man I know: I felt confident that my home base, as it were, was covered by having Bob in on my HIV status. I had brought my eventual disease home, as it were, to Bob.

Ward and Peter accepted my wish that I would determine when we would talk about my health. I told them every several months what Dr. Caceres was telling me and how I was feeling, but I made these discussions to the point and brief. I felt fine during the first several years of my infection—or I should say, in the first several years that I knew I was infected; I may have been infected many years before—and in 1989 I was far more concerned about Blitz.

I told no one else in Boston, and only a few friends in California—Andrew, Paul, and Arthur—not because I distrusted others but because I didn't want to add years of worry to the lives of any additional people. I saw no reason to tell my father and my new stepmother, since I was feeling good and I realized that eventually, when my HIV infection moved on to full-blown AIDS and the revelation of it became unavoidable, they would be told about my condition. I rationalized this as consideration for *them*—for friends, for family, for colleagues—but I know that my reticence also served *my* need, which was to keep private that which was now in a very significant way central to my life. The fewer there were who knew the truth, the less my life would become a tragedy in the estimation of people for whom I cared greatly.

I experienced a few symptoms of the oncoming horrors, among them diarrhea, which became a daily event and resulted in a weight loss of about fifteen pounds over the several years that I was treated primarily in Washington. A common AIDS manifestation, "wasting," found in great numbers of people with HIV in Africa and to a lesser extent in America, was not quite yet an appropriate label for what was ailing me. Tests for parasites, which can cause diarrhea and weight loss, proved negative, and the diarrhea sometimes eased without drugs or, later, with a daily Imodium tablet. I tried to cram myself with high-calorie foods and even toyed with the idea of returning to heavy drinking: alcohol is chock full of empty calories that often lead to what we refer to as a beer belly. For the first time in my life, I actually wanted to appear fat, or at least bulky. My outlook during that time was that I could live a fairly normal life, keep my private business out of the public eye, and get on with my work. But since the common image of AIDS-infected people is that of the rail-thin, emaciated person, some of the people with whom I spent time began to ask leading questions, seeing my weight loss as a clue. Of course I shoved all that aside with my habitual response: "I'm fine, really, fine."

Another frequent illness of people infected with HIV, thrush, a fungal infection in the mouth, was easily dealt with by

daily tablets of Mycelex, an inexpensive drug. Like the diarrhea, thrush was more a nuisance than anything else, and I went
through the fairly standard course of medications employed as
delaying tactics between infection and fully diagnosed AIDS.
This included a drug called ddI and a similar drug, ddC,
though Dr. Caceres warned me that sometimes people on one
or the other of these experience peripheral neuropathy, meaning pain in the feet or sometimes the hands, or, infrequently, in
both. Since every drug appears to have side effects, I didn't pay
much attention to the warning, hoping that the odds were with
me. Because every possibly useful anti-AIDS drug eventually
disappointed patients and doctors, and with the understandable
desire to give anything new a try, many HIV-positive people,
like me, weighed the possibility of neuropathy against the
chance that ddI or ddC might prove useful.

I seemed to be in excellent health, though I was thin—
scrawny even, at times almost frail. Over two years my weight
dropped from 175 to 157. Frequent workouts gave my body
some muscularity, and since I was always well enough not to
need to take sick days at work, most people assumed I was
healthy. When asked, I simply lied. If only wishes were facts.
Until my condition dramatically worsened during the late summer of 1994, I wasn't out sick from work for a year and a half.

"Longtime nonprogressers" is the chic term these days for
people who are HIV-positive but don't actually get—or at least
don't yet have—AIDS. People generally judge others' likelihood of being HIV-positive on the simple basis of how they
look, often with disastrous consequences for those who resist
taking precautions. Increasingly, the medical profession is coming to believe that people are often infected years before they
have any reason to think that having an AIDS antibody test is
wise. And since AIDS has become the most political of diseases,

with significant resistance by activists to broadening the scope of those who are urged to be tested, great numbers of infected but unaware people may well be among us, going about their business, including having unprotected sex, without the slightest thought that they may be carriers.

As awkward as coming to terms with my sexuality may have been in the repressed 1950s, at least I never had to confront what today's teenagers, both homosexual and heterosexual, face. As cases of AIDS are developing in people in their early and mid-twenties, the chance is overwhelming that young people might have been or soon will be infected in their mid-teens. Adolescents usually think that they're invulnerable, and the prospect that a newly sexually active fifteen-year-old needs an AIDS test seems preposterous. However, the incidence of AIDS among young heterosexuals is on the rise, though rarely discussed among the general population. The early tactic of AIDS advocates who proclaimed that everybody is at risk, even that everybody is at the *same* risk, of contracting AIDS has, mercifully, backfired. Mother Teresa isn't at risk for AIDS. I was. But the reaction to such propagandistic overkill from the activists had been a kind of national denial, an insistence that straight kids are just plain not going to get AIDS. This fantasy, which has even led to vitriolic opposition to urging young people to use condoms if they're sexually active, has already led to results that are horrific for many young people and for those who love them.

I believed that I had created a cocoon to protect me, with Dr. Caceres in Washington, Dr. Cohen in Boston, Blitz (until his death), and Bob, Ward, and Peter in Boston. It wasn't until I learned that my cousin Neil, the proponent in our family of coming out and nudging others to come out about being gay, had developed AIDS that I decided to tell my aunt and uncle about my own condition. My father, I was told, had been grief-stricken when he learned that his nephew, the son of his beloved sister Kathie, was HIV-positive. Kathie and her husband, Herb, and I talked now and again about whether and when I should tell my father and stepmother, and we concluded that the inevitable day could be postponed.

I continued with my full load of work: two or more movie columns weekly for the large *Tab* newspaper chain in Massachusetts, political pieces for the *Boston Herald,* travel articles for the *Boston Globe,* and television. My radio ratings remained preeminent in New England talk, and as I lived an archetypal Type A nonstop existence, I felt that maybe I would be one of those longterm nonprogressers. I spent my late forties and early fifties as the man who could do anything. I was invincible. I was not going to die of AIDS.

I was, of course, the dumbest of men when things got really rough during the late summer of 1994. Until then, nothing could have convinced me that I wasn't going to beat the odds. The Sunday supplements frequently carried features on groups of the fortunate few, and I would devour those stories, imagining myself into their tales of well-being. When friends confided in me that they were HIV-positive, I didn't reciprocate. Keeping their secrets was simple, and I offered advice about getting treatment early to two colleagues at WBZ, who were among those who told me about their condition. I was the man from Help—to others; to them I was Mr. HIV-negative. There is a positive side to not having reciprocated with tales of my own condition, but it didn't do much to bring others into my life.

I was going to endure this, whatever precisely it was, without a public revelation. If not telling is a lie, then I lied; if not specifically saying that I wasn't HIV-positive is a lie by omission, *tant pis*. I didn't owe anybody any tales from the medical front, or so I continued to tell myself. Mr. Impervious to the ordinary guy's need to spill his guts was acting true to form. My financial dealings were premised on long-term survival. I saved intelligently, imagining a ripe old retirement, behaving in general like a farsighted planner instead of like somebody who was going to make a premature exit from life. I didn't really believe that I would live for decades, but I considered the simple act of behaving as if I would to be a positive step. In little ways, then in larger ways, we fool ourselves.

Throughout the 1980s and early 1990s, Ward Cromer and I took trips to many places: twice to South Africa, once each to Holland, Morocco, Scotland, Russia, Sweden, Finland. With my then producer on radio, Jon Keller, and one of my former interns from television days, a Frenchman, Bertrand Soret, I went to Ireland and broadcast from the Dublin studios of Radioteleviseiran, the state-run broadcast media center. With another pal from TV days, Don Davis, I roamed around in Turkey. I traveled to Europe with Dick Fletcher and others and on my own traveled extensively in South and Central America, and on assignment I reported from Israel and South Africa. I loved going places, always had.

For years Ward had been urging me to visit Japan again—a natural destination, you would have thought, since my AFS summer in Japan had presented me with aspirations and eventually with career plans and had brought me into my own. Yet something kept me from returning to Japan, as if I had a mental image of the country that would inevitably be overshadowed, even perhaps erased, by the reality of today. But without emphasizing my HIV status, Ward led me to realize that I might have only a few more years left in which to make the great voyages that he knew I wanted to undertake. Finally his subtle proddings took root and I agreed to visit Kyoto in November 1993. Kyoto, the twelve-hundred-year-old city, the capital before Tokyo and a repository of glorious gardens and temples, was the perfect place for my second visit, after an absence of thirty-six years, to the country that had so radically altered my future.

Things went well in Kyoto until I began to feel some pain in my feet. At first I thought that the discomfort was simply caused by walking too much. I'm the kind who prefers cabs; Ward hikes; we compromise on his terms. Ward gave me a pair of his running shoes, veterans of a Boston marathon, and while these were more comfortable than my own, my feet continued to hurt. I immediately stopped taking the ddI, and when I got home I reported the problem to Dr. Caceres, who told me that it almost surely was the dreaded neuropathy. For the next eight months the pain increased in severity instead of subsiding, as it often does in people who stop taking the drug. I found no relief, and Dr. Caceres made me aware that while neuropathy can go away of its own accord, it is just as likely to linger, possibly forever. Not a happy prospect. Naturally, I wondered if I was finally experiencing an undeniable, even incurable, symptom of "it." By mid-September 1994 my feet were hurting constantly, but the tricky little mental adjustment of denial clicked in and I simply would not accept what was obvious: that I had entered a nasty new phase of being HIV-positive. I was fine, really, just fine.

I began taking sick days, after nineteen months without one, and using a cane to get about at work, and I required help getting up and down stairs. I was in so much pain that even during the six minutes of news at the top of each of my radio hours, I lacked the energy to go upstairs to get something from the cafeteria. I had returned to teaching a few years earlier, in

183

1990, in the College of Communication at Boston University, where my course in media criticism was popular, and I had at last realized the old dream of having some part of my life be centered on teaching. But in the autumn of 1994 I began to miss classes because I was weak and feverish and I hobbled, a cripple in all but name. Then began an impossibly lingering flu—at least, I thought it was flu. I was coughing and hacking continually, though I had none of the stomach ailments that we associate with genuine influenza. I was hardly able to move, leaning against walls while trying to get around at the radio and TV station and at the university, wheezing as if I had a serious inflammation in the lungs (which I later learned I suffered from and which turned out to be the same pneumonia that had killed Blitz). Dr. Caceres knew nothing of this, since I had visited him in Washington in July and the new symptoms developed just after that. My Boston physician tried futilely to get me to check into a hospital for tests, sending me to a neurologist at Mass. General for my neuropathy and later to an infectious disease specialist at New England Deaconess Hospital. Both tried to impress upon me how sick I was; both failed. I wouldn't let mere facts interfere with my magnificent case of denial.

Nobody who encountered me could help but see a sick man who kept insisting that he was healthy. I thought the doctors were alarmists, practitioners of medico-babble; they didn't realize how tough I was and how this flu would go away and I would be fine once again. At WBZ, the news and programming director, Brian Whittemore, and my producer, Kevin Myron, among many others, including my Boston University chairman, David Anable, tried repeatedly to get me to see how serious my condition was, but even blunt descriptions of my sickly color and emaciated appearance made no impression. My

184

feet began to turn purplish, not just little striations of color but the whole foot, both feet. And I got another symptom that only somebody in high denial could have brushed off; I woke one day and noticed that my calves and thighs suddenly had grown plumper, almost shapely, like those of a young athlete. Well now, I said to myself, I'm turning into Carl Lewis; isn't that nice. There I was with purple feet and the legs of somebody thirty years my junior, and still I refused to check into a hospital.

Strangers, friends, and colleagues kept insisting that I was heading for a complete physical collapse. My longtime buddy Joseph Curran, known to everybody as Papa Joe, went into his preacher mode and delivered his sermon whenever he saw me, insisting that the best thing for me was to check into a hospital immediately and let modern medicine work its wonders. No dice. Kevin was apoplectic about my condition, trying again and again to get me to take more nights off from work; on some nights he either sent me home before the program began or just yanked me off the air mid-show. The first time he did it I resisted, demanding to be left alone to decide whether or not I was too ill to continue, but on later occasions I accepted his decision; I was too weak to resist, too stubborn to put two and two together and admit to myself that I was headed for a catastrophe. I thought, *Well, I'm OK, but obviously Kevin needs to think I'm ill; it'll make him feel better if I go home.* I, of course, was fine. When I finally agreed to undergo a spinal tap, an MRI exam, and an echocardiogram, they yielded no conclusive results, and I continued to go through the motions of teaching and doing my media work. I humored those who thought I was sick. I lied to myself, which made what I said to others the truth; at least, I thought I was being truthful. You had to be there.

185

By late October I was hacking and coughing continually, feeling nausea and frequent dizziness, loss of appetite—I was barely eating breakfast, usually skipping lunch, frequently forgetting dinner—and I couldn't walk without holding onto walls and got from here to there on purple feet and bloated legs. I had nightly sweats. I had to use the freight elevator at the university to get to my second-floor classroom. I had no energy for exercise at the gym, even though my legs looked as if I spent two hours daily working on them. Much later I learned that the condition is called edema, but I remained ignorant of what it was and continued to avoid anybody who might tell me things I didn't want to hear. Even I could see that my reflection in the mirror had taken on a cadaverous cast, but this fifty-four-year-old purple-footed fellow stumbling around the halls and falling into bushes and eating practically nothing was just fine.

Dr. John Doweiko, the infectious diseases specialist at Deaconess to whom Dr. Cohen had sent me for examination, called me often, trying to get me to check into the hospital or at least to visit him again. Finally I agreed, reluctantly, to see him the following Wednesday. On the Monday before that scheduled visit, Kevin and Tony Nesbitt, my master control producer (the person who processes the calls and directs the flow of the program), conferred and decided to take me off the air immediately, and Kevin also arranged, without telling me, to have me off-air for the rest of the week. Tuesday morning I went to teach my class and delivered what I believed was a brilliant lecture, though I couldn't for the life of me seem to remember what I had said. My students sat transfixed, or so I thought.

After class Ward visited me and tried yet again to convince me to check into a hospital. He gave me cold drinks, cool compresses for my forehead, and insisted that I agree to let him take me to see Dr. Doweiko the next morning. Too weak, feverish, sopping wet, and muddled to know what I was saying, I agreed, and Ward then returned to his home four blocks away, promising to come back in a few hours and spend the night with me. He left, and despite feeling that I should be doing something—working on a lecture for Thursday or grading papers, *something*—I wandered around my rooms and then tried to rest. I couldn't sleep. I felt pangs of guilt about becoming a slug-abed in the middle of the day, knowing that this nasty flu would pass and I would go on with my life. I looked out my bedroom windows late that afternoon, and I saw what I remember as softening colors shimmering somehow in the light, a warm gray brightened here and there by pinks. A clearer head would have seen all that simply as sunset, however lovely, but I was swimming in a reverie, miserable in body but taken by the gorgeousness of the colors outside my window. I remember one last thing before everything went dark: I wondered how anybody could think that *I* was looking gray. I was fine, just fine, *really*.

As people who know me will tell you, control—of my own life, certainly, and of others' not infrequently—has been central to the way I function, or at least functioned. Once in Texas, in 1964, when Patricia and I took a group of our students to a performance by the New York City Ballet, I turned into a wild man because I had forgotten my watch at home, looked futilely at my naked wrist constantly, the portrait of a man whose control of time had slipped away. Of course, to my mind, always knowing what time it is is nothing unusual. I consider people who don't wear watches to be perilously close to irresponsible. Don't they know they might be late? Don't they care? In any case, the lack of a way to tell time played as much a part in the confusions abounding in my hospitalization as al-most anything else. The torture lasted for nearly two months after that final Tuesday in the classroom.

The first nine days of my hospitalization are completely miss-ing from my memory. I could just as well have been off in the cosmos visiting space creatures with L. Ron Hubbard, or in an alien craft with Louis Farrakhan, who claims to have been there with the twenty-years-dead Elijah Muhammad. I know the outlines of my life during those days only because doctors and what I came to think of as my Gang of Five—the five friends who were with me every day during my unconscious period and with me as well throughout my hospitalization—have told me what went on. I've no recollection of those days, not even a dream-state flashback, nothing; my body was present, but my mind was wherever minds go when all memory and conscious-ness are blocked, and even hearing from others what happened during those days somehow rings hollow, as if it were a sad story about someone else. My brain simply wasn't computing. By the time I learned what had happened to me, I was no longer in a state of denial, but still I couldn't imagine that what I was hearing was true. I had never had a memory loss before, never experienced a time when I couldn't account for every day. Now I was supposed to believe that I was missing nine days and would never get them back.

That I recovered at all from what hospital personnel believed to be an unsurvivable illness remains in large part unexplained to this day, and while I've been told that I should be glad that I have no memories from those nine days, that they would be an unbearable nightmare, I still hope now and again that someday a clearer recollection might wend its way to the surface of my mind. My control of my life would return, I think, if only I could retrieve those nine days.

This I've been told: after Ward left my house in the early evening on Tuesday, I evidently ambled about outside for a while, then lurched back into my building and collapsed in the lobby. I was helped to my door by the concierge, who called the building superintendent, Peter Clancy, who called 911 and asked for an ambulance, which came and took me to the nearest hospital. When Ward returned a short time later, intending to spend the night, he learned what had happened, called 911, and found that I had been taken to the emergency room at Mass. General. He went to his car, which he had parked in front of my building earlier in the day, and found that it had been broken into—welcome to the national capital of car theft—so he caught a cab and rushed to the ER, where he told the doctors, who couldn't figure out what was wrong with me, that I was HIV-positive. Since my lungs were in dreadful shape, the doctors took a chance and introduced Bactrim, a drug for *Pneumocystis carinii* pneumonia, found often in people with AIDS. This stabilized me. If I hadn't told Ward years before about my HIV status, if he hadn't planned to spend the night in my apartment and take me to the hospital the next day, if he hadn't returned to my place shortly after the ambulance came for me, if he hadn't ignored protocol and rushed to the emergency room, if he hadn't interfered and told the doctors of my HIV status, I would have died less than a half-hour after arrival.

Of all the people who carried me in their hearts and in their thoughts throughout the months of my hospitalization and who knew long before I did that I wasn't "fine, just fine," none was more aware and more burdened by that awareness than Ward. We had met on Cape Cod in 1973 and gradually, over several years, developed an intensely supportive friendship. We took to spending part of most summer weekends together when I had a house on the beach in Provincetown, within sight of his across

189

the bay in Truro. Had I been an early riser, I could have enjoyed the seaside sunrises that at dusk turned into Ward's gorgeous sunsets, but I rarely made the leap out of bed, so the
Ward View, as I thought of it, was my most frequent companionship with the sun.

I had begun living part of each week on the Cape three years
before I met Ward, first as a weekend boarder, then in a rented
cottage, and finally in the beach house I bought and enjoyed
for half a dozen years. I used to get into my car at midnight on
Friday, right after my radio show on WHDH and then on
WRKO, drive to the Cape, get some approximation of a
night's sleep, then cram as much as I could into the weekend,
returning to Boston on Monday afternoon. When I began
working at WBZ, six instead of five nights each week—talk
hosts on 'BZ were thought of as disc jockeys with ideas and
given the six-day schedules long familiar to music stations—the
prospect of arriving on the Cape early Sunday morning and
leaving the next day made my house seem more a burden than
a pleasure. I gradually weaned myself of it, first renting it out
during the season and then, in 1989, selling it.

By then Ward and I had become closer than ever, and we
took to fairly regular Sunday night dinners when he returned
from Truro. A psychologist, Ward inspires confidences from his
friends as well as from his patients, and I suppose I bored him
silly with sad tales of the increasingly bizarre Blitz, my own
various insecurities, my (I like to think) harmless neuroses.
Ward also saw me often in the years when I drank too much,
and a joke with a serious side had it that you could hardly get
through a dinner party with me when I didn't take a nap, just
to "rest my eyes," on Ward's or somebody else's couch, and
sack out for the night. Ward never complained, about either my

neediness or my heavy drinking. In an earlier age he would have been referred to as a saint.

Ward's professional training and his empathic nature gave him inescapable evidence of my emotional decline, however slight for the first few years, and in the months before my collapse, of the near-totality of my denial. He is not a pusher; he is a suggester, and he tried to get me to recognize that I was sicker than I could admit to myself. In a sense, my collapse and hospitalization made it impossible, once I began to recover, for me to deny any longer what had happened.

Ward and I both knew that a relatively symptom-free life wouldn't last long and that eventually something would put me into a new stage, although neither of us imagined quite the traumatic near-death experience that transpired. In his quiet, deliberate, usually unspoken approach to easing the almost certain hard times ahead, Ward attempted to make my apartment more conducive to the life of somebody who might well become housebound. For Christmas one year he gave me a microwave oven. He urged me to get a fax machine, which immediately became invaluable. Invariably, Ward knew and knows the right thing to do, and although sometimes I resisted obstinately long beyond the point when resistance made any sense at all, usually I let myself be guided and directed by him.

It was he who later explained to Kevin that as I was getting sicker day by day, I seemed to be, as he put it, "absenting" myself from my own health—not just denying what was undeniable to a fully engaged mind, unlike my own, but regarding any advice from doctors as somehow meant for another person, not for me. He phrased my approach to my body's manifest deterioration as a kind of nonparticipatory sense of concern, an abstract interest in the health of that body down there below my brain rather than a full acceptance of the fact that the body *was* mine, the departing health was mine, the resulting horror would be mine too. Ward became the preparer, asking Peter for his home and office numbers, something I didn't even think to tell him. He knew how to reach Kevin, with whom he had become a running and cycling buddy, and more, a close friend, which pleased me greatly, because I like having my friends like each other: somehow that helps order my life, helps me control my environment. Ward knew how to reach Patricia Kennedy and Jon Keller, my radio producer for five years at WHDH and WRKO and for many years an intimate buddy. All this he took upon himself, knowing that I would probably react hostilely if he asked me how he could reach these other close friends; of course, I thought of myself as in the pink of health. Ward became my silent partner, many steps ahead of me in what he was doing. I was drifting into another world long before I was hospitalized, and the real world was the one Ward inhabited. If I wouldn't prepare for the worst, Ward would, and did.

Ward had come with me to Deaconess Hospital when I had my MRI, spinal tap, and echocardiogram and convinced Deaconess to transmit my records to Mass. General immediately. The day after my collapse he showed the documents giving him my power of attorney and health proxy, and from then on the doctors consulted him about every significant decision concerning my well-being. Dr. Cromer, psychologist, became a kind of attending physician, adding that role to that of best friend and, in short order, guardian angel as well as guardian of the gates, so to speak. It was he who decided who could visit me and who could not. This all happened in the nine days missing from my recollection, but by the time I was conscious again, everybody had agreed that the final decisions on anything concerning me had to be made with Ward's participation.

Ward knew everything about my twice- or thrice-yearly vis-

192

its to see Dr. Caceres in Washington and my semimonthly visits to Dr. Cohen to have my blood taken. He got Mass. General to contact both doctors and add to its store of data about me. The prognosis at first was so grim, and the improvement so tentative, that Ward and the others were continually sad. Ward told me much later that he cried every day for weeks. Even I finally recognized that he was living two lives, his and mine. He was with me daily, in the morning bringing doughnuts and coffee, and again after work for a long visit. He was handling my personal affairs, even ones I'd given no thought to at all. While Kevin was holding down the WBZ fort, Peter and Jon were handling the media, and Patricia was giving me her particular brand of tender loving care, Ward coordinated everything and guided the others without my ever having a clue.

Ward asked that I be given as much medication as possible, to induce amnesia about what was happening during those first nine days. Sometimes in subsequent weeks, even months, one or the other of my Gang of Five let slip a hint to me of how tense and fearful they had been, how much the burden of keeping me alive had devolved upon them as well as on doctors of whom I had no knowledge. Of course, I had no knowledge of anything whatsoever.

I was as good as dead but didn't know it. My blood pressure, normally roughly 120 over 80, was 70 over undetectable. My breathing rate was forty breaths per minute; the normal is about sixteen. The ER team arranged for chest X-rays and blood tests and concluded that I was suffering from congestive heart failure as well as pneumonia and had abnormal liver functions—a "shocked" liver related to the heart problem, which later was diagnosed as cardiomyopathy. I had heard that term once before, when a young Boston Celtics player, Reggie Lewis, collapsed during a preseason practice session and died almost instantly. Whether my cardiomyopathy was occasioned by HIV is still undetermined, one of several mysteries about my medical condition.

In addition to the Bactrim, I was given steroids to reduce the inflammation in my lungs—and steroids often have severe side effects, as do many of the drugs I was given then and many of those I'm on now, I have learned the hard way. I also received the first of many ongoing morphine drips to sedate me, then I was intubated: a thick tube was inserted through my mouth into the lung membranes to drain the fluid that had built up. This remained in place for nine days, while the morphine kept me unconscious. While I clung to life, the ICU team, under the general direction of cardiology specialist Dr. Hammayoun Kazemi, did what they could and my friends kept watch. I had never imagined that one of my favorite Gershwin songs, "Someone to Watch Over Me," would one day become my anthem.

One crucial decision involved removing the tube that had been extracting the heavy volume of fluids in my lung membranes. I would either come through it, begin breathing on my own, and continue recovering, or my body would convulse and I would die. I might succumb; or my body might endure the extubation but suffer damage of my vocal cords, destroying any chance of returning to my radio work; or, as happened, I might recover, my voice gradually regaining its timbre. That moment of deciding whether and when to extubate me was Ward's most critical and, though I didn't know it, mine as well.

Ward insisted that he be notified when the extubation was to occur so he could be there. He was surprised by how slowly and gradually the process happened, having assumed that it was a one-two-three kind of thing: tube out, David lives or David dies. The doctors told him that even with my improvement

194

during the nine days in the coma, my body would now be faced with having to function without artificial breathing, and often a body in a condition like mine simply couldn't survive the shift from assisted to natural breathing. A CAT scan had not conclusively shown whether I had been brain-damaged, and nobody knew—at least Ward didn't know—if I had experienced any subconscious understanding of what had been going on during those days. He didn't know whether, if I started breathing successfully on my own, I would be angry, maybe even infuriated that all of this *stuff* had been done to me—for me.

One night shortly before my collapse, Peter Meade heard my interview with David Halberstam, one of the best radio guests either of us had ever entertained, and my questioning was inept; worse, my interview was at times unlistenable. Peter called Tony Nesbitt, my master control producer, to say that he would come in and replace me if I wanted, but of course I didn't. I was too vital to the station—to the world?—to be taken off the air just because of some piddling illness like the flu. The next day Peter gave me a chewing-out. You're scaring people, he said; something's terribly wrong, he insisted; you have to get medical help, he implored. I was the deaf wall: I heard nothing that Peter said. I couldn't hear it.

Peter and I met in 1986, when I was first hired at WBZ Radio. He had been at the station for a few years, and for a while we were direct rivals when I was at WRKO. At 'BZ, Peter's hours were six to nine; my hours followed his, nine to one. We became a kind of dynamic duo of Boston's nighttime radio, six days each week, providing a liberal-conservative one-two punch, though the terms mean less in our case than usual and became less accurate in describing either of us, or both, as

195

time passed. Peter likes to say that he was born Democratic and baptized Catholic; I was neither. We kept the airwave sparks flying, debating things from the film version of *The Last Temptation of Christ,* which he condemned without seeing and I defended, to the death penalty, which he opposed, to drug legalization and much else. We became an unbeatable evening radio tag team, and since we had enough areas of real disagreement about policies of one sort or another, we didn't have to make up radio feuds to spice up our back-to-back shows.

On occasion, Peter's friendship with me has led to his being accused of being my gay lover. He survives this nonsense with amusement, sometimes teasing obnoxious questioners by saying simply that his sexuality is nobody's business but his own. Early on during my hospitalization, one reporter asked, "How close to David are you?" Peter replied, "Close enough so that if he's sick I get a phone call. Are you asking something else?" The reporter backed off, but only a few weeks later, when the full truth of my illness was known, the Peter-and-David-are-lovers rumor started to circulate. I was on the critical list at Mass. General, still struggling for life, unknowingly at death's doorway, and Peter Meade was being saddled with a new sexual identity by people whose obsession with homosexuality leads to all sorts of brilliant conclusions, among them that a heterosexual with a gay friend is probably gay.

Peter's hours were changed after a couple of years, and later he accepted a position outside of broadcasting, but our friendship continued. Still, he retains a valued connection to the station as a political commentator, and he has filled in for me when I've had to be off. On election nights we are reunited on-air again. I'm fairly scrawny, and Peter, an ex-Marine, is powerfully built. I think now that he probably pondered the idea of just picking me up and carting me off to a hospital. Would that he had.

Peter had been watching the debate between his friend Ted Kennedy and Republican challenger Mitt Romney on Tuesday the twenty-fifth of October, 1994. When the phone rang, he thought it was his fiancée calling. When he heard Ward's voice instead, he knew right away that something was wrong. Like Kevin, Peter was convinced that I was heading for a crisis, and he went immediately to the hospital to join Ward. Peter's arrival there began almost surrealistically. The first person he saw, even before joining Ward, was Ted Kennedy, whom he had just been watching on TV. Ted asked Peter how he had found out. *What Fellini movie am I in?* Peter wondered; how had Ted known about David's condition? The senator asked if the press knew already, and again Peter was taken aback by his concern. Finally they realized that they were at Mass. General on different missions. Ted's wife, Vicki, had fallen after the debate and required stitches, but for a minute the two old friends were unable to explain each other's presence in the emergency room.

That night began Peter's participation in the nine-day vigil. It was the second time that he and his best childhood pal, now the Reverend James Hickey, had prayed in connection to me. In 1989, when Blitz died of AIDS, Peter and Father Jim had asked me if I would like a mass said for my friend, whom Peter knew well and whom Jimmy had met once. There we were at Peter's house with his family, Ward, Kevin, another WBZ pal, Ricardo (Ric) Duarte, and me, an agnostic Jew, celebrating a mass for my dead friend, another agnostic Jew. I don't know if that's entirely kosher according to Vatican II, but it meant a tremendous amount to me. Religious ceremonies starring me had amounted to two: my circumcision, which, mercifully, I don't remember, and my bar mitzvah, shortly after which I lost interest and belief in such events and eventually in organized religion entirely. Now here was a third important ceremony, and as if it were the wake (in Peter's tradition) or the seven days of visiting the bereaved (in mine), we talked warmly, recalling happy memories and funny stories about our absent friend. Ric, whom Blitz liked best of all my Boston buddies, joked, as I did, about Blitz's compounded looniness. And I rambled on, as I'm sure I did to the soldier in that bus the evening I learned of my mother's death.

The night of my hospitalization, Peter called Jimmy, and this time they prayed for me. Weeks later, when I was at Spaulding Rehabilitation Hospital to continue my recovery, Jimmy visited and regaled me with easy jokes and, more seriously, explained his faith that prayer, even for a nonbeliever, had efficacy, *clout,* in God's eyes. I asked him if I could spread the word that a priest friend had visited, in the hope that I might be spared at least one of the hospital clergy visits. And I expressed my doubt that the hundreds of letters I had gotten from people who said they were praying for me actually had any effect except making me feel better emotionally. Jim insisted that yes, prayers help, but I still had to pay my own mortgage. I didn't know then and found out only much later, that when I first told Peter of my diagnosis in the late 1980s, he had been so jolted by the news that when we parted that afternoon he returned to his car and wept.

Ward and Peter strategized a policy for handling the media. Two years earlier, in 1992, when I had fainted during my program in a particularly tense time in my life, TV coverage showed me being taken in an ambulance from WBZ to the nearest hospital. Though I recovered immediately and was back on the air the next night, the media coverage of that short-lived, probably insignificant event was extensive. Knowing that the media would be all over the story of this much more serious matter, Peter and Ward decided to tell reporters about my heart condition and pneumonia and leave it at that for the moment.

The first few days of my induced coma brought no hint of good news, and on the third day the doctors began discussions with Ward, and Ward with Peter, about what, if anything, the hospital could do. They suggested, not forcefully but with the belief that what they proposed was best, that my friends ought to consider the possibility that perhaps they ought simply to let me go. I'm not given to having extensive discussions about which impediments would be worse than death for me, but both Peter and Ward knew that I was clear about not wanting to live under vegetative conditions. Peter asked the doctors a simple question: will David eventually be well enough to walk down Commonwealth Avenue? Meaning, would my quality of life be worthy by my own lights? The doctors didn't know; for some weeks thereafter nobody knew, including, once I was conscious again, me. Peter wondered then if I would resent not having been detached from those machines and allowed to die.

Ward and Peter were in agreement—give David a chance—and since Ward was my health proxy, the decision to urge the doctors to do that was his. This was the second occasion on which Ward quite literally saved my life. The decision to keep trying was the right one, but during the third day after my collapse the question wasn't so easily answered. I've had moments thinking about when, if ever, the matter will come up again, not that I'm holding my breath in anticipation. Anybody with AIDS who doesn't contemplate it is in an even greater state of denial than I was for so many weeks in September and October.

My body began to rally on the fourth and fifth days, and chances of some degree of recovery improved. But the first few days after I was extubated and brought back to consciousness, which allowed the staff to wean me from the morphine, weren't particularly lovely. I remained in the ICU for four days more, apparently grumbling about everything. I kept insisting that I be allowed to walk to the bathroom, not knowing that I couldn't walk at all, even though I knew that tubes were coming into and going out of me. Two clocks on the wall puzzled me. The times were different, so I accused the nurses of trying to drive me mad. (One was a real clock; the other was used for timing some procedures, but without my glasses I couldn't quite see them, and I couldn't figure out what was going on or understand the explanations that people were giving me.) Ward told me that my first words after I came out of the unconscious state were to the effect that I wanted to go to the bathroom. I guess that became something of a refrain.

Other than my Gang of Five, the first people I saw were my Aunt Kathie and Uncle Herb, and I assumed somehow that I had been taken to Minneapolis, where they lived, since I couldn't figure out why they were at the hospital. I learned that they had been in New York to see their daughters and they had spoken with my father and come up to see me. I remember that they planned to go to dinner with Ward and another good friend, Dr. Harry Sobel, after visiting me, and I asked why I couldn't go too. Their explanation, that I was bedridden and couldn't possibly be allowed out of the hospital, wasn't very persuasive. I felt simply that *things,* all the *things* that made up my life, had been yanked out of my hands and I was no longer in control. I was right, but I had no idea how serious my condition was.

The seemingly eternal daylight of the ICU, or rather the lack of any correlation between real day and night, on the one hand, and the artificial light in the ICU, on the other, confused me. One day I had been promised that at one o'clock a particular intravenous drip would be removed. When I demanded at one o'clock that it be done, I was told that the time then was one *A.M.* and the IV would be removed at one *P.M.* I felt as if I were in my own Fellini movie, and because I didn't know how sick I was, I couldn't understand why they didn't just let me get up, dress, and go home. I've seen this sort of incident on TV many times and always thought that the patient was being ridiculous; wouldn't he *know* that he was seriously ill? Now I was living in a bad TV movie. I hallucinated ghastly conversations among medical personnel who took great care of me by day but became fiends by night. I was visited in my nightmares by monsters, the human kind, people who came back to torment me for my sins, as I hovered halfway between a morphine state and a dawning awareness of my situation. I felt genuine terror and couldn't figure out what was real; my darkest dreams somehow conveyed reality more vividly than my life hooked up to machines.

I told Ward about one of the more terrifying hallucinations and began weeping, so convinced was I that it had happened. Ward was doubtful, suggesting that I had imagined it all, that my faithful moviegoing had gotten the better of me and I was remembering some horrid film. While floating on a sea of narcotics I experienced the whole range of dreams, all of different kinds, of a Technicolor vibrancy more overwhelming than any I had had during any of my acid trips. One day I thought that I must be going mad, or the world was crazy and I was the last sane man alive.

I recall beginning to fear that I wouldn't "make it," as I kept saying. I felt absolute terror, convinced that I would never leave that bed alive. One evening when the Gang of Five came to visit, the tears flowed, and mixed with my sense of impending doom I felt acute embarrassment that I was crying, and I couldn't stop crying, which made me only more embarrassed. This was compounded by an ongoing fury that I was being treated like an invalid, subjected to bedpans and impaled by needles and catheters. I remember beginning to shake; I felt like a prisoner in that bed, that room, in a state of sickness that nobody had as yet been able to describe to me so that I fully understood. I began regressing to a juvenile state of fear and despair, and I remember that Jon Keller came to my side and kissed my forehead. I must have dozed off at that point, because the next thing I knew it was the following day and my head had cleared. For the first time since my arrival in the hospital, I asked to see the newspapers and started talking about things happening outside my enclosed little world.

Ward never told me during my six or seven weeks of increasing illness before my collapse, though he did tell Kevin, that he thought I might be willing my own destruction, passively experiencing my own decline, maybe trying to rush myself to death. He wondered if perhaps my collapse on that Tuesday in October was my way of reaching out for help, of somehow deciding that I wasn't convinced that I wanted to die, that maybe I wanted a chance to survive. I don't know if there's anything to that or not—denial again?—but I know that for Ward and the others, my determination to get well, my determination to do almost everything the nurses and doctors told me to do, was a relief: David was going to fight, not flee. What for nine days had been a question simply of surviving or succumbing became a question of how to return to a functioning life.

If anybody over the years has been completely level-headed about my priorities, about my emphasis on working and enjoying every moment of my work, it is Ward, who became the manager as well as the guardian. One day in the hospital he asked if there was anything I could think of that we hadn't talked about. I cheerfully—blithely, actually—said no, everything is under control, isn't it? He smiled and said that I had bills to pay, that he had found my checkbook and was dutifully paying them for me. I had become so accustomed to having my guardian do everything, I didn't realize how extensive "everything" was. Ward also contacted my father and stepmother every day, with part of the story, and talked with Kathie and Herb about the full story. When I had told Ward about my HIV condition years earlier, he had volunteered to be there for me, in whatever ways became necessary, through the last moment of my life. This was no empty promise, no dramatic rehearsal for a poignant deathbed scene, and it was nothing I asked of him; it was Ward's decision to be, as might be said in the Bible, my rod and my staff. That he was. That he remains.

Meanwhile, the erstwhile best little boy in the world was just trying to become the best AIDS patient in the hospital, to get well and strong, to get home and get back to work on radio and on TV and at the university and in the newspapers, to get back to being all that I had been.

EIGHT

Where's the
Rest of Me?

Television and the movies often teach us as much about life as we learn from living itself. As a reviewer, I have seen too many thousands of films over the years not to find myself sliding effortlessly into the terminology of the movies and a cinematic approach even to elements of my own life. And to a large extent, I realized that my sense of what happens to a seriously ill patient in a hospital is conditioned by the way medical crises are handled in movies and on television: the patient arrives in a hospital and is placed on a gurney, he is the picture of doom, and within a few heart-stopping (if not heartrending) minutes of TV or movie time the patient either dies and everybody dissolves into tears or he recovers. The End.

No such luck for this boy, the would-be best little AIDS patient at Mass. General. I became the bedridden man who came to dinner: I lingered on and on, clearly destined neither to recover nor to succumb. I learned later that my case was so unusual, it was used as an instructional tool in medical rounds, the periodic gathering of a hospital's medical personnel to discuss some particular case. It's nice, I guess, to be unique, but as W. C. Fields's tombstone inscription says, on the whole I'd rather have been in Philadelphia.

My doctors have told me that a considerable part of my recovery had to do with having a good outlook. My memories are that I was a wretched patient, grumbling and whining and so unclear about the extent of my illness that I behaved like somebody being held against his will in a prison. I remember saying once in the ICU, after the extubation, that the doctors and nurses there were all commies and I was captive in their gulag. Everybody tells me that my memories are flawed, that actually I was some kind of patient from paradise—loving, considerate, thoughtful about the needs of others, and ready to do all that I was told to do—and that once I was out of the ICU and had begun to regain my emotional equanimity, I turned into a role model for the good patient syndrome. Guess who strikes again.

On Saturday the fifth of November I was liberated from the ICU and moved to Phillips House, the most luxurious patient area at MGH. Distances seem vast when you're flat on your back and are wheeled along what appear to be miles of corridors by apparently mute orderlies. The room overlooked the Charles River and parts of Boston and Cambridge, and I arrived just at sunset. That particular sunset was breathtaking, outlandishly vibrant swirls of red, bolts of purple, highlights of gold interspersed with cascades of pinkish grays—a sunset for the ages, like those Ward and I had often enjoyed over Cape Cod Bay. I don't think that there's anything significant about remembering a beautiful sky late in the day on the evening of my collapse and this magnificent extravaganza on the day I was liberated from the terrifying ICU and ensconced in Phillips

House, room 2020. But for whatever reasons, my last memory before the collapse and my first on the day that I was by all accounts heading for some degree of recovery were of the gorgeous vision outside my windows. I didn't become a painter, however much I enjoyed studying art and puttering around on a canvas and drawing nude models at the Minneapolis Institute of Art as a kid, but I have a keen appreciation of beauty, and those two sunsets come back to me in memory again and again even now. I was entering a new phase in my hospitalization, and somehow I felt as if the sunset were a good omen.

Once I was settled into Phillips House, which seemed more like a hotel suite than a hospital room, and arranged for the TV to provide me with every channel available, Kevin summed up the new arrangement in a simple, apt phrase. He told a friend on the day of my move to Phillips 2020 that he had good news and bad news. The good news: David's out of the ICU and getting better. The bad news: he has a telephone! The joke worked its way around town; who was I to deny the truth of it?

When I discovered that only a few days remained until the elections on November 8, I insisted that I simply had to be released from the hospital in time to do the election coverage with Peter Meade and our news team on WBZ. Since 1974 I had been involved in coverage of all federal, state, and local elections but one, either on TV or on radio, sometimes on both. Couldn't I please get up and go home? Whether everybody stifled a guffaw or a snort of amusement I don't know, but I remember being told gently that I probably shouldn't set my heart on being back at work in three days, election or no election. Still, how could America feel properly informed about the senatorial, congressional, and gubernatorial elections without me? Three days later, I sat in bed, tears streaming

206

down my cheeks, as I listened to Peter and our news anchor, Gary LaPierre, doing the coverage on radio and watched my TV colleagues somehow soldiering on in their task of reporting the election returns without any input at all from the indispensable me. Denial didn't disappear all at once—maybe it never really disappears—but I suppose that since I couldn't deny that I had been forbidden to do what everybody knew I loved doing, I finally had to accept the seriousness of my illness. This wasn't one of those things I could bluff my way out of or will myself to overcome.

That first evening out of the ICU, my Gang of Five eased me into some slight understanding of the truth of my condition. Like the others, Kevin Myron was relieved by the prognosis of a partial, maybe even a substantial, recovery. A bright, handsome, eager twenty-six-year-old given to deadpan ironics when he came to WBZ in 1987, Kevin began to work on Peter's and my shows and eventually became our coordinating producer and finally mine alone, when Peter's hours shifted. He had been frustrated for weeks as I sickened but thunderously resisted any notion that I needed help. He told me months later that he was almost relieved when Ward called him at home that first night and told him that I was in the hospital. "I thought that the way you went, passed out and near death, scraped up from the ground and put in an ambulance, was the only way you were going to get to a hospital and finally get the attention you needed. *Your* way!"

Kevin learned that I was HIV-positive from Ward almost immediately after I was hospitalized, and he realized that I had been that way throughout most of our years working together. That helped him understand some of my behavior, which he now saw as fear transmuted into anger instead of any hostility toward him. I used to kid Kevin that he and I were like the

207

Bickersons, a radio couple that had come and gone long before Kevin was aware of radio or anything else. Strong-willed, both of us. Our mutual task—to make my program the best on the air—put us often at odds: the micromanaging Bruds was incapable of imagining that every single detail of the show didn't require my superintending brilliance; the more sensible Kevin was doing a fine job but going crazy with his host calling him at least fifty times a day to fret. But Bickersonian or not, the relationship matured into a firm friendship, one that grew until I was included in Kevin's family. Working as closely as we did, and do, we had our moments of madness, fights so furious that outsiders must have thought we hated each other. Once, when I had been badgering Kevin about something that was probably inconsequential but that to my Type A personality seemed crucial, he finally lost his habitual cool and yelled at me—at *me,* the infallible Brudnoy—to stop calling him at work a hundred times each day, the job was getting done, he didn't need a babysitter, I should get a life! I finally got a whiff of the aroma of compulsiveness I was blowing in his direction. It was a moment that had arisen before, but this time I began to grasp the nasty fact that I was becoming a kind of nut case and that he was right. I had to acknowledge that the success of my program, which dominated its day-part, was to a great degree due to his excellent producing. Kevin did and does have a life; mine had become indistinguishable from my job, into which I put a nearly monastic single-mindedness. I had become a nudge, and I was driving this *mensch,* as Granny Brudnoy would have phrased it, up the proverbial wall.

The first days I was in the hospital were so woeful that Kevin told me later he actually sat down to write a eulogy for me—premature, of course, but a way to come to grips with my situation. I was so doped up that I heard nothing, saw nothing, consciously felt nothing, but Kevin hoped that if I lifted an eyebrow when he spoke to—at—me, it meant that I was comprehending him on some level. He joked about how he finally realized that my hair, which he had always assumed was a "weave," as he put it, was real, although thinning. He assumed that I might be so handicapped that I would be unable to groom myself and have to resort to wearing a beard, which I had told him long ago made me look like a rabbinical college dropout. In his frightened state of mind, even the super-calm, rational Kevin found himself veering between two contradictory assumptions: that I was about to die and that I was about to recover. "One thing I expected," Kevin said, recalling those first two weeks at Mass. General, "was that you would be suffering from a really severe depression. It never happened. Your attitude was so positive and you so quickly began to act like the old Bruds that I finally became convinced that your quality of life would be acceptable to *you* and sufficient for all of *us* once you left the hospital. I was finally sure that you would make it. And you did."

Of course, my affection for Kevin was based on more than the fact that he was the producer of our radio program, as I had with others on occasion—a television intern here, a radio colleague there—I felt a mentoring urge, maybe the desire to have a younger brother or even a son. A number of young men whom I had met through my work preceded Kevin in a similar role in this amorphous, nameless category. Each entered into a friendship with me that went well beyond casual but was not sexual. I think that I displaced some libido, if I've got the correct term, by befriending people who, since they weren't gay, could not become my lovers and were therefore safe. These relationships fulfilled a different need, and with all of them I have enjoyed being able to give dispassionate advice, extend a protective arm when necessary, and enjoy the proximity of my friends' youth and promise. I know this sounds as if I was or am a twisted jangle of frustrated yearnings, but it's not that at all. I have, of course, wondered, and friends have asked me specifically, why I don't have a lover, why I haven't had anyone in my life who could be said to occupy that role since my days in Texas. I say I'm busy. I say I'm too picky. Who could match up to the ideal men of my youth: Stephen, Paul, Andrew? I say I'm probably more the aesthete than a tiger in bed. (That's true enough, but so?) I don't say, because I am not sure I can believe it, much less say it, that I am just not interested romantically in most people and would rather have a good conversation with a pal.

Or perhaps I've rationalized away the need for intimacy and that thing called love, at least romantic love. When you've got an audience of millions, maybe that's enough. The fact is that I find ways to deny that someone who comes on to me is actually, strictly speaking, coming on to me; I find excuses for why a mash note is really just a fan letter, why a series of invitations to dinner or what-have-you is simply politeness, not an overture to romance, or at least to sex. I am successful, well known and well liked, affluent, intelligent, not bad-looking for a middle-aged myopic talk host, clever, witty, decently built—well, I do have AIDS, but what's that among friends? In my early days in the media and in full-time college teaching in the Boston area, I would pick up someone and have a brief hour, or less, of true lust. Friends knew what my sex life amounted to; my fans only suspected that I was gay. As the years went by, however, and certainly from the time I learned that I was HIV-positive, I found excuses for avoiding sex altogether.

I found myself more wrapped up in my work, if becoming more of a workaholic was possible, and I stopped going to gay bars, avoided gay gatherings, reminded myself that sometimes one's best friend, carnally as well as otherwise, is one's self. I took the bulk of my personal pleasure from friendships with fewer than a dozen terrific guys, mostly straight, and a few terrific women, invariably straight. Every adult knows that the years seem to fly by faster as time goes by, and mine were no exception. It seemed to me that one day I was with Andrew in Texas; the next day, thirty years later, I was the resigned bachelor in Boston. Somehow getting hooked up with one person didn't happen, not that in my own destined-to-fail way I haven't longed now and again for a true love.

I don't know if the people who mean so much to me realized the full extent of my gradual, albeit partial, withdrawal from sexual involvements and the accelerated significance they have played in my life. Younger friends like Kevin, who have filled a space in my life that could possibly, under very different circumstances, have been romantic, were something else entirely, something precious that filled in for other pleasures, now mostly deferred.

Though I still hadn't seen myself in a mirror and could barely move my torso in bed, I felt skinny arms, shriveled legs, and hollows in my cheeks. Later I learned that I had lost so much weight in a matter of days that I had gone from 155 or so, the last weight I remember before collapsing in October, to a recorded low of 125. But I felt no pain of any sort, and my voice began gradually to return nearly to normal, though it was scratchy and sometimes I found talking difficult.

Nurses brought in tiny paper cups filled with pills every hour or so, and I still had a breathing tube in my nose and about six intravenous needles along both arms—a major reduction in the number of things going into and coming out of me. That I

211

couldn't simply get up and walk around was explained by one of the doctors as the inconvenience brought on by all the tubes; I was told to relax, not that I had much choice in the matter. I felt lovingly surrounded by my Gang of Five and by a roving band of doctors and nurses, most of whose names I never learned, though increasingly I saw Dr. Deborah Cotton, an AIDS specialist, and her colleague Dr. Gregory Robbins. Clearly I was being eased into the AIDS treatment protocol, and though nobody said very much explicitly about the nature of my diseases, the unvoiced message was: you have AIDS, full-blown, and that's what we're dealing with now.

Santa Kevin arrived daily with bags of letters and gifts. At first the mail was the stuff that had poured in while I was unconscious; then, every day thereafter, a few hundred new letters or cards arrived. One afternoon I tried to answer a few that had come in from personal friends, but my handwriting was so shaky that even I could barely read what I had scrawled. Kevin had another plan entirely, which was to discard the envelope from every letter whose sender's name wasn't familiar to him, so that I wouldn't try to answer them as I had done for almost every letter that had come to me at WBZ before my collapse. At first I felt frustrated, irritated by Kevin, until I realized that even if I were well, I wouldn't live long enough to respond to all the letters, cards, and notifications that prayers were being said for me. Kevin was growing, making decisions that I was in too much of a muddle to make, and by taking away one part of my compulsive need to respond to every letter, he saved me both time and energy. And, he would add with a grin, "what's left of your sanity."

I had so little understanding of just how wretchedly ill I had been and still was that every step toward acceptance of the situation involved the destruction of a false (and hope-filled)

212

belief and its replacement by a hard, firm datum. I learned that my lungs and heart had nearly done me in and that I had brought on my own near-death by refusing treatment when everybody who saw me was imploring me to get to a hospital. The dread word "AIDS" firmly embedded itself in my brain, and I stopped thinking of myself as HIV-positive—the appetizer, as it were, to the main course. I learned that I would be hospitalized for many weeks more and that there was a serious expectation that at best I would have a few years before "it" took its toll. I assumed that I would learn to live as a person with AIDS and find a practical way to function. As Patricia began to bring me the daily newspapers, I realized that the public perception of my condition was simply that I had nearly died owing to cardiomyopathy and pneumonia; nothing was said of AIDS, which was how I wanted to keep it.

Aside from my weeping jag in the ICU and the self-pitying scene I made as I watched the TV coverage of the elections, only one incident at Mass. General hit me so hard that I regressed to a childlike state of total fear. I was asleep on Monday night, November 7, when a man I had never seen before came in, sat down on the bed, gently awakened me, and introduced himself as a neurologist. He spoke his name clearly, but I forgot it immediately and have repressed it ever since. He wasn't inconveniencing me very much, he hoped, but might he take a few minutes to examine me? What could I say to my late-night visitor? Sure, Doc, examine away, said the instantly gregarious patient, wondering what a neurologist would have to examine in *me*. My problems weren't neurological, were they? No, he said, not entirely, certainly, but he just wanted to look at my feet. *I* hadn't looked at my feet in two weeks; I hadn't even felt my feet or thought about them. Odd: before I was hospitalized,

213

my feet hurt terribly; now I had no pain. Suddenly it dawned on me that I had no feeling at all. What the hell was going on?

The doctor, pensive, quiet, fondled my toes, asking me to move them this way, that way, any way at all. I tried but could not. He asked me to touch various parts of one foot with the other foot and then with one or both hands. He did some simple tests of my nerve responses—touch nose with index finger, stuff like that—and again and again prodded my feet. I felt something in my calves but not in my ankles, and he took out a probe with a point and gently touched me on various parts of my feet. Still I felt nothing, but sweat was pouring down my face, not because anything was hurting but because *nothing* was hurting, nothing below the ankles was *feeling,* nothing at all was responding to his touch—not the toes or the balls of my feet or the arch; nothing.

This went on for about forty-five minutes. I was saying nothing except "no, no, no" to his questions about whether I was feeling anything where he was touching, and then he stopped asking me anything and began to murmur what sounded like "mm" or "hm" or "ah, um," and I suddenly imagined myself in Ronald Reagan's part in *King's Row,* where he cries out, "Where's the rest of me?" Finally, I asked, "Doctor, will I walk again?"

His response was not encouraging. He said that he thought not, and I was too stunned to ask whether he meant that I wouldn't walk with crutches or canes or something or that I wouldn't walk under any circumstances at all. Now suddenly I realized why my requests to get out of bed were routinely diverted into discussions of something else. I didn't know if my friends were aware of this—I learned in due course that they weren't—but Dr. Robbins told me months later that the doctors were aware that my neuropathy had gone into a phase of

total paralysis, which sometimes happens during long hospital-
izations. But I had been at Mass. General for only two weeks,
and my feet, which had been agonizing before I was hospitalized, now had no sensation whatsoever.

I couldn't even speak after the doctor casually let out his
prognosis. I couldn't say goodbye to him or anything, and I
don't recall whether I even shook his hand, whether I, the
good citizen, was minding my manners. I lay there, breathing
furiously, sopping wet not from my illness but from fear, wondering if I had experienced a phantom visitor, hoping that the
neurologist was a figment of a twisted imagination, feeling that
maybe he hadn't been there beside me at all. But I remembered
that the doctor had put a cup down on the table next to my
bed. He forgot to take it with him when he left. The cup was
there. His visit *had* happened. I pulled myself up with the metal
triangle over my bed, and I tried to lift myself, but I couldn't
budge. I swung or at least thrust my legs outward, toward the
left, intending to stand up then and there and walk out of that
bed and out of that room and out of that hospital, out of that
nightmare. I got my legs over the side of the bed and put them
down on the floor. I felt nothing. No touch of the feet on the
cold floor; at least, I assumed it was cold, though it might have
been heated by coals. I felt normal from my head down my
trunk and into my thighs, but nothing below my knees. Slowly
I pulled my legs back into bed, shaking now with terror. I
remember trying to make a sound, a holler, something, and all
I could do was gasp.

I told myself this couldn't be happening and frantically
flipped on the TV and found the Channel 5 news, at which I
had been a commentator for two years, and which was running
later than usual because of Monday night football. The
coanchor, Chet Curtis, was closing with a little personal news

about me. "We've just learned that our friend David Brudnoy has been released from intensive care at Mass. General Hospital, that his condition has been upgraded from critical to stable and he's resting comfortably. We wish him a speedy recovery. We're all bucking for you, David." I felt that I was caught up in some futuristic horror show where the TV characters begin talking directly, by name, to somebody sitting there innocently watching. I kept trying to piece this together. Had the doctor actually been there? Was Chet actually mentioning me on the news? I'll just stay tuned until *Nightline* comes on; I'll just clear my head and this bad dream will end. But I knew this was no dream. I started heaving with emotion, trying to control myself. Fleeting visions of life in a wheelchair floated into and out of my mind, in the garish colors and preposterous excesses of a bad horror flick. Unless I speak to somebody about this right now, I was yelling silently to myself, I will collapse.

I called WCVB and got Chet Curtis on the line and told him, or half told him, what had just happened. Chet was calm and said something that I heard repeatedly in the next days and weeks: you won't give up, you'll do what it takes to walk again; don't take this one doctor's opinion as gospel. He heard me out, and though I know he was less sanguine than he sounded, he kept the level of his voice even and repeated his belief that I would beat this thing, whatever "this thing" was. He talked me down to a level of calmness, to quiet if not to contentment, and kept repeating that he and his wife and coanchor, Natalie Jacobson, and everybody else at Channel 5 were with me.

I turned off the TV set, still breathing heavily, still trying to find a way around what I had been told, a way that would make it not have happened, a way that would allow me to think that I had dreamed the whole episode. My thoughts turned wildly to Franklin Roosevelt, functioning in his paralyzed condition for decades; to the former mayor of Boston John Collins, who had governed the city for years from his wheelchair and with whom I had occasionally done television chat shows; to people I had met and admired who had come to grips with a late-life paralysis and hadn't given up either hope or their continued pursuit of the work they loved. I was rushing ahead of the situation, convinced one moment that I would be wheelchair-bound forever, hopeful the next that I would get over this thing—people do; people did; I could, couldn't I?—and walk again. I didn't try to touch my feet or move. If I just go to sleep now, if I don't think about this, I'll get up in the morning and everything will be the way it used to be. I'll walk tomorrow. It's a hallucination. Too many days in this hospital. I've seen too many bad movies and I'm living in one right now. I'll walk tomorrow. I am not going to be crippled. I'll walk tomorrow. I *will* walk, tomorrow.

Twelve days had passed between the night I collapsed and was taken to the hospital and the moment when my late-night visitor delivered his prognosis. This informed opinion by the neurologist came as the most devastating news I had ever experienced—worse than my diagnosis of the virus itself, since I had had half a decade to come to grips with the fact that I too would die of AIDS. I was prepared, I thought, for death; I often quoted Woody Allen's line "It's not that I'm afraid of dying. I just don't want to be there when it happens." But paralysis! Death would come, but I now feared it would come to a man who could no longer walk.

Months later, when the national media began to chronicle my illness and recovery, I met ABC's John Hockenberry, who had been paralyzed at age nineteen in an auto accident that left him a T-5 paraplegic, limited from just below the nipples to the tips of his toes. A gutsy, wackily funny man, he tells his story with wit and hardheaded realism in *Moving Violations,* graced on the cover with a joyful photograph of him doing wheelies in his chair. My introduction to John came the day his producer and crew began their morning with me at my Boston University class. We went back to my place and waited for John to fly in from New York; he had a cell phone with him and would call us when he arrived. But no call came. An hour, two hours passed, and finally I suggested that we go downstairs and see if anything was wrong. John was sitting in his wheelchair in front of my building; his cellular phone batteries had died, and nobody had asked if he needed help. He sat there in the drizzle for over an hour, but he smiled when he saw us, brushing off the inconvenience. I saw it as a horror; to John, this was just another day in the rain. The crew lifted him up the seven steps into the building and we went upstairs in the elevator. I shuddered for John and the situations he endures, and I shuddered in retrospect for myself, recognizing what my life would have been like if I had not overcome the neuropathy—and in prospect, perhaps, since the antiviral drugs I'm now on may impinge on my feet once more. I was beginning to learn about disability, both from experience and from an emerging empathy, and I began agitating then and there for the retrofitting of our building to comply with the Americans with Disabilities Act. It takes one to know one, evidently, and I was beginning to see myself as disabled, although I had been rescued for the moment from anything even remotely comparable to Hockenberry's condition.

My radio interview with John about his book was one of my best, and his book is easily the best I've read on the subject; I assigned *Moving Violations* to my media criticism students for a take on how the media deal with handicapped topics and peo-

ple. But when the neurologist visited me months earlier, I
knew nothing of John Hockenberry and his valiant and successful efforts to triumph over what I was sure would have
destroyed me. In the first days after the neurologist's visit, I
didn't know if I could take paralysis, could accept any limitations as severe as that. I imagined only that even if I survived
the immune destruction of AIDS for a few years more, I would
be locked into all-encompassing physical chains and might prefer an early death. I was wild with foreboding and fortunately
short-lived self-pity.

Mica Rie, a physical therapist who had been among the
many Mass. General personnel who had visited me when I was
in the ICU, came again to see me the morning after my visit
from the morose neurologist, all smiles, filled with encouragement. She was having none of my morbidity, and though she
didn't precisely declare "You will walk again, I guarantee it,"
that was the tenor of her visit. Mica explained that she would
put me into the hands of one of the hospital's best therapists
and one of her own most accomplished students, Suzanne Garden.

Suzanne spent part of every day with me and became the
most important person in my life until I transferred eleven days
later to Spaulding Rehabilitation Hospital. She introduced me
to the walker even before the end of election day and urged me
to stand on my own, clutching the sides and just remaining
stationary. I had lost so much muscle mass and had been bedridden for so long that when I stood I shook, and I immediately fell back into the chair. Suzanne insisted that I try again,
and when I did finally manage to stand, I clutched the walker as
if it were salvation itself. I whooped with an intense joy I had
never experienced before. My hands ached just from the exer-
tion of holding on to the walker, reminding me of a cross-

country skiing episode in Vermont with Ward when I was so awkward that my fingers had to be literally pried off the poles. Now, years later, as I tried to stand and steady myself on the walker, my body was Jell-o but my hands evinced the grasp of steel.

In the next days I stood repeatedly, holding on to the walker and gradually feeling confident that I would remain upright. Eventually I was able to lurch ponderously across the hospital room, like the just enlivened monster of Dr. Frankenstein. I could go fifteen feet at most and was fatigued almost to nausea, but I was determined to keep going until I could do it without Suzanne's supervision. Proud of this tiny move toward disproving the neurologist's prognosis and almost giddy with delight in showing off to my friends, I called my little routine my Stupid Human Trick. Some of my visitors feared I would tumble to the floor and break some bones, which, with skin, was about all I amounted to just then, but they humored me and praised me as if I were a kid learning to remain steady on his first two-wheel bike. I soon learned how to sit down by backing into a chair, feeling the seat at the back of my thighs, and easing myself downward into it, and against orders from Mica and Suzanne I practiced this when I was alone. If I could stand, "walk," and sit down, I wouldn't be the crip, to use John Hockenberry's favored term, I feared I would become.

Within a week I had become a slow-motion whiz, getting up, "walking," turning around, keeping my back straighter than I ever had before, providing the balance that would keep me from cascading onto the floor, and sitting and getting up again and again. By the time I left for Spaulding on November eighteenth to undergo intensive work on my feet, Suzanne had me taking six steps in the hall without the walker, one hand holding a cane and the other loose at my side. Of course I was

220

delirious with joy and wanted to do it over and over again, but Suzanne had proved her point: in time I would probably walk without any support, and this was the best news of my stay. Six months to the day after the neurologist first sent me into despair, I did my own mini-Lourdes and cast away my now superfluous cane—well, retired it to my umbrella stand—and I haven't used it since.

Just before leaving Mass. General, I was subjected to a battery of tests to determine what muscle functions remained in my feet and to search for signals from the spine to my feet. People told me that these were painful tests, but since I had no feeling in my feet, the hours of prodding every millimeter of those nearly useless appendages involved no pain at all, just the sensation of the technician's hands placing probes on me. The results: there were then no working nerves in either of my feet, though my left calf had some nerve sensation and the right one, more severely damaged, had minimal feeling just below the knee. Both thighs were okay, and no neuropathy was apparent then, or later, in my hands. One doctor said that if and when I learned to walk again, my leg muscles would probably do all the work while my mind translated the leg activity into a memory of sensation in the feet. It would be something like the phantom pain that many amputees feel, a false sensation of appendages no longer in existence, in my case of feet that felt nothing. I determined to find a way to walk even if I never had another nerve functioning in my feet. Even the prospect that my peripheral neuropathy might eventually affect my hands seemed less than horrendous, since if I could in some sense walk, I could still live an independent life.

The chief of the cardiopulmonary unit at Mass. General, Dr. Kazemi, said that he would have released me from the hospital and let me go home except that I couldn't walk. My lungs and

221

heart were improving nicely, and my spirits were high once I had concluded that I would have some mobility after all. Moreover, I continued to believe that the etiology of my cardiomyopathy and pneumonia, namely HIV, wouldn't become public knowledge. Every step of the way from collapse to my eventual return home and to work was accompanied by my adroit ability to go into denial when I was unable to handle reality, compounded by nearly equal doses of willpower on the one hand and fairly massive ignorance on the other.

My friends, especially the Gang of Five, tried to balance their desire to ease me into a sense of confidence about my prognosis with their belief—quite accurate, of course—that I needed to know the full extent of my illness if I were to construct a rational course of action for whatever time I had left. Patricia had many gay friends and had seen a few die of AIDS, and while the subject of my health never led to *the* question, my collapse and the fact that it was owing to AIDS didn't surprise her. She used to joke with me about keeping the carpets clean at my condo because she would inherit it when I dropped dead and didn't relish the prospect of having to replace the rugs. But Patricia, who feared that AIDS might take me eventually, was equally concerned that my high-powered, controlling approach to life would lead to a heart attack, which was just as likely as anything else to do me in. She told me later that months before I collapsed, she saw my body as ravaged, and like other of her friends who had died of AIDS, I seemed doomed. She knew that telling me her fears would only anger me and that I would dismiss her concern as foolish. I was, after all, fine, just fine, really.

Like Kevin, Pat thought that if I lifted an eyebrow while she spoke to me in the ICU, maybe I was hearing her. She wondered what "unconscious" really meant, at least what it meant for me. She kept babbling to me, even though I wasn't responding. She later told me how she had gone over things that had happened to us and outings we had had, our adventures in Texas, our trip together to Egypt; she had been getting things off her chest and wondering if I heard her somehow. She also tried to help me come to terms with all the anger I had manifested, anger that she felt almost certainly came out of me because of fear as I sickened. All of this to an unconscious patient hovering between life and death; all in hopes that I could somehow hear her words or at least comprehend, on whatever level, her love.

Even as my condition improved and I was released from the ICU, Pat knew that everything was going to be different, permanently. She knew that I had to accept the ongoing nightmare of coping with AIDS, but she had known me longer than any other of my friends in Boston—thirty years—and understood that for me, life was a marathon. Slowing down was out of the question; mine was the life of a person who had places to go, people to see, things to do. I liked it that way, and Pat, ever tolerant of if never passive about what she was convinced was a prescription for my early death, had no choice but to stifle her warnings and pleadings that I ease up and let what would happen, happen.

When I was well enough to hear it, Pat told me that she was trying to come to grips with the realization that a facet of her life was about to change forever. She knew that I was going to die and was trying to deal with that even as it drained all her energy. She told Kevin, who repeated it to me, that just going through the motions of physically getting on with work each day took everything she had. Pat didn't know how she could tell her children, who regarded me as a surrogate father. The

223

twins have no memories of a time when I wasn't a part of their lives.

One of the sadder parts of living with AIDS is what it does to others. I'm glad that I chose not to shove the HIV diagnosis into the minds of everybody who means something to me. I inflicted it on only a few, and I'd do the same today if I had it to live over again. So many people suffer when one person sickens. In some ways it is a confirmation of the Buddhist belief, which I first learned of when living in Japan, that life itself lies in suffering. Pain and joy, fear and hope, desperation and determination, are always joined.

During my hospital stay I was visited by doctors who listened to my program and just wanted to come in and talk about radio or movies or whatever. Other acts of kindness nearly saved me at times when I felt terribly debilitated, so much a nuisance to others and to myself, so doomed. There were moments when I felt so in need of a warm touch that I embraced a nurse's aide, just hugged her, like a child with a scraped knee running to Mother, and I was never rebuffed. Mary made my introduction to a catheter bearable—twice in one night, when I was having urinary problems. This is not the most dignified of all hospital procedures, but Mary had a clever way of joking with me until I gave up my fear of what was about to happen, and as I laughed, she swiftly inserted the wretched thing. My primary day nurse, Susan Bardzik, has the healing touch and a radiant smile, and when she realized my passion for chocolate, she brought me huge amounts on a daily basis, the better to fatten me up, we agreed. Each small act of kindness gave me a measure of optimism. I was a very scared fellow indeed, and every kind word, every unforced touch (surely some of the staff must have feared that even touching a man with AIDS could endanger them), was a blessing.

Mica and Suzanne and the doctors and others who attended to my unending needs convinced me that I would in due course learn to walk and got me to believe that nowhere was it written in the Book of Life and Death that *this* hospitalization must mean that I would *soon* be dead. I needed honest encouragement, not fairy tales, as each day I realized that my head was clearing, that the hallucinations were over, and that though I couldn't get up and go out into the world just then, I could and must begin to take back the reins of my own life. Near the end of my third week at Mass. General, I was contentedly into a routine of medications, therapy for my feet, gargantuan meals to help me regain my thirty lost pounds, visits from friends throughout the day, including, invariably, the Gang of Five. I came to accept, day by day, little by little, just how sick I had been and how tenuous my condition still was.

By the time I left Mass. General, I had asked Deborah Cotton, my first female doctor ever, and Greg Robbins if they would become my principal physicians. I was sure that living with AIDS would be more bearable than otherwise if I had Deborah and Greg to shepherd me through. I talked at length, almost embarrassedly, about this with Ward, fearing that it might be presumptuous for somebody in my condition to have preferences about physicians. Ward long ago grew used to my odd mixture of chutzpah in some situations and painful shyness in others, and he laughed and assured me (how does he always know these things?) that of course they would agree to what I asked. And they did.

I had one fervent wish: that I could keep the fact that I had AIDS out of the public consciousness. I wanted the thousands who had reached out to me with letters and the dozens of journalists who had written articles in the local papers about me and the radio and TV commentators who had discussed me with kindness and concern in their broadcasts to be satisfied knowing that I had succumbed to pneumonia and cardiomyopathy without knowing about the syndrome that had occasioned those diseases. I was pretty much back into my controlling mode, figuring that I would be out of the hospital in a few weeks, mobile again if not quite a marathon runner, back in my classroom at the university and in my radio and TV jobs, managing the various AIDS diseases as they came along—they always come along as the syndrome progresses—and maintaining my privacy. The closest of friends would know that I had AIDS, but outsiders would have no idea. Dream on.

NINE

Revelation

Peter Meade put a quick stop to my fantasy. One afternoon about two weeks into my hospitalization, I took our discussion into the subject of when, if ever, I would have to tell Dad and my stepmother, Audrey, about "the AIDS thing," as I tended to call it. Mutual friends had begun to ask him whether my problem went beyond pneumonia and cardiomyopathy, inching their way toward the truth. I was living in a dream when I thought I could just keep plugging on, ease back into my work, and let AIDS be a matter between me, my doctors, and the Gang of Five.

And why not? Why, I asked Peter with childlike (or dumb) innocence, couldn't my health problems remain my business alone? As with politicians who feel that they're obliged to fling their tax returns before *hoi polloi,* public figures who insist on spilling their guts to the public always struck me as obsequious, lacking in discretion. If I were not now known as a person with AIDS, I wouldn't have dreamed of writing this book (at my tender age). Necessity is the mother of invention, true enough, but also sometimes the precursor to revelation. Would the media maggots (I forgot that I too am a media maggot of sorts) not be satisfied with just enough of the story to know that I'd been miserably ill? Peter gave me one of his "you've got to be kidding" smiles and said, in almost these words, You're a public figure, Bruds; what else have they [the media] to do but write stories about their own? Oh, said I, with astounding comprehension.

And so it came to pass that on the fifteen of November, Susan Bickelhaupt, radio critic for the *Boston Globe,* called me at the hospital and politely but insistently brought up the matter. She had heard rumors, she said; well founded, she implied; from sources unnamed, she teased me. So, David, tell me: are they true? I slid around the question, committing, as the logicians put it, an *ignoratio elenchi*—an evasion, with a wink, of the main point—by tossing off the truthful "Well, I haven't had any AIDS test here," hoping that she would take that as an answer. So, no AIDS test at Mass. General, she said; how about elsewhere? No, I said, a bald-faced lie. Does that mean you absolutely don't have AIDS? Pinocchio Brudnoy compounded his sin: now I was on record denying the truth. Susan asked me whether it would be okay if she tossed a little item into her column. *Would that be okay!* I screamed inside my skull. Was that iceberg ahead of us on the *Titanic* okay? Go ahead if you must, said I, shaking and beginning to sweat, knowing that even the most offhand, tentative item in Susan's well-read column would fuel the fire or fan the flames or whatever the cliché is. But what could I do except lie? And what could Susan do but serve her journalistic demons and print the item? There it was left for a few heart-stopping minutes, though she called back later and we danced around the matter again; I should say, I danced around it. Susan knew that she had the story. It was up to her now. She could "out" old Bruds as an AIDS sufferer or accept what she was certain was a lie from a pal whom she wouldn't want to hurt for the world.

At which point Jon and Ward arrived, joined soon by Kevin and then by Peggy Slasman, Mass. General's director of development and public information, who gave me the oh-so-welcome news that she had been getting calls asking the same questions. The master of naïveté said something like "Well, I guess there's nothing we can do about it; Susan's going to run a 'denied' rumor tomorrow." Jon, political commentator for the local Warner Bros. TV channel, columnist for the *Globe,* my radio producer for five years during the late seventies and early eighties, one of the Gang of Five, and a very savvy guy, said, "No, there is *not* nothing we can do about it. We can negotiate with the *Globe*—we don't have to just let things happen. We can trade with the paper: it spikes the gossip item and we give the whole story to one of its star writers. It's doable, David, and the *Globe* will [expletive deleted] in its L. L. Bean trousers to get the story from the horse's mouth."

Suddenly everything changed. Of course I knew that newspapers prefer exclusive confirmed stories to rumors, and I was hamburger now, sizzle meat for the journalistic griddle. Jon and Kevin knew what to do; I should have known but was too sick and confused to focus. Jon called the paper and went down the food chain from the editor to the executive editor to the features editor, Nick King, who, unlike the others, was still at his desk. Coached by Jon, I began the trading: "So, Nick, would you prefer a feature exclusive to a gossip item?" You know the answer.

It was arranged in a matter of minutes. Nick asked whom I wanted to write the piece, letting me know that Jack Thomas, one of the very best feature writers at the *Globe,* was already assigned a piece on me, and now, with the AIDS dimension, he had his hook. Would Jack be okay with me? More than okay, I said. Call Jack at home and set it up, Nick instructed, asking only that the *Globe* have a media exclusive, with one exception: if WBZ Radio and TV wanted the story, they could have it for the same morning, two days hence. Kevin went into gear, calling our boss, Brian Whittemore, and spilling the beans about my AIDS, whereupon Brian said he'd arrange for a taped interview with me the next morning, to run the following day. So there it was, inescapable, upcoming in hours: the revelation scene I thought I could slide away from, the burial of the fantasy that my AIDS wouldn't become public information.

Peggy then asked whether I wanted a series of one-on-one interviews Thursday morning, after Thomas's piece hit the stands, or one big press conference. *Press conference?* I asked incredulously. What do you mean, *press conference?* Who would care? She, Kevin, Jon, Peter, and Ward cast their glances heavenward and took the matter out of my hands. Somehow I was still flapping my wings, desperately trying to fly right back into denial. Peggy departed with "It'll be a morning to remember." Ah, yes, I thought, just what the doctor ordered, a morning to remember. As she left, I asked Peggy how many reporters she expected; I imagined two or three. "This'll be standing room only," she shot back. "I've got to find someplace big enough to hold them all." My heart was racing, I think, and my head started aching. I was being dragged by events into something I did not want. The immensity of the moment began to register in my brain, and I lurched nearly into panic. It was getting out of hand; hell, it was going to be a catastrophe. Not so, Kevin insisted; it'll be the best way to handle the media. Besides, Jon said, everything will turn out just fine. Oh yes, *fine, just fine:* where had I heard *that* phrase before?

I called Pat to give her a heads up, and Peter to get his take on the matter. He laughed, already aware, as I had not been just an hour earlier, that my AIDS story couldn't stay a secret forever. This is all for the best, Peter said in his avuncular voice, soothing wee Davy's panic. Pat said little; she easily went into her silent mode, letting me talk on and on, realizing that I was scared shitless and needed her calmness to get me down from the ceiling. In anticipation of my public revelation, I needed their support all the way. I had been relying on my friends as a buffer between me and the outside world; now I needed them, in a sense, to protect me from myself.

The next morning Brian arrived with our morning WBZ anchor, Gary LaPierre, who taped twenty-five minutes with me, no holds barred. I sounded awful but told Gary everything he wanted to know or at least felt comfortable asking. This wasn't an inquisition, it was a profile of the best-known evening guy in town by the best-known morning man. Gary calmly eased me into a frank revelation of precisely what I was suffering from, of why I had kept my HIV status secret for so long, and of what I expected to do in the time remaining to me. Gary has the quintessential radio voice, firm, clear, muscular, precise; I was racing into the answers, leaving off concluding elements of my sentences, sometimes losing track of my responses, but nevertheless, I did it. One of the city's major media figures had come out to the public with news of his AIDS. After the taping, Brian shouted, "He's back! Bruds is back!" Not quite, but we all got the point: I was finally being honest about myself, as I insisted on being about those whose stories were fodder for my show. One thing that morning gave

231

me was the certain knowledge that I *would* return to radio—
and that was enough for me.

Jack Thomas arrived soon after, bringing me doughnuts and
a big coffee—everybody knows the path to my heart begins at
Dunkin' Donuts—and taped for over an hour. He also convinced me to let a photographer come, which was against hospital regulations (the photographer hid his equipment under his
parka). The color photos made the front page and the first page
of the Living section the next day and included one of me
sitting like a mummy with a plastic urinal bottle attached to my
chair. Jack finished our interview, the photographer hid his
toys and departed, and I began calling friends to give them
advance notice.

Now it was time to communicate with Minneapolis—that is,
finally to tell my parents. My dad has army buddies in the
Boston area, which meant my news would reach Minneapolis
on the heels of the paper's release. I knew it was better for them
to hear it from me than from somebody else, but it was also
terrifying to have to do the telling. I called my Aunt Kathie
first, and we worked out an arrangement. She would stop by
my folks' apartment and gently lead them into what was coming, then at a set time I would call. I feared because of my dad's
advanced age—eighty-six—and conjured up a nightmare scenario: I tell Dad, he gets a heart attack and expires on the
phone. The fact of the matter was less gruesome. At our prear-
ranged time, I spoke, my heart racing, my temples thumping,
my tongue nearly cleaving to the roof of my mouth: "Dad,
Audrey, I think you know more or less why I'm calling. Yes,
I'm at Mass. General Hospital, as you already know, because
my heart and lungs nearly gave out. But the reason they did was
because I'm HIV-positive. I've got AIDS."

Dad took this calmly; at least, his voice was calm, though I can imagine what pain he must have been in. We had never spoken about my sexuality. There were times when Dad was still practicing dentistry when I'd come home and go in for a checkup. While I was numb with anaesthetic and unable to answer, he'd gently probe: "Had any interesting dates, son? What are the girls like back in Boston?" Hardly a birds-and-bees discussion—we'd never had one of those either—but an indication that he was tentatively trying to open a heart-to-heart. That's as far as it ever went. He obviously knew that I was gay; if nothing else would clue him, my many unmarried, middle-aged male friends were an unmistakable giveaway. Once when he and Audrey were visiting me in Provincetown, two of my pals had a garden party in large part in their honor. The guest list was not exactly what they were used to in Minneapolis. They *knew;* we just didn't discuss it—a familiar story in the lives of homosexuals. But my health had never been a topic of concern for him, and the sudden news that I had AIDS must have been overwhelming.

But it was Audrey who surprised me. She was angry. Why didn't you tell us earlier? Didn't you think we could handle it? I tried to reassure her, explaining that I had intended to tell them if things got rough. Now things were rough, and the news would be all over New England by morning. Audrey was not to be consoled, and she remained angry at me. Ward explained that she wasn't angry at me, she was furious at the disease. Though I was rattled by her reproaches, I kept cool and let her vent, while insisting that I loved them both but had kept my AIDS secret to protect them from the news. Audrey was brutal in her denunciations, though two days later she came around, reverting to her loving ways, and she became my greatest champion from then until her death, of lung cancer, late in April 1996.

Night had fallen, and I had fallen into despair, assuming that the next day would be a catastrophe, the end of my privacy—and the end of the false belief that I was straight. Though the "gay thing" was no secret in New England, many listeners, especially in the thirty-eight additional states that get the WBZ signal after sundown, might well have no idea; the topic rarely came up, and on only a handful of occasions had a discussion of gay matters led to a question about my own sexuality. Still, even for those who could be expected to know, "knowing" and *knowing* aren't always the same thing. What would the Bible Belt think now? Even more pressing was the end of my image as free of AIDS—an image I clung to—and the beginning of what I feared would be either recriminations from the closet police on the gay left about not having shouted my HIV status as soon as I learned of it or moralistic prattling from the sanctimonious saints on the right. In any case, I would be turned into a poster boy for AIDS.

I never believed that my audience would flee and my broadcast career would end, though the David Brudnoy of tomorrow would forever be quite a switch from the David Brudnoy of yesterday. I learned of my HIV diagnosis in the era of Ryan White; my coming out occurred in the era of Magic Johnson. I told myself that my anxiety was due to my certain knowledge that once I was depicted as an AIDS "victim," I'd never hear the end of it. I would turn into a clichéd phrase, like "Watergate ex-convict Charles Colson" or "one-time presidential candidate George McGovern"; I would be "AIDS victim David Brudnoy." In retrospect I realize that what was really terrifying about coming out with the news was accepting it myself. Denial had ceased to be an option. Just as I had attempted to fool others about how sick I was by first fooling myself, so I would have to be frank with others by being frank with myself

Evening wore on, and among my callers was Dean Johnson, Susan Bickelhaupt's counterpart on the *Boston Herald*—a sweet guy, one of the princes in the Boston media royal court, and a friend. He had heard rumors, among them both that I had AIDS and that the *Globe* was running with the story the next day. Dean knew the rumors were true, and he knew that my denials were from Desperation City, but my agreement with the *Globe* demanded print exclusivity on the story. Giving voice to a lie so preposterous that it's embedded in my mind, I categorically denied that anything at all was being published the next morning in the biggest newspaper northeast of New York.

No sooner did Dean hang up than another *Herald* staffer, my buddy Margery Eagan, with whom I had done point-counter-point on WBZ-TV, called, wanting stuff for *her* column. I let Peter handle this one. Rather, he told me, sotto voce, to get lost, and he told Margery that I was out of the room with a therapist working on my feet and I couldn't be interrupted. Whereupon Peter, who had not made any agreement with the *Globe* and could say whatever he wanted, did. The next day Margery's column had an exclusive from the Brudnoy bunker at Mass. General with Bruds's longtime friend the estimable Peter Meade.

Dean was on the phone again soon, but with Peter answering, I was able to avoid him for the second time. Known always as the man who suffered not only fools but hypocrisy poorly, as the talk host who insisted on the truth come what may, I had become a categorical, if not quite a congenital, liar. Somehow I fell asleep, interrupted only by wild dreams of being torn apart by media monsters.

The next morning I was given a shower and awaited Ward's

morning visit with the papers. There it was on the front pages. Pensive Brudnoy, in color, topped the *Globe,* headlined "Brudnoy's Battle," then leaped into the Living section with "David Brudnoy's Secret Struggle," subheaded "The broadcaster goes public with his private life as a gay man with AIDS." Jack Thomas's column was a warts-and-all piece of revelation journalism, and a valentine too. I emerged as valiant, not as a sneak—as a man who bore up more or less alone under a terrible weight for five years, now confronting my fate with dignity.

The *Herald* ran its piece—I should say pieces—as well: the front-page story out-and-out lifted twenty-four of Jack Thomas's paragraphs from the *Globe*'s earliest edition, half acknowledging that the material had come from its rival. Peter's talk with Margery Eagan panned out nicely; her column's head was "Public, private man gets to take a second bite of the apple." Medical editor Michael Lasalandra did what he could with medical opinions given by doctors who didn't know me, but it was Dean Johnson who more or less owned the *Herald* that morning, weighing in with yet another story, this one headlined "Radio Community Expresses Shock, Sadness," which contained a remark from radio analyst Clark Smidt that consoled me: "He's kept his personal life to himself and has always conducted programs with the utmost professionalism. . . . New Englanders respect a person for what he's capable of on the air, and I don't think David has ever let his audience down. Why should this [the AIDS revelation] hurt him? He can still be a conservative talk host—and a very good one."

Peggy Slasman said that the press conference, called for eleven A.M., would be packed. I scoffed. My WBZ-TV and WBZ Radio bosses arranged for one of our anchorwomen, Kasey Kaufman, to come a bit early and get an advance interview; she also brought her makeup kit and modified as best she could my look of having slept in Dracula's coffin or just undergone the seventy-day Egyptian mummification procedures. I looked ghastly, and there was only so much that Kasey could do. At eleven I was wheeled down to a solarium and then, at my insistence, got up from the chair and rose to clutch the walker. I was dressed in a loose sweater, not that that fooled anybody about my severe weight loss, and I slowly entered the room on my own legs, precisely ten days after the morose neurologist had doubted that this would ever be possible.

The room *was* packed, SRO, with about seven TV cameras and crews, countless print journalists, my editor at the *Tab* chain, Greg Reibman, Jon Keller, a variety of other familiar faces, and Dean Johnson and Susan Bickelhaupt, who I hoped forgave me my lies. The TV crews were accompanied by their remote vans, antennas stretched as high as they could go to feed the material back to the stations for the noon news. I didn't actually see this jam in the main entranceway of the hospital, but I saw it on TV throughout the day. I held things together adroitly that morning, sitting between Dr. Kazemi and my nurse Susan Bardzik, congratulating my media colleagues for turning up so early even without coffee and croissants to temper their jangled morning nerves. I was all smiles on entering the room, clearly in good spirits. The questions were softballs, by and large: Are you feeling better, David? Do you intend to continue working on TV and radio when you're back home? Friendly stuff, supportive stuff, the stuff of which media dreams, not media nightmares, are made. These men and women really *cared,* and for one horrible moment I felt myself reaching for Sally Field's unforgettable moment, when she got one of her two Oscars and gushed, "You like me! You really like me!" I resisted the temptation.

But the thing is, they did like me, and the press conference became an educational session for me, allowing me finally to talk about the foolishness of those who don't listen to their bodies and get into situations as serious as mine out of a fear of facing reality; about the need for people to be very careful when doing things that could lead them to contract HIV; about my determination to live as full a life as possible and as filled as ever with the work I loved. As I left the solarium—I was ordered by Dr. Kazemi to get into bed then and there and take a long nap—I passed close by my friend from the *Herald* and said, "Good to see you, Dean; I haven't talked with you since I lied to you on the phone." I was tingling with excitement. My fears that this event would be miserable had been washed away, and I was certain then that I could be completely out, as a gay man with AIDS. It's an overused cliché, but a weight did indeed lift off my shoulders.

I cheated (this was becoming habitual) and instead of going to sleep flipped around on the dial to see how various stations were dealing with the matter during their noon news. I did disconnect the phone afterward for a few hours and try to sleep, but I couldn't. As soon as I reconnected the phone the calls started coming, and a near-deluge of new plants arrived throughout the day, enough for a mob boss's funeral but for me a tribute of kindness.

In the following days, *Herald* stories included interviews with gay activists, some of whom griped that I hadn't come shouting to the world that I was HIV-positive way back when. The paper's Saturday edition featured an editorial called "A Private Man Goes Public," a love letter from the hard-boiled tabloid. A number of radio programs devoted time to my situation; on one, the *Jerry Williams Show* on WRKO, I first heard a self-described conservative read me out of the movement because I had the wrong sexuality and the wrong disease. A UHF cable show on Thursday evening had a graphic of me looking as if I were dead on a slab; its host, Chuck Adler, took calls about whether or not I should have been "outed," which seemed to fascinate people. On my own program, guest host Steve Le-Veille played the entirety of Gary's twenty-five-minute interview at the top and the bottom of the show and announced that when I returned I would discuss the matter further but that the *David Brudnoy Show* would now revert to what it was designed to be, a program about news, not about its host. Every night for months thereafter Steve took a few seconds to give an update on my condition and then went right into holding the fort.

I certainly couldn't be said to lack media savvy. I've long understood the appeal of talk radio, whose hosts become part of their audience's family, of their lives. When I reviewed Eric Bogosian's gut-clenching movie *Talk Radio* in the *Boston Globe,* I noted that radio talk shows have become the last neighborhood in town. Through radio, even more than through my television appearances since 1971, I had become a celebrity long before I was ushered into the Age of AIDS, and though we don't find in radio talk shows a contemporary incarnation of Plato and the lads in the agora or at the Academy, tens of millions of people hear our programs, among them many who invite us into their lives. When I realized in mid-November that I had no choice but to let the whole story come out, I knew that the people who listen to my programs wouldn't desert me, but what surprised me and everybody else was the intensity, depth, and scope of the response to my situation. If the Arbitron ratings, by which we are judged and which sales departments use to peddle their wares, are a fair indication of success, then my sexual orientation didn't seem to matter to most listeners.

I opened a few furiously angry letters, of course, and once in a while some oaf would call the show and thunder a question clearly weeks in formulation: "ARE YOU A HO-MO-SEX-YU-AL, you PERVERT, you!?" To which, if I was in the mood, I tended to say, "Only on my better days," and in another frame of mind, "Well, no, actually, but thanks for the proposition." Overwhelmingly, the audience response has been indifference to that facet of my life, which I never paraded around on-air or off. I found no abiding discomfort in being discreet but not closeted, and I've tried, futilely, to explain to some gay zealots that I too, in my quiet way, may have done some service to the cause of acceptance, by just being at ease with myself.

Friends, colleagues in the media and the universities, and the movers and shakers in politics rushed to my side in person or by mail, but most touching to me was the support from listeners, viewers, and readers of my columns, whose missives to me numbered seventeen thousand within three months of my collapse. Only a few of these were of the "Burn in hell, faggot" sort; one of the more memorable went on for two pages of invective, beginning with the lines "Hi Davey, Ya look pretty good on TV. Are you STARTING TO *ROT?* Rock Baby [Hudson, I presume] sure looked Good at the End, Didn't he? Fucking lovely! Were you Born QUEER? Are you a 'cocksucker' or a 'bum-fucker'?" So there were the exceptions, like this charming item, which I'll donate in its entirety to any library that might want my papers. But the response was overwhelmingly supportive.

It took me back to the time in 1990 when my first four-year contract with WBZ was running into its last months. Unbeknown to me for quite a while, management was finalizing an arrangement between 'BZ and Tom Snyder's syndicated evening talk program for—can you guess?—*my* hours. In one of his cantatas, Bach had put the words of Isaiah, borrowed famously by Martin Luther: "The people that walked in darkness have seen a great light." I had always believed that my eyes were fully open to the light of reality, but that too demonstrated my denial. Before I had a chance to see the light of this reality, local newspapers went into overdrive. "WBZ's David Brudnoy: I'm Being Fired" headed Dean Johnson's front-page *Herald* story on June 19, 1990. In the *Patriot Ledger,* same day: "Talk Show Host Brudnoy Leaving WBZ Radio." The *Globe,* often scooped on radio stories, got into it soon, joining the chorus, and in the next two weeks the rush was on. Jack Thomas wrote *(Boston Globe,* June 25): "The possibility that WBZ would fire David Brudnoy in favor of syndicated programming makes you wonder if WBZ has fallen into hostile hands determined to destroy what used to be the most respected radio station in Boston." The *Herald*'s Norma Nathan, a columnist whose ability to write either viciously or kindly was remarkable and who I had feared earlier would be the one to expose my visits to the Mass. General AIDS clinic if she knew, was on my side now: "Bad Luck for Brudnoy. Bad Luck for Listeners" (Friday, July 13).

Author Robert Parker said on-air with me, "Do we have time to bad-mouth 'BZ for letting you go? The people who run this station are stupid." Boston University president John Silber, not renowned for being wishy-washy, was quoted as saying, "It's regrettable that more canned stuff will be coming in by people who know nothing about the community, to replace a figure who has become a real personality in Boston." Financial consultant John Spooner resigned from his commentary position on WBZ, writing to the station: "You'll regret it when Brudnoy beats the brains in of Tom Snyder on a competing station."

Jack Thomas ran a second piece in the *Globe,* "A Rare Gentleman Leaves 'BZ Tomorrow," noting that the morale at 'BZ owing to the general manager's decision was "lower than the Thresher." The finale: "Don't underestimate Brudnoy, though. He's too much of a gentleman to embarrass WBZ tomorrow night, but from ten to midnight, he'll take no calls. Instead, he'll reflect on fifteen years in talk radio in Boston, and it's certain to be worth hearing." The station management didn't even think to get me off the air and out the door the day the first article appeared. And then, on the day before my last show, the station had a party for me. There, as if finally responding viscerally to the reality of my departure, I promptly began to choke on a piece of beef that lodged in my throat. Norma Nathan quoted me in her *Herald* column: "People didn't understand what was happening to me. Even though I couldn't swallow. The meat was going nowhere. I couldn't get it out. And everyone was standing, chatting, drinking. I was turning blue and pointed to my throat. Kevin Myron is shorter than I and couldn't do the Heimlich. Finally, [General Manager] John Irwin comes up behind me and gives me a real pouff [I meant that *he* knew the Heimlich maneuver] and out comes this big chunk of uneaten meat. 'John, you could just have let me die. Then you wouldn't have had to fire me!' "

The next night I did as Jack Thomas indicated, ruminating about my fifteen years on radio, saying not one critical word about 'BZ. I've long since learned—Connie Chung, take note—that in the media, if you can't be fired without making a fuss, nobody else can comfortably hire you. The last day, the *Herald* published my op-ed piece on my experiences with talk radio, a reflective piece without any rancor. Local cartoonists expressed their revulsion over what had happened, and an irritated Mike Barnicle of the *Globe* asked in his Sunday piece, "Now that they've fired David Brudnoy in favor of canned programming, why don't the bosses just move the station to Wichita Falls, Texas?"

In the next several weeks, the articles increased in frequency, the buzz was heavy in the air, and even Tom Snyder, whose hours were now ten P.M. to two A.M. following Peter's new hours, six to ten, said on-air, "I can't tell you how relieved I am to hear we have one listener on WBZ. I know I replaced a very popular program there. I know I'm swimming upstream." A caller warmed to this and said, "It's difficult to let go of David; he's terrific, bright and informed," and Tom, bless his honorable heart, said, "If you miss him enough, you'll get him back and I'll be gone."

I'd been around; I had seen good people cast aside like out-of-fashion clothing; I'd seen the bright young things brought in to rescue a station with falling ratings, or just because they were young and the castoffs weren't; I'd seen the crazes in programming change. I knew that this kind of thing happens. But my ratings were superb, and I had frequently been assured by John Irwin that he'd get around to renewing my contract. And now, out of the blue, I was being "downsized." Or did the matter have something to do with John's reputed traditionalist Christian beliefs? Was I too gay for John Irwin's radio station? Or was it just that he wanted to save money by canning a local show and putting on a less costly syndicated program? I felt humiliated, as I had when, seven years earlier, new management at Channel 7 had decided to downgrade the station in a vain effort to make it more . . . what? cool? Then I had been moved from the six o'clock news to the noon news and eventually out the door. That availed Channel 7 nothing but bad press. This thing at WBZ seemed preposterous on its face. Everything ventured (by 'BZ); nothing gained, except what happened next.

One day shortly after I entered the ranks of the unemployed, the morning after I had been interviewed by *other* radio stations about the Robert Mapplethorpe photography exhibit which was then causing a flurry of local commentary, I was approached by Fred Davis, a respected businessman, cause activist, and charity organizer, who was infuriated by WBZ's betrayal of listeners' expectations and who asked if he could create a Bring Back Brudnoy movement. Sure, said I, though I thought that this Davis person might be one or two doughnuts shy of a dozen. He was anything but, and though we didn't meet until months later, we fast became phone mates. The *Boston Herald* wrote about the BBB movement and gave its mailbox number, and fans by the hundreds sent letters immediately. *Inside Radio,* a national broadcasting industry newsletter, noted that "WBZ-AM, Boston, Slits Its Own Throat Late-Night," and Jack Thomas and Dean Johnson and others kept up the drumbeat. *Adweek*'s Charles Jackson asked, "Why is David Brudnoy suddenly the hottest topic in the usually unflappable Boston media market?" and the *Herald* even wrote a lead editorial: "David Brudnoy is a Boston institution, and all of us—really, *all* of us— miss him."

In August I filled in for two weeks on WHDH, my first radio station. This was a wake-up call to WBZ—if 'BZ was through with Brudnoy, mightn't other stations find him just the ticket?—and later that month I wrote a long piece in the *Globe* on the ways that talk radio is portrayed in the movies, keeping my name front and center. Meanwhile, a friend with a spy in Westinghouse Broadcasting's New York headquarters

244

kept me informed on a daily basis, reporting that the big boys in Gotham were getting a deluge of mail; Bring Back Brudnoy was shipping thousands of letters off to New York, and Fred Davis was invited at last to confer with John Irwin at WBZ. Poor John was beginning to understand that Boston isn't just Indiana on the coast (no disrespect intended to Indiana), and as offers were coming in to me from other cities, with even *Variety* hyping the story, the worm turned.

By early September I was headed back to WBZ, courtesy of John Irwin, who called me one day and said, in essence, "Let's erase this 'mistake.' " I learned that human resources (the p.c. term for personnel) had never expunged me from the active files. One of the HR people said that she couldn't believe my departure from WBZ would be permanent, so why bother to go through the whole mess of reentering me into the computer instead of just leaving me there all along? Good question, but not one I would have asked as I departed on July 13. Michael Blowen wrote in the *Globe,* "Brudnoy may be the Jane Pauley of local radio. Like Pauley, who didn't know how popular she was until NBC dropped her from the *Today Show,* David's appeal is reaching new heights."

So, four years before I revealed my AIDS, Tom Snyder lost one of his stations—mine—as did another syndicated radio host, Sally Jessy Raphael, who had also been plunked onto WBZ's airwaves by John Irwin, and the rondelet that is Boston media continued. Even *Group W News,* the Westinghouse newsletter (October 1990), made a virtue of necessity and praised WBZ for listening to its listeners. This whole thing was unprecedented. When radio fires or doesn't renew, radio never admits its mistake. Until my rehiring. And I, who couldn't resist, reported in the *Herald* on December 30 in a column about resolutions that "I resolve to help Westinghouse sell as many light bulbs as possible to restrain their tendency to fire people." The last word, happily, was mine.

I know that all my nine lives won't have as happy an ending as the episode in 1990 had. This current life, the AIDS life, won't end happily. And although I was blameless in the 1990 affair, not everything crummy that happens to me is somebody else's fault. My survival on radio has been due to many things, among them, prominently, the support of my listeners. In my second brush with banishment from the Garden of Media Eden, I had to learn a lesson, at times a harsh lesson indeed, which demonstrated the precariousness of a media career.

One afternoon in March 1992, I attended a small lunch sponsored by *Boston* magazine, for which I had been film critic, restaurant critic, and occasional essayist years before. The purpose was to get into some intelligent discussion about a few of our city's problems. The group was mixed racially and included some media types, some from the political world, others from the world of letters. I was not a naif on race in America, but I was more naive than I should have been about the acceptable parameters of discussion. Karen Holmes, host of a black-oriented weekly public affairs program on WCVB-TV, the station where I was doing my point-counterpoint with Mike Barnicle, remarked that violence doesn't get much attention until it spills over from the black community into the white. I responded, "You're absolutely right. Remember the days when people used to talk about 'the Saturday-night specials up in Niggertown'?"

Everybody agreed that this was all I said. The magazine's editor, Mike Roberts, was quoted later as saying, "I don't think it was a racist remark, but it was not in the best of taste." There is no dispute about the exact wording, which found its way into a big *Globe* article shortly thereafter. My remark was a historical reference to a mixed group of sophisticated people who I assumed would recall the reference; I thought they would know that the term "Saturday-night special," for those cheap handguns that cause such misery in America, was once associated solely or primarily with blacks, and that "Niggertown" was a standard pejorative, never said kindly, in an era now, mercifully, past. Had I been given to racist rhetoric, I would hardly have used that expression in that assemblage of Bostonians. It was precisely because we were mixed company that I thought my intent would be perfectly clear.

Nothing is perfectly clear. I was innocent of what I was charged with—a racist intent to offend my lunch companions—but I was not innocently unaware of the temper of the times and should have realized how the area of permissible discourse had narrowed, owing in no small measure to the particular agenda of political correctness, broadly understood, and especially to discourse connected in any way to race, specifically having to do with blacks. Race matters *matter*; they matter and become bones of serious contention even when no slight is intended. The fault, however, to paraphrase the bard, is not in our stars, it is in ourselves. In myself.

Though nobody said anything about it at the lunch and discussion went on to a variety of topics, I found the next day, when I went into WCVB to tape my commentaries for the week, that Karen had been incensed and hurt by the remark and had mentioned it to friends, who evidently urged her to bring it to public attention, which in Boston means first and foremost the *Globe*. I was greeted at WCVB by the publicity director, who asked that I return a call to Ed Siegel, then the paper's television columnist. When I did, I was stunned to learn that my remark had taken on a life of its own, and though I explained the context to Ed and he agreed that other accounts confirmed what I had just told him, he said it was the *Globe*'s opinion that a significant piece on the incident should be published.

When I got to WBZ, I received a call from a local black activist, a friend of Karen Holmes, and she was livid; our discussion satisfied her in no way but alerted me to what I feared was coming: a feeding frenzy of a kind quite different from that in 1990. I had been moving away from the standard liberal line on racial matters, having learned at Texas Southern University that white liberal patronization of blacks was neither the best way to advance racial harmony nor the best way to advance the cause of equal opportunity for all. My objections to affirmative action and quotas were well known, and I scoffed at the latest theories of Afrocentrist "history." A black lawyer who has subsequently become our first female black state senator confronted me on a TV program well before this incident with her insistence that Cleopatra, Beethoven, Haydn, and President Eisenhower's mother were all blacks. She mocked me for not believing the "documented truth" that these worthies were indeed black. I had staked out my territory in strict libertarian terms, opposing all special rights for anybody and demanding equal rights for all; this, as you know, is not universally accepted as proper, and quotas for certain minorities are considered by many to be consistent with an egalitarian notion of how America ought to be organized. Some of the wilder gay activists have just about fallen into that quagmire for themselves as well as for blacks, Hispanics, women, and selected other groups. Leftist homosexuals generally despise me because I reject their claim that being homosexual and conservative is impossible, and some found the occasion in the "Niggertown" incident to unmuzzle their fangs and have it out. I had long insisted that Louis Farrakhan and his bizarre mélange of Muslim and Afro nationalist ideas, coupled with a strong dose of anti-Semitism, were simply rotten. I had the local Black Muslim honchos barking at my heels on more than one occasion, and in the years that witnessed the rise of Jesse Jackson as a would-be presidential nominee, I had made good use of his tendency to stick his foot in his mouth (look who's talking). I reminded my listeners for a while that his remark about "Hymietown" was made to an all-black gathering, to which he had said, "Let's talk black talk." It was a black reporter, Milton Coleman of the *Washington Post,* who publicized the "Hymies" and "Hymietown" verbiage, for which he was attacked by some blacks as a "white man's Tom."

I was unequivocally on record as no fan of black extremism or of white extremism, for that matter: Klansmen, neo-Nazis, and the like came in for a hefty dose of bashing from me. But I was on record not only with defensible (if arguable) political and social positions; I had also made one terrible, stupid joke in 1989, a comment that in a few seconds nearly obliterated any validity of the bulk of my opinions on race. I apologized for it immediately and then at greater length the next night at the beginning of my program, but it seared itself in the memories of many people and returned to torment me and escalate further in the aftermath of my "Niggertown" remark.

It happened during a few minutes of chitchat when Peter Meade handed off his show to me at nine P.M. We were talking about Reaganite appointments to the bench, rambling on about the good and the bad ones. Peter said, "There may be a new Dred Scott decision." I said, "I don't think they're going to go back to slavery, but if they do I, I wonder if I and my broker can buy me a couple."

Peter immediately realized the significance of this idiotic remark and saw by my offhand attitude that I simply was talking for the sake of talking, meaning no harm but doing more harm in a few seconds than probably I had ever done before. It didn't require a genius to get the message that Peter's face was giving to me, and I struggled for a way to erase the damage. "How do I get out of that one?" I said lamely to a million listeners; to which Peter, wiser than me by far, said, "Plead insanity."

I knew it was a wretched, thoughtless, even pointless remark—Peter and I could do a hand-off about the telephone book, if need be; I wasn't in desperate search for a comment, I was just going bonkers on the air—and my apology, although sincere, was insufficient; more, it was deficient. Little was said to me about the incident, and nothing reached the papers. But a great deal was said about me at the station. A petition condemning me and demanding, if not quite my head, then the rest of me, skewered, was drawn up and signed by about 90 percent of the black staffers. Among the signers were people I had known and been cordial with for years. This was painful for me, chillingly demonstrating what in my brain I knew but with my tongue I could and did forget. And it outraged and was profoundly hurtful to a great many who heard it and still others who heard of it. I soon came to see what I avoided seeing for the few days immediately following the remark: that my cavalierly tossed-off "joke" had inflicted gratuitous wounds on many people—my colleagues, whom I esteemed, and my audience, black and white alike, people who deserved and expected to be well served by me, not scandalized, not offended, not savaged with grotesque remarks.

It was I, not some enemy trying to derail my career, who made the comment. It left no mark in the newspapers, which routinely quoted people on TV and radio for our every *bon mot,* witticism, or stupidity, but it left an indelible mark in the memories of more people than I imagined. Friends—*friends,* mind you—sometimes would, out of the blue, ask me if I'd bought any good slaves lately. Twice callers trying to embarrass me, and succeeding, brought up the remark as I was interviewing a black guest. But eventually it seemed to go away; that is, I wished it had. It arose in conjunction with the media overkill on the "Saturday-night specials up in Niggertown" remark, and the two incidents were conjoined so as to depict a "pattern" of "insensitivity," if not outright racism, from me. The issue blew up into an Incident, and everybody any media outlet could find was asked to comment on it. Liz Walker, a WBZ-TV coanchor who is black, said to the *Globe,* "If David is as progressive as he thinks he is, he should know the harm that the word ['nigger'] causes." Karen Holmes said, "I am still upset if he hasn't learned the harm that those comments cause or make." Defenders arose, attackers pressed on; I simply wanted to fade into the woodwork. My news director at WCVB-TV, Emily Rooney, knew from her father Andy's travails how these things can balloon, and she asked Karen and me to meet with her, which we did. Karen, a gracious woman, was noncommittal about whether or not she accepted my apology for the remark at lunch, which was, as I had said, a historical reference, though the effect of it was to open up a great sore in the souls of those who read of it, especially when the 1989 incident was brought up again and considered in a context that made them seem to be of the same stripe.

I was also asked to comment on the matter in my regular spot on WCVB-TV, usually my point-counterpoint with Mike Barnicle. This was to be my solo. Then the powers decided that that would be too much, perhaps making more of the incident than it deserved; then the powers decided that I *should* do it,

251

and I did, on March 31, on the eleven o'clock news. I said, *inter alia,* this:

> Without intending to wound and cause pain, without intending to evoke anger, I have done both. A recent remark of mine and a dumb joke from three years ago have awakened stirrings of resentment against me and have become the ingredients in an ongoing media event. What had been implied . . . is that . . . the essence of me is a few offhand remarks, for which I sincerely apologize. . . . My commitment to integration and equality is lifelong. Honorable people differ on how we get to the fullest achievement of those goals. My approach may not necessarily be yours. But it is genuine. It is defensible. It is what I believe. I stand on my views. I uphold my values. Sometimes, however, I also cause enormous hurt without intending to do so. For that I apologize.

I had done what I was asked to do, but that was insufficient, and the next day's column by Derrick Z. Jackson, a *Globe* op-ed page columnist, catalogued a number of other hurtful remarks made by white people and chastised my employers for not firing me: "Silence equals support of Brudnoy and his remarks. It makes WBZ and Channel 5 equal partners with Brudnoy in mocking African Americans." The weekly *Bay State Banner,* serving Boston's black community, weighed in a couple of times with a rehash of the incident; the *Herald*'s Leonard Greene followed, tossing me into an assemblage of people who dared to criticize affirmative action, which to him automatically meant that we were racist. Because of my remark, for which I alone was responsible, I received a deluge of criticism that went far beyond the understandable fury at the 1989 slavery comment and a misunderstanding of the historical reference at the lunch. My political stances, especially my opposition to affirmative action and my frequent booking of *conserva-*

tive black guests with whom I was in agreement, all became fodder for the attacks on me. I had opened my big mouth and now I was eating . . . well, you know the rest of that phrase.

The backlash against those criticizing me began with a column by the *Herald*'s Beverly Beckham—"David Brudnoy Hit by Hate-Filled Attack"—which laid into Derrick Z. Jackson: "Your words are poison and they injure us all. You hate too much. . . . Do you actually believe [David] said this to intimidate his host or to make [Karen Holmes] feel uncomfortable? . . . You used this incident as a jumping board to attack Brudnoy for a comment he made three years ago. . . . Brudnoy shouldn't have said this. It was insensitive and stupid. But it was not mean. . . . Do you hate David Brudnoy so much, a man without a racist bone in his body? Or is it because he is white that you hate him?" Others chimed in. Columnist William Buchanan attacked the "ultra-liberal *Globe,* [which perhaps] is not too happy with Brudnoy's longtime conservative opinions!" My publisher at the *Tab* newspaper chain, Russel Pergament, who saw the issue going far beyond my remarks and into the emerging world of political correctness, called up the *Globe*'s Ed Siegel and asked him if he believed I was a racist. "No, I don't," Siegel answered. "Then why, if you know he's no racist, did you write two articles implying he is?" asked Russel. "I'm not sure that the articles did imply that," Siegel responded. But the damage had been done. *When something's in the papers, it's got to be true.*

Letters to the papers damned me, praised me, scoffed at the Jackson and Greene columns, lauded those columns, branched off into wild theorizing both about racism in general and about liberal media bias. In his letter to the *Globe,* Ric Duarte, who had offered so much support during the mass for Blitz in 1989, branded Jackson's column "uncalled for and definitely unfair

. . . filled with so much hate for someone he has never met or spoken to. I am black, educated, and a friend and colleague of David Brudnoy. I also produce his program every night on WBZ Radio. I have worked with him for six years and know him better than any of these people who are screaming for his head. I have nothing but respect and admiration for him and consider him one of my closest friends. David Brudnoy is not a racist. You didn't even have the courtesy to give Brudnoy a call to get his side of the story. I think you need to check your own back yard and see just who the racist might be."

There was no end in sight. Syndicated TV columnist Daniel M. Kimmel opined that "the reaction from the *Globe* has bordered on the irresponsible. . . . Channel 5 did no better. Instead of backing up Brudnoy and pointing out that he had done nothing wrong, they instead put him on the air last week to apologize. Brudnoy did not retract his remarks but said he was sorry for any pain they may have inadvertently caused. . . . If Brudnoy had made a racist remark, he should have been condemned. But he did not—he stated a historical fact."

I accepted an invitation from the American Jewish Committee to speak about the matter in a session open to the public, but the evening following my speech I fainted during my program and was carted off in an ambulance. I remained unconscious for several minutes. At the hospital my blood pressure was found to be extraordinarily high, but no other indices of illness were found, and I went back on-air the next evening. I was quoted in the *Herald* as saying, "I have not been the engineer of my own train the last three weeks. It seems to me my body was saying 'I've had just about enough emotional turmoil for a while.' "

On April 23, a few days after I fainted, the *Bay State Banner* reported that a committee of black activists was agitating to get me fired from radio and TV, and the Boston chapter of the national Black MBA Association wrote to WBZ demanding that it recognize that my views were "contemptuous." And in August, *Boston* magazine came up with a split decision, designating me the best radio talk-show host while branding Mike Barnicle and me the worst TV commentators: "One guy you can't take out to lunch, while the other guy is *always* out to lunch."

Finally, at my suggestion, I met with a small group of black employees at WBZ to try to clear the air. I was hoping to open discussion about what had happened and to restore some of our relationships. Sadly, few of those who had petitioned against me in 1989 or who expressed their anger in 1992 showed up. I think the session went some way toward making real amends, though I would have liked to talk also with those who chose not to come to that meeting. To this day, some of my colleagues look the other way when we pass in the halls at 'BZ. At times I feel that as a slight beyond reason; at other times I think I know, at least a little, how they feel. The incident finally fell out of the media maw, as other incidents came forward to get attention. But it was not insignificant, either in and of itself or as an instance of the cruelties I have committed and have felt it incumbent on me to recall in this narrative.

I do know that if I could remove two episodes, and only two, from what I have done in my life, I would wish not to have lived whatever moment it was in which I contracted HIV and not to have lived the three seconds in which I said words that were intended as a joke but became a firestorm, hurting enormous numbers of people and nearly destroying me. I hope that the rehearsals of my life—the episodes that revealed things both good and anything but good about me—are over, and that I have become more thoughtful, or at least more aware of my

255

thoughtlessness. Maybe being consumed by the memory of this event is not the worst thing; maybe it has served as a reminder, however painful, and is thereby useful. Of all the cruelties I have inflicted upon others, the two remarks, in combination, turned into a weapon against me. But it was a weapon I had fashioned myself.

I survived in 1990, going back triumphantly to WBZ Radio after nine weeks in Tom Snyder limbo. I survived in 1992, when the media overkill and the overreaching to get me fired inspired a strong reaction. Still, I had no idea in 1994–95, during my time of trouble—the most trouble I have ever been in— that I would be bolstered yet again by that large family of listeners, viewers, and readers who know what I believe— hope—is the real me. I don't have a great radio voice; I have a slight speech impediment, a hard time with the *s* sound, and sometimes when I'm excited I appear to squeak, not just to speak. My memory is faulty and I am given to pontificating. But I have one virtue: I say what I mean and mean what I say— except, of course, for the occasional joke, benign or wretched—and the current state of American discourse encompasses fewer and fewer people like that. Do we believe the ever-shifting positions of our politicans? Is celebrity the best approximation we can find for heroism?

I survived and even prospered, whether my homosexuality was known or just suspected, my status as an AIDS "victim" notwithstanding. I even received increased ratings once the AIDS thing entered public consciousness. I was not fired and was not the *plat du jour* in a desired feast featuring not-yet-dead white males. There's a lesson for us here, perhaps a small lesson about acceptance in America, something more positive and deservedly optimistic than what we are so often told is the pre-

256

dominant mode today. But even as I bathed in the warm glow of thousands of supportive letters and became convinced that I would somehow walk again, I was attacked by a medical set-back that terrified and unnerved me. For the first time in the saga of my experiences of living with AIDS, I wanted to die.

TEN

Thanksgiving

Whatever most of my visitors thought—they saw a frail, gaunt, nearly emaciated person inching his way down the hall in slow motion—*I* knew that I would disprove the gloomy neurologist's prognostication and walk again. Mass. General wasn't equipped to deal with long-term rehabilitation therapy, and though I missed the luxury and felt squeezed in the tiny rooms of Spaulding Rehabilitation Hospital, it was there that I experienced both my greatest physical triumph and my greatest physical and emotional misery.

I had hoped that as soon as I moved to Spaulding, therapists would begin a grueling schedule of all-day sessions. I was fortunate that they didn't, because my energy level was low, and at first even a half-hour of therapy wiped me out for the rest of the day. Most of the first weekend was filled either with naps or with repetitious orientation meetings. I wanted so much to be well and back home, I could taste the experience. I would be the patient from paradise. But Spaulding's therapists and the magnificent doctor who tended me, Gerald Kassels, director of the Complex Medical Program, knew that I wasn't strong enough to go whole hog into therapy.

Of course I imagined that if I worked my tail off, I could be home soon, back on the air by December. Dr. Kassels tried to lower my expectation of an early release and get me to see that I couldn't be sent home until I was functionally independent—able to shower and dress myself, amble around my apartment, pick myself up if I fell. And though I may have been well enough (comparatively) in terms of my heart and lungs, I was a typical hospital denizen, picking up nosocomial infections—the fancy word for infections that abound in hospitals and spread to patients rather regularly—and providing a daily illustration of my fragility. My blood pressure was erratic, fluctuating wildly, normal or near normal when I was lying down, dropping significantly the minute I sat or stood up. The adrenaline burst that occurs when somebody with a weak heart sits, much less stands up, contributed for days to abnormal blood pressure.

My muscles were atrophied and weak, owing not only to my many weeks of illness during my denial period but also to nine days of floating on the morphine plane and two weeks more of limited movement. For years I'd been a regular at the gym, and I was rather muscular for somebody in his fifties. Now I was scrawny, puny, quick to become exhausted, tired most of the day. My muscular atrophy dovetailed with my heart and lung deficiencies, and I was anything but an appealing physical specimen. And because of my neuropathy, blood and fluids tended to build up, causing swelling and impairing the flow of blood to other areas of the body. Such is edema, one of the symptoms that even I should have recognized during my denial period, a symptom of serious physical illness.

Just what every one of my symptoms was caused by, I never

felt confident that I knew. Early on, Dr. Robbins had explained that the answer to many questions about seriously ill patients was "We don't know." I'm the kind who needs to know, who catalogues, files into sections, chases down until I have learned the answer. Spaulding, like Mass. General, was incapable of feeding my appetite to understand all that had happened and was happening to me, and sometimes I completely misunderstood what doctors told me. One time, at Mass. General, I told a reporter that I had a hole in my heart and tuberculosis. No hole, no TB, but a sorely damaged heart and plenty of pneumonia. Because I was in a cancer ward at Spaulding—there was room for me there, no other reason—I feared that I also had cancer. I mentioned this to a visitor, a doctor friend, who asked a nurse, who evidently asked Gerry Kassels, and I learned that I didn't have cancer. My ears heard what doctors told me, but my brain got much of it scrambled. My vocal cords spewed out nonsense.

The therapy, however, was encouraging. My primary physical therapist, Sharyn Levine, explained that my lightheadedness resulted from the cardiopulmonary problems and also from the great amounts of bed rest I had enjoyed (or endured). The dilemma: I needed hour upon hour of rest, but the more rest I experienced, the less fit I was for exercise, and the less I exercised, the slower my recovery would be. I wanted to go home, but I couldn't until I was walking or doing a functional substitute for walking. Sharyn told me that my body was working as hard as possible and, as important, that my attitude, my desire to overcome this disability and get on with my life, would help my rehabilitation.

I was given a brace to wear on my right leg whenever I walked, which sometimes put me off-balance, which increased my blood pressure. Eventually, however, I got used to the brace and to an even more intrusive cast that was strapped to my right leg during the night. I graduated from the walker and was given a four-pronged cane, a step up (no pun) from the walker but still not where we were aiming to be within some weeks. I learned that "occupational therapy" doesn't mean therapy to do your job again—therapy to preach over the radio?—but therapy to do the quotidian tasks that most people need: bathing, getting up and down stairs, cooking or at least microwaving, picking up your clothes, grooming yourself. Jennifer Feenan, my primary occupational therapist, added to Sharyn's supportiveness, saying that my desire to get well was adding to my speedy progress, though she often had to slow me down, to keep my blood pressure at a healthy level and to make me see this experience as long-term or at least middle-term in length, not a week of hard labor and then off to the races. As usual, I had become a model patient, accepting the routine at Spaulding as well as its pacing. I was lent some cassettes and a player by the hospital librarian, and a friend brought me Tina Turner doing her voluptuous song about taking it easy, *real . . . easy.* Oh yes. This was not a metamorphosis from Mr. Type A to the Laid-back Kid, but after about five weeks in hospitals, I began to see that I would have to slow down permanently, and that progress could come in little turtle steps as well as in rapid rabbit leaps, and that I, the Energizer bunny, would have to become more the tortoise and stop feeling guilty about it.

Because germs congregate so easily and dangerously in carpets, patient areas usually have no carpets, only well-scrubbed floors, which meant that I couldn't walk without shoes, so even hobbling the two feet from my bed to the toilet meant that I had to find and put on my shoes, which was sometimes impossible without help. Maybe an unstated part of Spaulding's therapeutic technique involved getting patients to accept their limitations as well as aspire to overcome them. Having to call a nurse to help me put on a shoe, or both shoes, embarrassed me, but having to acknowledge that as the way things were just then and the way they would remain for many days, or weeks, knocked a little sense into me. Unlike Blanche DuBois, I had never depended upon the kindness of strangers. Now, helpless without the kindness of strangers, I had to (as the shrinks put it) own my condition and come to accept it.

The significance of friends' visits and letters and cards and phone calls in creating my positive attitude can't be underestimated. The Gang of Five was there, daily or pretty close to daily, and others who were dear to me finally got Guardian Ward's blessing to come. My oldest male friend in Boston, Dick Fletcher, who had exercised with me at the YMCA at seven A.M. back in the sixties, came to visit. My pal Papa Joe Curran, who had visited me in an absolutely convincing hallucination at Mass. General before he turned up in the flesh (he became known then as the Phantom Visitor), came bearing candy, pounds of it, daily reinforcements of it, finally finding me a willing recipient of anything that would add pounds to my frame. I was rarely alone, as friends from TV, from radio, from the newspaper world, from whichever part of my life, came to call. Mike Barnicle got in even without Ward's blessing, because, he said, he looked like the help. I took to showing off: with my walker first, then my four-pronged cane, finally my regular cane. I would hobble down the hall and usher my visitors into the lounge—my room was too tiny for more than one visitor at a time—and though I couldn't open the hall toilet door by myself and needed help with a door that rivals that at St. Peter's in Rome for heft, I began to believe what I had been told by Mica back in Mass. General: I would walk again.

Kevin with the mailbags; Peter and his fiancée, Rosanne Bacon, with tales from the world outside; Patricia with mail from home; Jon with Inez and drawings by their preadolescent sons, my buddies Barney and Jared, to brighten up my room; Ward with doughnuts and coffee; and, unendingly, the plants, one from AmFAR, the American Foundation for AIDS Research, chaired by Elizabeth Taylor (for a moment I hoped that maybe she would come in person), which was so huge it looked to be a refugee from *The Little Shop of Horrors*—all came and took my thoughts away from my fears of what AIDS would do to me in time. I hired a temporary secretary to help me answer letters from personal friends, which relieved a little of the guilt I was experiencing over being such a crummy correspondent; the best little boy in the world lives within me even now. Papa Joe, the Phantom, delighted in tormenting me with his "I told you so" routine, and yes, yes, yes, he had told me so, told me to get to a hospital months earlier, but I never listened. I was showered with love and concern, and the newspapers speculated not on whether but on when I would return to my program. I even felt confident enough to assure my Boston University chairman that I would be ready to teach my course in the spring term, beginning in mid-January.

Spaulding got me up on my feet and out of my slump; my spirits sometimes sank, though I don't think I ever suffered from clinical depression. Every moment was a new experience—a kick, some of those moments; others more a knock on my head. In Dr. Kassels I had an ally who insisted that I get my shower every morning at six A.M., a procedure I worked into a minor miracle of conciseness: a nurse's aide would wheel me down to the shower room, and then I, alone, shampooed my hair and washed myself, all except my back, which I needed help with at first. I faced the day not fresh as a daisy but not stinking, not covered with the sweat that visited me almost nightly. Jennifer told Kevin that I was "one tough cookie." I was beginning to admire myself, after a long time of feeling like a worm, and my primary nurse, Sharon Donohue, told Kevin that I was gracious 100 percent of the time, though my memory is that I was a pain in the butt. I was up to my old tricks: entertaining the troops. Lifting my spirits by trying to be the best little patient at Spaulding.

Since I was staying on the cancer ward, I witnessed people in far worse shape than I was—people who would never walk, people who would soon be dead, people who cried out in the night with certain knowledge of their coming death—and in the darkest hours I sometimes pondered my fate too. I did not pray, but I conversed with (I presume) myself, uttering over and over what had become my mantra: *I will walk, I will walk, I will go home, I will go home, I will return to my jobs, I will work at my jobs, and I will survive AIDS for some time yet to come.* A favorite statue on the Commonwealth Avenue mall near my home is that of William Lloyd Garrison, the early nineteenth-century antislavery activist, journalist, and bane of the existence of the comfortable people of Boston, because he railed against slavery in the South and against the collusion of northern businessmen in the odious practice. I imagined that at my best I was Garrison's spiritual heir, speaking out without fear, defying the Powers to stifle me. At my worst I was just a pain. Garrison's two favorite aphorisms grace the base of his statute: "My country is the world; my countrymen are all mankind" and "I am in earnest. I will not equivocate. I will not excuse. I will not retreat a single inch, and I will be heard!" I revere Garrison and have taken that last quotation as my motto. I was going to make it. But not quite yet.

❑ ❑ ❑ ❑

I was getting better in my therapy sessions, insisting on week-end workouts with the backup crew, not wanting to lose even one day on my sure path from hospitalization to freedom. I could shave without falling over; I ate everything, gluttonously, ordering huge meals and devouring all the candy that Papa Joe brought to tempt me. At night, when I was lowest in spirits, one of the nurse's aides would come in and rub my back and legs and sorry feet with a soft, creamy lotion, telling me tales of her own life and letting me hold on to her now and again. Things were going well; I was a busy boy, getting close to the day when I would be discharged and return to real life.

And then I was faced with a new and entirely unexpected horror. What I didn't realize was that it had started back at Mass. General when I felt bumps on my right buttock one morning. I assumed, since I hadn't spent any long time in a hospital since childhood, that these bumps were bedsores. An inexperienced intern dismissed the bumps as a rash, but Dr. Robbins examined me and made the diagnosis of shingles, which he confirmed with a biopsy. Shingles? That weirdly named thing my great-aunt Jenny often whined about when I was a kid? Herpes zoster, or shingles, is the chicken pox virus, which most people experience in childhood and which then goes into hiding, so to speak; sometimes it comes out again in adulthood, more often in old people than in the middle-aged, and most frequently in immune-suppressed people. It tends to be but isn't always confined to one side of the body, most often the lower back or the abdomen. Jon Keller, Pat Kennedy, and Blitz had all experienced brutal bouts of shingles, and while I thought the name was silly, I didn't know how ghastly shingles could be.

At Mass. General, my case of shingles was easy. Greg located the telltale bumps both on my right buttock and on a part of my penis and right testicle, ordered that my room be quarantined against any visitor or medical person who hadn't had chicken pox, and hooked me up to another intravenous drip to infuse me with acyclovir, or Zovirax, the best-known (in essence, the only) drug for the initial stages of shingles. I was on so many drugs, including painkillers, during that period of my hospitalization that those first days of shingles seemed more a nuisance than anything else. I guess I wasn't paying close enough attention when Greg explained that immune-suppressed people sometimes experience a later stage, a "post-herpetic neuralgia," which is what the name says: a nerve pain following the herpes.

I went to Spaulding thinking that my shingles was fully on the wane and that my only debility would be the limitations in physical activity brought on by my peripheral neuropathy. Neuralgia and neuropathy sounded similar, and I concentrated on my semiparalyzed feet. Gerry Kassels was aware that I had shingles, and like Greg Robbins and Deborah Cotton, he tried to prepare me for this post-herpetic thingamabob, just in case. Just in case of *what?* I asked. Just in case you get it, because, he said, it can be rough.

Rough. The first indication that I was heading right into the post-herpetic stage was an intense itching in my right buttock, which I scratched to no avail, though I opened wounds that took months to heal. Little did I know that that was the least of it. Suddenly one day I felt a rumbling in my groin and buttocks that turned instantly into a convulsive eruption of such extreme intensity that I shrieked. I clutched one of the bed railings and began hyperventilating, yelping for help, shaking throughout my body, my leg veins bulging as if they were about to blow up. I was so frightened and confused that I didn't notice at first that I had completely lost my bowel control. Then for a second

266

or two I felt as if I were being morphed into a horror movie and that the David who had soiled himself wasn't really me. This wasn't a one-time event. Day after day, without notice, the thing took hold of me, and I was useless to stop it, though sometimes I could yell at visitors to run out of the room because I didn't want them to see what was coming next. And come next it did, four or five times a day. I made it to the bathroom twice, but most of the time the pain, the convulsions, the shaking, the terror, and the soiled clothing gave this experience its standard pattern. I couldn't imagine putting up with this forever.

No matter how intensely painful my neuropathy had been before I was hospitalized, no matter how frightened I had been at Mass. General when I learned just how seriously ill I was, I had never lost confidence that somehow I would recover, even if only for a brief period, and that the pains were bearable. But when this post-herpetic neuralgia had taken its toll for a full week of terror, filthy bowel explosions, convulsing, shaking, and screaming, I remember calling out to God, whose existence I doubt, that I couldn't stand it anymore. I looked out the window of my seventh-floor room at the Fleet Center under construction below, thinking that throwing myself to my death couldn't possibly be more unbearable than what was happening to me. I have felt suicidal only once in my life: this was it.

The attacks—I called them the Beast in the Bowels—lasted only thirty or forty seconds from the first rumblings in my body to the end of the convulsions, and none of the nurses and aides admitted to finding the nasty business of cleaning me up nearly as disgusting as I found it. Dr. Kassels had warned me about the neuralgia and had said that sometimes it lasts a lifetime, and in reading about it later I found that enormous numbers of people kill themselves rather than abide their symptoms for very long. In my own case, the post-herpetic neuralgia was complicated by another little infection, infectious colitis, in which a toxin, Colodsia difficilia or C-Diff, inspires a kind of instantaneous, explosive diarrhea. When this toxin was produced in me, my body expelled it as quickly as possible, so the neuralgia, painful as it was, was magnified by the colitis and C-Diff.

In the past year I've talked with hundreds of people on-air about shingles and post-herpetic neuralgia, and while most of the stories are horrible, none is identical to anybody else's. The virus is astoundingly resilient, I've learned, sometimes striking for no discernible reason, sometimes coming and then going eventually, though my "eventually" is yet to occur. There is no painkiller that works for it, and dozens of people have sent me their "cures," all of which I've tried, futilely. A great many people who've had chicken pox in childhood get shingles as adults, and of them, a significant percentage get post-herpetic neuralgia; of that group, a not inconsiderable number live with it for the rest of their lives or end their lives rather than bear it. None of this is unique to people with AIDS, but our immune systems are so fragile, so shot to hell by the time we die, that this virus evidently feels right at home visiting and tormenting us.

How could I have been what the nurses and therapists said I was: of good cheer most of the time, rarely a nuisance, an ideal patient? I still sometimes hear myself screaming during those days; the experience comes back to me as a cursed visitor during the night, as a dream, of course, from which I wake shaking. Eventually the Beast abandoned my bowels and became a habitual jolt of pain, one that I decided I could put up with. The agony was frequently rough, but I stopped soiling myself and my clothes, and one night I even counted the attacks of intense pain in my genitals and right buttock: from eleven P.M. to seven A.M., on an evening when I couldn't seem to sleep, I had over four hundred attacks. Gradually this too eased, until I had fewer episodes; the pain in my rear returned to an incessant itching, and the pain in my genitals was like being nipped at by small pliers over and over again. Any movement, any touch, and we were off. That too began to ease, and I learned to control what had been my involuntary little yelps of pain when the Beast came to visit, so I could be out in company and not reveal to anybody just how much pain I was feeling. The suicidal urge ended, but if what we've learned about AIDS is to be my fate too, I expect that I'll have other torments, each in its season. I have had, I know, a preview of coming attractions.

Until I felt certain that I could control my bowels, I knew that going home was out of the question, but I had to give leaving the hospital a try, and the occasion came along when Jon Keller asked me to spend Thanksgiving with him and his family at his parents' house, where I had celebrated the holiday several times in past years. Negotiating this was easier than I thought; Dr. Kassels said that if Jon would come by early and have a lesson in how to get me into and out of a car and into and out of a house, I could have my Cinderella evening. I warned Jon and Inez, and asked them to tell his parents, that we could have an accident, though I was now five days away from my last explosive bowel eruption. Jon dutifully came by for an instructional session with my therapists: wheelchair to car, patient eased into car, patient eased out of car onto walker, friend accompanying patient into house and any time that patient got up to go anywhere . . . well, you get the gist of this thing. This was the most thankful Thanksgiving of my life, with good friends and away from the hospital. And on top of it all, my longtime barber, John Clark, had called two days before and volunteered to come to the hospital Thanksgiving morning to give me a haircut, which I hadn't had for two months. So I was spiffed up for the event.

Thanksgiving 1994 was a lifesaver. It gave me a tremendous boost. And I couldn't help but recall that Jon may have saved my life years before, when I had come close to being murdered. In 1983, my stepmother had called me at WRKO to say that my father had suffered a heart attack and was in intensive care in Minneapolis. I said I'd be home the next day, but she insisted that the doctors felt there was no point in that. Dad recognized nobody and would either die without regaining consciousness—sound familiar?—or recover. It was as if I were back on the bus trip the evening that Kathie called to tell me my mother had died. I was suddenly overwhelmed by a desire to have sex; I was Camus's *étranger* once again. Having been told not to go home until further notice, I left the station after my shift and went on a frantic prowl to find a partner for the night. I drove downtown, ambled into a gay bar, then out, and on the street I encountered a handsome, open-faced, olive-skinned twenty-two-year-old, Donny, who fit the bill. We were at my place in minutes, and as we sat talking on the couch Jon called, asking if I'd heard anything more from Audrey about my dad. After Jon and I spoke, Donny asked what the problem was; I told him about my father's heart attack. He expressed concern and went on for quite a while about his own father, who had died years before.

Later, after we were in bed, Donny got up and wandered through my apartment. I got out of bed and there was Donny, his eyes wide, almost bulging. He was clutching a letter opener and shrieking that he was going to kill me. I've little experience with psychopaths or with people high on drugs—I was well off psychedelics by then and had never become interested in co-caine or heroin—and instead of taking the gamble that I might be able to beat him if I started pounding him, I felt only fear and a sense that I was best off obeying rather than confronting him. He pushed me back into the bedroom, cut a phone cord and bound my hands with it, then tied me to the bed with a couple of my neckties, rambling for an hour or so as he paced around the room, incoherently telling me of his miseries and how he hated me and was going to "stick" me till I bled to death. So often we read of scenes like this, or what we presume is a scene like this: middle-aged bachelor found stabbed or bludgeoned or strangled to death, no sign of forced entry, po-lice have no clues, probably some fag out for a nice time. My nice time turned into a nightmare as Donny babbled on. I tried to remember what I had learned in psych courses, racing back in memory to the scene with the young man in Minneapolis, and I spewed out major bullshit: you're so handsome, Donny, so beautiful, I love you, you wouldn't want to hurt me, I know you wouldn't, just take anything you like from the house and enjoy yourself, just don't hurt me, Donny, I'd never hurt you. It was as if I were having an out-of-body experience—this scene going on with a person who looked like me could not really be me!—one that was so intensely horrifying that I could feel my body shaking, my heart racing, sweat pouring down my face, my back, my chest. I was sure that I would piss or shit then and there.

Donny had taken a pillowcase and filled it with some items, including a camera, some money, a few trinkets, and he heaved a deep sigh and just sank into a chair at the side of my bed, shaking. He lifted a pair of scissors into the air, his eyes bulging, his head wobbling; I thought of Anthony Perkins in *Psycho,* dressed as Mama and propelling that knife into Janet Leigh.

271

Suddenly everything changed. Swiftly down came the scissors, but not into me, into Donny's *own thigh,* which spurted blood. He winced and cried out; he was bleeding profusely, nearly convulsing. The fight went out of him; the look of madness turned into that of a child in great fear of something, and even the tone of his voice went back to what it had been when we met on the street an hour earlier. Donny hugged me and apologized and said that because he knew that I was worried about my father—Jon's call had alerted him to that—he had decided not to kill me. He switched instantly from raving maniac to whimpering, pathetic character, politely asking me if he could have a pair of my trousers to replace his own blood-soaked pair. I volunteered to bandage him if he would untie me. He kissed me again, and again I put on the great theatrical act of my life, but he still wouldn't let me loose. He wandered around the apartment, dripping blood on the carpet, talking to himself, periodically running back to apologize for his actions, then demanding my car keys and again expressing the hope that my dad would recover. Then he went to the living room and I heard the front door open and shut.

I couldn't see into the living room and feared that he was still there somewhere, waiting for me to free myself and then landing on me again and finishing the job that he had begun. *Psycho* came to mind once more. I called his name several times, then was silent, then called his name again and again, and after an hour or so I decided that he was either the most patient of madmen or had actually left. I struggled with the phone cord and the neckties that bound me, and in a half-hour I managed to free myself from Donny's amateur shackles. I called out again, as if he might be in the living room or my library or the kitchen. Then, still naked and shaking, I crept into the living room, looked everywhere I could think of where he might have hidden himself, and locked the door. I found a note on a table: "Sorry," it said, then mentioned where he would leave the car.

The time was four A.M. I called Patricia first, then Jon, and told them what had happened, remarking to Jon that perhaps his call had given Donny pause, enough at least to find somebody else to torment. Who knows? The whole thing (except for stabbing himself) may have been a ruse, a pretence of psychopathic behavior to scare me out of my wits and into submission. It worked, whatever it was, and I was scared for months afterward. For nearly a year I was unable to meet any stranger in a gay environment and take him home. I kept the severed phone cord and the note, though Patricia thought I was being obsessive and tried to throw the stuff away. I have those items to this day.

The next day I reported the car stolen and indicated where I "thought" it might be. Then I voted—it was mayoral primary day—and ran into Bob Cord, to whom I spilled out my story and from whom, as expected, I got tremendous emotional support. Later in the week I went to look at mug shots at police headquarters, where I found many a familiar face, but not Donny's. I searched for weeks for clues about who this young man was, and finally saw his picture in a gay newspaper which advised people to watch out for the person pictured. A few years later I saw him again. He came up to me in a bar, smiled, apologized again for his actions, attributed them to cocaine, and asked if I would like to go home and continue our "date." I bought him a beer but begged off renewing our "friendship," though I did give him a hug and said I forgave him. That night in 1983 marked the beginning of my gradual withdrawal from wild sex with improper strangers. And I believe to this day that without knowing it, Jon saved my life that night.

Jon, however, thinks that I had or have a death wish, and while he has never referred to *l'affaire Donny,* he certainly must have thought back to that night as I lay dying in the hospital. When Kevin phoned Jon to tell him what was happening, my old friend said to himself, as he later told Kevin, "Good job, David. Mission accomplished. You've finally killed yourself." Jon had seen weeks before that I was denying my illness, falling apart physically, and on the night Kevin took me off the air after one hour, it was Jon who came in to finish my show. He was as convinced as anyone that my "flu" had to be more than I said it was, more than I was able to acknowledge, and when I finally told him in the hospital that it was AIDS, he wasn't surprised.

Jon joined Pat and Kevin in having one-way conversations with me in the intensive care unit, and said later that he thought talking to me in my unconscious state might have served a purpose for those doing the talking, been a way of reconciling themselves to what was considered a near certainty. Like the others, Jon saw that I indeed did have a family of friends as well as strangers, people who cared and who made the absence of a lover in my life something I could accept. He took some comfort from the words of a nurse who said that of course David was hearing him and everybody else. She went over to me, I am informed, put her head face-to-face with mine, and said, as much to Jon as to me, I'm sure, "Hey, Dave, how ya doin'? You got company." I wish I had been there.

Only a few weeks transpired between the twenty-fifth of October and Thanksgiving, but they were the weeks that took me from death's door to the Kellers' for my favorite holiday. Jon had seen me unconscious, had spoken to or at least at me, and had been among those who sat in my room two days after I had been extubated; it was he who had kissed me on the forehead when I had fallen into a morose reverie while anticipating my death. Like the others, Jon knew that Ward had to decide whether to have me taken off life supports or to insist that I be given more time to rally. None of them had reason to hope, though reason and hope are often inconsistent experiences, and so hope triumphed over reason, and eventually they all agreed that I just might be cantankerous (or lucky) enough to survive those days in the coma.

Jon believes that I wanted to kill myself, that my denial, however unconscious on one level, was deliberate, a way of becoming so sick that I couldn't pull back from death. Maybe so. My behavior in September and October 1994 could as easily and accurately be interpreted as a deliberate march to death as simply a terrified person's denial. My self-image is wounded by thinking that this may be so; I am too much a man of reason, too much in love with life, too energetic to want to escape from life prematurely. Or was I actually a coward, too fearful of the agonies of late-stage AIDS to remain on the scene to experience them?

I have always spoken out in favor of the right to die, by which I mean the right of a rational person to find a convenient, painless way to shuffle off this mortal coil without having to seek the approval of doctors or the government or anybody else. Some states now perform capital punishment by means of lethal injection, but none permits a noncriminal to have access to the same procedure. Strange world, strange country; strange indeed. But my intellectualizing about the matter on radio, on TV, and in newspaper columns was always an argument in the abstract. I was not validating a conscious decision to do away with myself. I have always wanted to be onstage for the final act, to take a proud bow at a very advanced age and toddle off to death one quiet evening in my bed, painlessly, noiselessly, and with no fuss or muss for others. Were Jon not such a superb analyst of behavior and such a loving friend, I might think that he was off the mark in his evaluation of what I was doing to myself, what I was not doing for myself, in those months before my collapse. I am brought up short by his views. They ring all too true.

I had my furlough day with Jon and the rest of the Kellers, and Cinderella got back to Spaulding before the clock struck midnight, demonstrating to myself as well as to Gerry Kassels that it was no longer true that you couldn't take David anywhere. I could be taken home, and after my therapists took me home for an inspection tour, to see if anything needed retrofitting to accommodate my disabilities, and after a bathing chair and a secure railing had been installed in my shower, Dr. Kassels and I sat down and had the big talk. Could I leave and feel capable of independence? Was my progress in walking with a cane enough to get me up the building's external stairs? Would there be somebody in the building who could keep a daily eye out for me? Of course: Bob Cord, and finally I wouldn't be so resistant to talking about my health. Could Ward and the others be counted on to let the doctor know if I experienced anything unusual, since it was plain that I was on the upper high of an optimism phase, post-herpetic neuralgia notwithstanding, and was unlikely to complain about anything until it might be too late?

Gerry Kassels made it plain that he wasn't throwing me out of the hospital, that the insurance ogres hadn't demanded that I be cast out; he was releasing me because he was convinced I was ready. My blood pressure was stabilizing, my degree of functionability was acceptable, my attitude was positive, and the therapists' report on my living space was encouraging: I had plenty of room, easy access to the kitchen and bathrooms, a supportive staff in my building to help me in whatever way became necessary, and of course I had the Gang of Five. With the complete approval of his colleagues at Mass. General— Deborah, Greg, and Dr. Bill Dec, who became my cardiologist—Gerry concluded that nothing was holding me back. My mental stability was excellent; my attitude was upbeat, though sometimes a patient who is very upbeat is actually in denial, and denial was not an unfamiliar presence in my life. I wasn't living in a dream state, he concluded, and since the Beast from the Bowels had abandoned me to lesser torments, I would be able to keep myself clean and resist additional infections. When I entered Spaulding, I weighed 135 pounds, up from the bottom of 125 or so in Mass. General. The day I was discharged, Sunday, December 4, a day that will live for me not in infamy but in eternal thanksgiving, I tipped the scales at 141. Still skinny, but I was moving in the right direction.

On that day, my two months of hospitalization came to an end. I was ushered out with affectionate farewells from the nurses and doctors and aides, accompanied by Kevin and Ward, who carried my bags as I, with my cane in one hand, did all the walking from the hospital's front door to Ward's car and then to my building. I eased myself up the steps to my building, and then, just at the last step, the one without a railing, I slowly began to fall backwards. Ward, who was behind me, said it was like slow-motion football on the TV instant replay; he saw me gently falling onto granite stairs, right onto the haggard buttocks that had played unwilling host to the Beast from the Bowels, possibly adding to that horror a broken back. He caught me—is he eternally condemned to save me?—and I was barely aware of what had occurred until a visibly shaken Kevin and a panting Ward got me into the building, up the elevator, and into my apartment.

I was back. My life could begin again. I had delayed death's claim on me and was determined to live life all the way—no more rehearsals, no more deferring pleasures and experiences until later. My "later" would be short; my todays were all that mattered.

EPILOGUE

Life Is Not
a Rehearsal

During my long journey, I did not find God. I wasn't looking. I found instead resources in myself that I thought didn't exist. I found that I could tolerate more pain than I had ever imagined and that I could at times even regard my troubles as an educational experience, as if I were studying myself from far away. No, this was not an out-of-body experience; except when I was hallucinating right after being brought out of the nine-day coma, I retained a cogent sense of being the David to whom all this was happening. I finally saw the patterns of behavior, however unconscious, however unintended, that had formed my life, and in learning to accept the help offered by others without my habitual insistence on self-reliance, I realized that Donne was on the money: no man is an island, entire of itself. My neediness over the many years during which I chose to pretend to myself that I needed little, if any, help from others was a delusion. The truth is painful many times, and at first I resented what was clear: that I could be independent only to an extent, that there is no shame in asking for help, no commandment from on high that would validate the traditional male fantasy that a *man* is a solitary individual beholden to none other. I had one primary goal: to get better, to get as well as a person with AIDS can be, and to make the most of the life remaining to me. I had often rehearsed an existence that would place me away from, even above, the concerns of others, in which what I did was a matter not only of choice but solely of *my* choice. I now know that no one can function without the frequent aid of others, that one's expectations seldom resemble one's actual circumstances much. Life, Trollope wrote in *Phineas Finn,* is so unlike theory.

Every step in my recovery was a collective act, a combination of the assistance of others and my own endeavors. Nature blessed us with the gentlest winter in years, unlike that of 1993–94, which amounted to blizzard after blizzard, icy streets that were hazardous for walking and impossible, I imagine, for hobbling on with a cane. But the winter of my discharge from the hospital and my growing contentment in the life I now had to lead was almost like a second spring. Maybe somebody up there likes me; the least of my problems was simply getting out and about. On December 4, 1994, Ward, Kevin, and I celebrated my release from hospitalization by walking two blocks to a restaurant, enjoying food with taste, and walking home again. This was my gesture of optimism, a mere amble of short distance that said to my friends that I was determined to get back into the swing of life and to myself that much was possible. The more I struck out into the living of life, the less I would be defined in my own mind by disease.

During the month before my planned return to the airwaves, I was visited every day by a nurse, Christine FitzPatrick, who tended my medical needs, and by a therapist, Sandra Juan, who worked with me on my walking, devising exercises to strengthen my muscles and stimulate nerve regeneration. The first day that Sandra and I left my apartment and walked around the block demonstrated what I could expect if progress continued, a life again *in* the world, not just on its fringes. My acupuncturist, Joe Burstein, who had cured my sciatica a decade before and to whom I went for general maintenance thereafter, offered to come to my house for treatments. We were running a little hospice just for me, and I found that I came to accept this home care without much fuss. The need was apparent; the response had to be suited to my low energy level. Only my weekly or twice-weekly visits to Dr. Robbins and Dr. Cotton took me into the hospital setting again, and the more walking I did, the easier walking became. I was being monitored carefully, tended kindly, encouraged continually. I did what I was told and felt pride in my accomplishments and gratitude for the help offered by others. My friend Juanita Tarnowski designated herself Shopping Lady, doing the supermarket routine every Wednesday, and Ward turned into Refrigerator Monitor to make sure that I was eating the nutritious food Juanita delivered. Many friends came bearing lunches; my moviegoing pal Tex Golden brought suppers (he'll make somebody a wonderfully useful husband one day); I went out to dine. I began to go to movie screenings again and then to write my film column, at first half-time and then full-time. As long as I had a couple of naps every day and slept soundly each night, I had the strength for a limited but gradually expanding schedule of work and play. Papa Joe got me out to South Boston for supper on many Saturdays, and I experienced my new notoriety in an unexpected setting: I wasn't precisely given a standing ovation when I hobbled into the Farragut House for dinner, but almost.

281

Brian Whittemore, Kevin, and I began strategizing my return to the air, Peter reintroduced me to our habitual political discussions, Jon began to use me again on his TV program, Patricia again became my morning wake-up caller, and Bob, who lived just above me, came by repeatedly to offer help. Often I accepted; when I felt that I was better off doing something for myself, I said thanks but no. However, I was no longer the helpless wretch who denied my illness, resenting offers to give me a hand. I wasn't quite transfigured, but I was transformed. I did the first of many TV interviews, with Paula Zahn on the CBS morning program, and a variety of cable interviews on national outlets. For the first time in my life, I wasn't surprised when truck drivers, cops, and others yelled encouragement to me as they drove by; not for the first time in my life, strangers rushed up to me on the street to shake my hand and urge me on. I was welcomed back to my habitual breakfast and lunch place, the Travis, by its owner, who refused any payment from me until I began to feel so guilty about sponging that I insisted on paying for my meals. These are small things, but they were large in my recovery, as the voluntary support and consideration of both friends and strangers washed over me. Kevin's mailbag was chock full every day. My month of recovery included no radio shows, but I felt sure that I knew what was coming when I returned. In reality, I had no inkling of how much was yet to come.

Brian thought that a month to recuperate would do me a world of good and that, not so coincidentally, the fifth of January, beginning the winter rating period, would be an ideal time to take up my duties at the station. Of course my first broadcast was to be a media event, with journalists and TV cameras in attendance. A lot of people, especially Papa Joe, suggested that I broadcast from my home, thinking that minimizing travel to and from the station and maximizing my opportunities to rest before the program and get to sleep immediately after it would be just the ticket. Deborah and Greg thought this was a splendid idea, and Brian agreed to the arrangement. We selected my library, with its floor-to-ceiling bookcases, its dark red walls covered with photos of politicians, movie celebrities, and my beloved Calvin Coolidge, and a zebra skin over the brown carpet, as the obvious choice for an in-home studio. NYNEX did its part, installing the appropriate phone lines, and our WBZ wizard of remote broadcasts, Warren Brown, assembled the equipment in my apartment. Until an hour before air, I wasn't confident that everything would be ready in time. An in-house studio is expensive and complex, and I had visions of talking into a microphone that broadcast nothing, a room full of reporters facing a talk host speaking into nobody's radio, impotence on the airwaves, the *Titanic* sinking.

Like a teenager getting gussied up for his first date, I tried on one suit, then another (too formal), then jeans and a sweatshirt (too slovenly), then an all-black outfit (too severe), then one in off-white (too virginal, ha), settling finally on a multicolored, multipatterned sweater that I knew would catch the television audience's eyes and look good in a color photo in the *Globe*. I had become a fashion plate at long last. Five camera crews and a dozen or so reporters squeezed into my little library as I sat alone, speaking live for the first time in nearly three months to my radio audience. I knew that I wanted to talk about what had happened to me and what I had done to myself and then open the lines for an hour of listener response, then have a few notables join me for the third hour. Brian wanted me to do just three of my regular five hours for a month or so, to conserve my energy, rather than go full tilt into twenty-five hours on

283

radio every week. I resisted, of course; he won, of course, and I'm grateful. Even three hours was a stretch at first.

My library, which I came to call the "smoking-, drinking-, and kick-off-your-shoes-friendly WBZ annex," filled up just before seven P.M. This would be my unrehearsed return to broadcast life, and for one moment I felt the nearly uncontrollable urge to put on a Gloria-Swanson-as-Norma-Desmond sneering smile and say, "I'm ready for my closeup now, Mr. DeMille." I was sailing, joy-filled, confident, knowing that what I was about to say would unlock any of the seemingly closed closets still containing me. I saw this night as essential, as the moment to put aside any doubts about my resolution to get back to work and back into life. The word had gone out from WBZ management to the columns, to other shows on the station, way back in November that when I returned, I would tell all. Everybody else had had his say, his take on my story, his theory. Now it was my turn to describe what had happened, what I had done to create what had happened, and what plans I had for myself from now on. Now it was also my turn to connect with my audience, who had heard only twenty-five minutes of me on-air, way back in mid-November, and only of, but not from, me ever since. I wanted this radio evening to be truthful, lacking any hint of coyness, serious, detailed.

Never before had I used the airwaves to get as intensely personal as I would this evening. Here was my opportunity to come back not only in style but in full awareness that New Englanders and people far away would be wondering how the last three months had changed me and what I intended to do with the last years of my life. Violating one of my cardinal rules as well as one of the sensible traditions on radio, of not devoting one's program to oneself, I took a deep breath, closed my eyes a moment, and began: "I think it's only fair in response to

284

enormous numbers of requests for this from listeners that I tell you what's been going on in my life in the last couple of months. I am a fifty-four-year-old homosexual and I was suffering the first attack of HIV—the AIDS virus." I told my listeners how much of what I did before my collapse was the result of a massive denial; I talked about my incomprehensible lecture at the university the morning of the day I collapsed and about how in the last three months many people had led me, as if leading a child by the hand through heavy traffic, to see the facts that I had tried desperately to avoid seeing. I explained how during my nine days in a coma "I did not see any bright lights; nothing awaited me at the end of a tunnel, beckoning me to come to God. I have no memory of anything [during] those nine lost days of my life." I went on to say that "I've always been very independent and think that if people were to describe me, they would say he's a loner, he's a self-starter, he does his own thing, he doesn't depend upon others very much. I realized that that's a delusion. . . . And one of the good things that has come out of this couple of months of very ungood things, severe illness and a very traumatic time, is the recognition of the dependence that I and I presume you at some point have or will have on one's friends. I can't tell you how important it was to me to wake up and find friends there, and I remember the second day or so I was out of the unconscious state, when the drugs had worn off or were beginning to wear off . . . ," and then I confessed, for the first time ever on radio, that I had cried in fear and confusion. "I had dissolved into a kind of infantile state . . . but they all assured me that I would live."

My voice did not constrict, nor did I sweat, even with the hot TV lights, nor was I unsure of myself for even a moment. This was not a rehearsed speech. I sat alone, revealing with a

285

straight-on bluntness the story of my most frightening moment, when the neurologist doubted that I would ever walk again. It came bubbling out of me as if I were talking with an old friend. My audience *was* an old friend of sorts, more a friend than I had ever realized. I hadn't planned the details of my solitary hour, but as I spoke I felt more liberated, freer. I was open now to a wider world, since I was a more complete person. This was my second experience in all this journey from denial to honesty of an almost giddy sense of openness: the first, the morning the news hit the papers and I hit the hospital's solarium for my press conference; this, the reunion with my radio listeners.

I was a frail, grossly underweight, still easily fatigued figure in a handsome but wildly colorful sweater sitting behind a small desk, talking into a microphone, and my voice alone, save for the clicking of the still cameras, broke the silence. I thought back to the day in early November when I woke in a strange bed in a place I didn't know, with Ward and doctors and nurses hovering over me, and of my fear on and off for days thereafter that I would surely never leave that place. Now, two months later, I was stripping off layers of my persona and becoming, fully, an integrated person.

"I had had a dream at one point that it might be fun to do a hiking tour in the Andes, but my dream then [in the first days of contending with my paralysis] was to be able to walk from the bathroom to the kitchen. The scope of one's desires begins to accord with the reality of one's circumstances. . . . Just to be able to do anything, when you're told you'll be able to do nothing, is a great advantage." I described the first time I was able to take a shower and shared the gruesome details of many hospital procedures, and as I unbuttoned the cloaks that had shielded me, I told of how I had gradually abandoned my ha-

286

bitual modesty and independence, coming to accept whatever help was needed. I told my audiences about shingles and about that ungodly post-herpetic neuralgia and about my fantasy that I could scoot out of Mass. General in time for the election and about the brisk blast of reality: I was crippled, very ill, likely never to walk or to do radio again.

I raced through the events of my hospitalization and of my progress during the month since I left Spaulding. I described the pain I was feeling as I spoke: "I have to live with [it]. It won't keep me from doing what I'm doing right now or from reading or from seeing movies or from reviewing things or from talking with friends and going out to dinner. . . . But it's a thing that lingers. . . . I'm not a brave or strong person, but I think I am able to be realistic about it, about my lot." I told of the blood transfusion I had had a few days earlier, which took seven hours to get two pints into me, and of "my gratitude for being alive and for having a second chance and for the tremendous support from friends," from the Gang of Five. "There are moments when I'm sad now. But by and large I'm optimistic and positive about it all."

I explained that I had told everything about my AIDS experience because I realized that rumors "not responded to" or allegations "ignored" would serve only to cast me, by my own evasions, as incapable of facing the reality of my situation, and once I decided to make the story public, I concluded that I must make the *whole* story public. I mentioned the oceans of ink wasted in speculation about whether I had been "outed" or had chosen to "out" myself as a person living with AIDS, and my worries about what Dad and Audrey would be able to handle and how much pain I would be bringing into their lives by letting them know the full story, and how for years I had been treated in Washington to maintain my privacy but now I was melding my life's parts into a coherent whole. And I explained that next only to my determination to do whatever I must do to restore my health, to the extent it could be restored, was my determination to get all vestiges of pretense out of my life. "I feel completely at ease with it all. There's never been a secret about my sexual orientation. . . . The disease is a different matter." And of course I closed with my usual invitation to listeners to become callers that evening, "to hear what you have to say about this, or anything else, right after this on WBZ, NewsRadio 1030."

We have six minutes of news at the top of each hour. As I finished the toughest radio hour of my life, and possibly the best, Kevin poked his head into the room, and I looked at him for encouragement or for his oh-too-ready grim expression when he thought I was off my game. He shot me a huge, gloriously happy smile and gave me *two* thumbs up. Some of the reporters and photographers actually cheered. I had done it, and I knew that it had been a triumphant hour. I am a media performer, nothing less, not much more, and I know when a performance, in this case a performance of truth-telling, has worked. I had before me—I *have* before me—adventures galore, successes in improving my health, declines, relapses, recoveries yet again, but having shared my life's darkest hours on the air, I had crossed one great hurdle. I was grateful for the opportunity to share my experiences with the world. As I spoke that night, I felt strength gathering in me, as if the very act of disclosure healed me.

The response from my callers was everything I could have hoped for: emotion, encouragement, joking, affection, even the inevitable complainer hoping that I would be gentler henceforth with President Clinton, or Bubba, as I affectionately called him. (I haven't been.) For half a decade I had withheld one part of my life, the part that will truncate my life. Now, however, I had found the context to bring what I had kept to myself into the life that had otherwise been frankly open to my listeners. AIDS had given me a curse, a horror, but also a great gift—several gifts: the knowledge that I was not alone in any way, I was a part of people's lives and more so than ever before, and the knowledge that what gave the entirety of me to others gave more of the strength of others to me. I wasn't a hypocrite about AIDS or about matters of interest to homosexuals. I always spoke from my convictions, not from my fears, as I had from the beginning of my media career in the late 1960s. I didn't pretend to have views that I actually despised nor disparage values and views that I cherished. But so much of that had been abstract, removed from the personal. I said it repeatedly in those first few weeks of my recovery, and I insist on it now: I am not solely a gay person or a person living with AIDS or a conservative talk host or what have you. Learning that I am not capable of functioning without help is not akin to collapsing into the infantile delusion that what makes each of us distinctive, unique, is to be ignored. And the right time for me to go public with my AIDS was not necessarily the right time for somebody else to do so.

They say in real estate that location is everything, in politics that timing is everything, and I say that in the outpouring of one's deepest feelings context is everything, or pretty damn near. I had begun to become more open, more honest, more willing to share myself with others. It hasn't been a tale full only of woe and fear; it is also a tale of regeneration. In the second hour I took calls; in the third, William F. Buckley, Jr., Mayor Tom Menino, and Senator Ted Kennedy were my guests. The program from then on returned to its real purpose,

289

discussing the things that matter most to our listeners. I was back in the world. All my rehearsals had led to that moment.

Later in the year, twelve months after I collapsed and nearly died, the March of Dimes gave me its lifetime achievement in radio award, which I accepted happily from the presenter, Mayor Menino, though as we kidded each other, I noted that I was perhaps a bit young for such notice. I enjoyed the media attention, the disruptions that come when a national network's crews come into your house and move everything, including yourself, around. I fussed less, fretted hardly at all, just took things as they came. I believe that Patricia has found me less tense, less frenzied, than before I took ill. Like the others in my Gang of Five, she worried that I wouldn't be able to handle any form of limitation on my activities or accept pity. She's right, of course. But I know that I'm easier to be with than I used to be; I am fonder of myself than I can ever remember being in recent years, less critical of my failings, more accepting. I cherish accomplishment, zeal, energy, and determination, but I've pulled away from some of the absolutes that ruled me before. I have not been a man of moderate opinions, but now I'm beginning to realize that absolutes are often walls that block understanding; now, though I remain more comfortable with absolutes than with relativities, I can at least *see* the grays, occasionally even admire them, though not quite yet fully embrace them. Give me time.

I'm more open, less compulsive, less guilt-ridden when, as happens frequently these days, I can't fulfill every social or civic obligation. I'm able to let a crummy movie come to town without bothering to see and review it, willing at last to skim a book whose author I'm interviewing rather than stay up to all hours to read every page. But evidently my habitual capacity

290

for denial is still alive and well, as evidenced by my third brush with death during these travels with AIDS. In April 1995 I had a relapse and didn't realize it until Ward, hearing me wheezing and insisting (again) that I was fine, just fine, called Dr. Cotton, shoved the phone into my face, and told me to let her hear my voice. She said, "Speak to me." I spoke to her, and she said, "Go to the emergency room immediately." I said, "Okay, right after my shower." She said, *"Now;* skip the shower," and I followed doctor's orders. I learned the next day that I had again been at death's door when I checked into the ER. Deborah said later that except for the fact that I hadn't passed out, my heart and lungs were in as bad shape then as when I collapsed in October 1994. Left to my own devices, I wouldn't have dreamed of bothering her to tell her that I was short of breath and woozy. Without Ward, I would have just died. Ward is evidently condemned by fate to rescue me fairly frequently. Perhaps it is fear that fuels my seemingly unlimited capacity for denial. I would like to believe instead that it's my seemingly unlimited desire for life.

On a beautiful April day, the Monday featuring the ninety-ninth running of Boston's world-renowned marathon, Ward took me home from the hospital after six days, and within a week I was back on the air and in my classroom. Three days after I left Mass. General I was doing a little skit with my WBZ buddy Joyce Kulhawik for an AmFAR fundraiser. We were quite debonaire, old smoothies performing a Bogart and Bergman routine, she in a slinky dress that shimmered, I in a trenchcoat and fedora, cigarette in my mouth. Joyce had the bigger part and was wonderful; I had one line—"Here's looking at you, kid"—after which I rose to embrace Joyce but, still weak, promptly fell on top of her. We tumbled to the stage, and of course everybody thought it was part of the act and gave us a standing ovation. I was indeed back.

My activities since my hospitalization have been geared to gathering strength. The post-herpetic neuralgia and the peripheral neuropathy in my feet remain with me but with a bit less pain. I get my daily naps, but if I miss one I'm not wiped out. Though my heart isn't in perfect shape and I'm back on all the medications that my cardiologist, Bill Dec, took me off during the third month after my long hospitalization, he gave me the go-ahead to return to the gym in June 1995, and today I am pumping more iron than before I was hospitalized. I'm a tiger at the Nautilus machine, that AIDS guy with biceps, and I've not only gained back all the weight I lost during my illness, I've added twenty pounds, to hit my goal of 180 pounds. One of my gym buddies said I was getting love handles. I liked hearing that: fat is good, at least in my case.

I missed the election of 1994, forced to be a passive observer in a hospital bed watching while others reported, analyzed, and bestowed media wisdom on a waiting world. I wasn't about to miss any more elections. In February 1996, Kevin and Papa Joe and I went to New Hampshire to broadcast for the primary, the first step in my return to political coverage. I have returned to the WBZ studios on Mondays, so that I can wallow in the office shmoozing that I missed, but I remain in my library studio the rest of the week, for convenience and because of Deborah's insistence that I eliminate stress whenever possible. I don't need my Boston University classes to pay the mortgage; I need them to feel in direct contact with people, not just to look at them through a TV camera or talk with them on the radio. I am a person once again *in* the world, not just gazing at it from a distance. I have learned and listened and returned to my audience energized, still waspish about politics, merry about the

292

pleasures to be had from the natural thrill that comes from hovering at the edge, this time not the edge of a six-story building, tripping on psychedelics, but the edge of what makes exciting radio. I play with ideas and remain tough-minded but with a larger element of compassion in me—I hope—and a truer sense of the direction I must go in.

I am not a wholly new man, but I am better for what I've gone through, and I am resigned to my fate. Each day is precious; each experience is meaningful, even the ones that attend my illnesses and the outlandishly large numbers of drugs and injections, self-administered, that keep me going. I bound into Mass. General for my office visits and blood tests, not fearful but relishing the fact that I can do it on my own two legs and am enjoying a period, however brief it may be, of stasis: the damn AIDS isn't going to get me just yet. This journey of discovery and acceptance continues, and while I know that I'll die earlier than the actuarial tables consider normal, I can handle it, knowing with absolute certainty that the rehearsals of my life are behind me.

Acknowledgments

Many people sustained me through my illness; many are featured by name in the text, though others deserve mention here. Space limitations forbid. I trust that the thousands of strangers (who became friends in a special way) who wrote with encouragement or called or prayed for me understand how grateful I am. Some, I hope, will see this book and understand what they have meant in my life.

Kevin Myron eagerly undertook the chore of interviewing friends and medical people who had important things to say but whom I felt hesitant about interviewing myself. I was too close to the story to find appropriate objectivity. Kevin did the job wonderfully, enhancing his interviewing skills and benefiting my book tremendously.

The vice president and general manager of WBZ radio—now the vice president for all our CBS-Westinghouse AM stations—is Ed Goldman; a more considerate boss would be difficult to locate. Ed's successor as WBZ general manager, Ted

Jordan, has continued what Ed began. Ed gave Brian Whittemore, then program/news director, now general manager of KDKA-AM in Pittsburgh, the go-ahead to take cues from me about when I was strong enough to go back on-air. Ed, Brian, Peter Casey, then our executive producer and now program/news director, and most of my colleagues, facilitated my return with regard for my reduced energy level.

Ed Symkus, my colleague at the *Tab*, and our editor, Greg Reibman, provided the same consideration for my unusual needs. Ed took over my movie column until I could get back to it, and Greg made clear that our newspaper chain, Community Newspapers, expected me to be doing the movie sections for years to come.

Rachelle Cohen, editorial page editor, and Guy Darst, chief editorial writer, at the *Boston Herald*, for which I frequently write op-ed pieces, expressed patience and concern; when I returned to writing columns, I felt as if I were coming home.

John O'Sullivan, editor, and Bill Buckley, editor-at-large, at *National Review*, authorized the Books and Manners section editor, David Klinghoffer, to invite me to do an extensive piece on my bout with AIDS—the first time my (and Ronald Reagan's) favorite magazine had treated the subject from within; that article was the first time I actually wrote about my story; this book is the second. Managing editor Linda Bridges, senior editor Priscilla Buckley, executive secretary Frances Bronson, and many friends at *NR* extended extra cordiality and affection.

David Anable, then the journalism chairman, and Brent Baker, the dean, at Boston University's College of Communication, did everything possible to keep my course in good hands (excellent hands, actually: my pal Michael Blowen took over my fall 1994 class) and welcomed me back to my classroom when I was ready. My students know the whole story and have been terrific. BU president John Silber, often unfairly considered hostile to gay people, though he and Katherine nursed their beloved son, David, at home in the year before David died of AIDS, did what his friends knew he would: he extended every courtesy and great affection to me.

Mike Paternostro and his colleagues at the Boston Sports Club helped get me back into physical shape (I call my body Muscles by Mike), and Leo Travis, whose Back Bay restaurant is my breakfast and lunch hangout, made sure that I was eating well. The Travis is a rare gem, a true neighborhood café without pretensions.

Scores of political friends—perhaps surprising to some, other than Mayor Tom Menino and Governor Bill Weld, Ted Kennedy and his nephew, my congressman, Joe Kennedy, are at the head of the list—expressed their good cheer. Even politicians whom I've savaged did this. Go figure.

The media world reached out to one of its own, making ideology irrelevant. From nearly the outermost fringes of the left to the analogous spot on the right side of the spectrum, these men and women rallied round. We're not all media maggots.

My colleagues in the Boston Society of Film Critics did me many kindnesses, including establishing the David Brudnoy Fund at the Intensive Care Unit at Mass. General. The hospital itself established the David Brudnoy AIDS Research Fund, assisting several area hospitals in funds acquisition. I've become a volunteer fundraiser, an unaccustomed role but it fits, now. Contributions are welcome.

Many doctors, nurses, aides, and others at both hospitals, in addition to those mentioned in the text, provided the best care available anywhere. This doctor's grandson is very thankful. My dad and Aunt Kathie and Uncle Herb, especially, among many family members, and countless personal friends rushed to my side. As Woody Allen reminds us, showing up is 80 percent of life. These people showed up.

Eugenia Mazariegos kept and keeps my house in order, and my plants lived, courtesy of Eugenia, even as my own survival was in serious doubt. Jack Armitage and his colleague, Loel Poor, included me in their exhibits of Loel's photographs of people with AIDS, allowing me to participate in a superb educational effort.

My agent, Stacey Woolf, directed me wisely into the hands of Doubleday, saying that she had a "feeling" that I would love working with Doubleday executive editor Elizabeth Lerner, who shepherded me through a zillion revisions of my story, each an improvement; the book is in large part hers. She also perceived something I hadn't. "It's really quite extraordinary how you managed to survive," she said. "One almost gets the feeling that your denial saved you." I'll always be grateful to Betsy, and I hope she'll edit many books by me in coming years.

Almost all of the names in the book are real; a few are pseudonyms. The three men who shared my life as lovers, when given the opportunity to be identified by first name only or by pseudonym, insisted that I use their full names.

Five greatly talented friends and role models, among them my beloved cousin, Neil Isbin, died of AIDS in recent years. The others are Terry Krieger, Randy Shilts, Paul Monette, and John E. Boswell. All of them are much missed.

Ward Cromer, to whom this book is dedicated, read early

versions and gave me support, advice, encouragement, as always. There is no better friend on earth.

Henry James, who spent a great deal of time in my neighborhood, said this: "Three things in human life are important. The first is to be kind. The second is to be kind. And the third is to be kind."

All these people were extraordinarily kind. It helped. It helped a lot.